Fugitive, Where Are You Running?

Critical South

The publication of this series is supported by the International Consortium of Critical Theory Programs funded by the Andrew W. Mellon Foundation.

Series editors: Natalia Brizuela, Victoria Collis-Buthelezi and Leticia Sabsay

Leonor Arfuch, *Memory and Autobiography*
Paula Biglieri and Luciana Cadahia, *Seven Essays on Populism*
Aimé Césaire, *Resolutely Black*
Bolívar Echeverría, *Modernity and "Whiteness"*
Diego Falconí Trávez, *From Ashes to Text*
Celso Furtado, *The Myth of Economic Development*
Eduardo Grüner, *The Haitian Revolution*
Karima Lazali, *Colonial Trauma*
Premesh Lalu, *Undoing Apartheid*
María Pia López, *Not One Less*
Achille Mbembe and Felwine Sarr, *The Politics of Time*
Achille Mbembe and Felwine Sarr, *To Write the Africa World*
Valentin-Yves Mudimbe, *The Scent of the Father*
Pablo Oyarzun, *Doing Justice*
Néstor Perlongher, *Plebeian Prose*
Bento Prado Jr., *Error, Illusion, Madness*
Nelly Richard, *Eruptions of Memory*
Silvia Rivera Cusicanqui, *Ch'ixinakax utxiwa*
Tendayi Sithole, *The Black Register*
Maboula Soumahoro, *Black is the Journey, Africana the Name*
Dénètem Touam Bona, *Fugitive, Where Are You Running?*

Fugitive, Where Are You Running?

Dénètem Touam Bona

Translated by Laura Hengehold

polity

Polity Press
65 Bridge Street
Cambridge CB2 1UR, UK

Polity Press
111 River Street
Hoboken, NJ 07030, USA

ISBN-13: 978-1-5095-5184-2 – hardback
ISBN-13: 978-1-5095-5185-9 – paperback

A catalogue record for this book is available from the British Library.

Library of Congress Control Number: 2022939967

Typeset in 10 on 12pt Sabon
by Fakenham Prepress Solutions, Fakenham, Norfolk NR21 8NL
Printed and bound in Great Britain by TJ Books Ltd, Padstow, Cornwall

The publisher has used its best endeavours to ensure that the URLs for external websites referred to in this book are correct and active at the time of going to press. However, the publisher has no responsibility for the websites and can make no guarantee that a site will remain live or that the content is or will remain appropriate.

Every effort has been made to trace all copyright holders, but if any have been overlooked the publisher will be pleased to include any necessary credits in any subsequent reprint or edition.

For further information on Polity, visit our website:
politybooks.com

Art is the strength to make reality say what it would not have been able to say by itself or, at least, what it might too easily have left unsaid. ... I argue that there should be another centre of the world, that there should be other reasons for naming things, other ways of breathing... because to be a poet nowadays is to want to ensure, with all one's strength, with all one's body and with all one's soul, that, in the face of guns, in the face of money (which in its turn becomes a gun), and above all in the face of received wisdom (upon which we poets have the authority to piss), no aspect of human reality is swept into the silence of history.

Sony Labou Tansi, "Foreword," in *The Seven Solitudes of Lorsa Lopez*, trans. Clive Wake. Oxford: Heinemann, 1995.

Contents

Introduction

Seloua Luste Boulbina

Rather than defending claims, the texts contained in *Fugitive, Where Are You Running?* propose perspectives. With a poetic hand steeped in practice, Dénètem Touam Bona follows a line of flight to the horizon that lends depth to the field of experience. Experience needs vanishing points to orient the gaze in a certain direction and to escape the order of a certain world. Where power consists in imposing immobility, movement is life preserving: "the *cimarrón* is a runaway slave" (p. 1). The fugitive runs, turning his back on the unjust fate reserved for him alone.

The converging lines of marronage and *lyannaj* are articulated on each other. Neither exists without the other. In fact, the maroon does not (re)discover the freedom that he originally lost in deportation and then, again, in servile work: he searches for an exit. He strives to escape a condition that oppresses and injures him. In doing so, he turns the forest, the world of lianas, into the space of his own emancipation. The author's pseudonym or alias, Dénètem Kilombo, was not chosen at random. What place, in fact, corresponds to the exit? And what action? Weaving bonds means sharing fertile moments of powerlessness. To accomplish this, one must sometimes just leave, narrowly escape, which already suggests the uncertain outline of a roundabout path and the sinuosities of a lengthy journey.

It takes intersections, the meeting of solitudes, to open one's eyes to what is possible and enjoy it rather than record the unhappy impossibilities of an infernal present. A whole logic of the ruse, indeed several, may develop, enabling one to ferret out, explore, and discover ways to exist together besides confinement – and thereby to advance. A form of resistance through feints and displacements, marronage involves extracting oneself from whatever enslaves by unbinding oneself, by hiding from the disciplinary eye that freezes and exploits, by transforming the body machine into a body subject in the act of secession, by burrowing through and into the forest's darkness, forming autonomous societies, inventing ways of being and styles of acting.

The limited margins of maneuver leave no room for rest. Dissemination weakens, but at the same time reinforces. The fugitive "fugues" more than he flees: "The rebel *nègres* do not flee, they fugue. Masters of subterfuge, they evade pursuit, beat around the bush, vanish into a cloud of tricks: false paths, lures, stratagems, ruses of every kind. As they escape, the runaway warriors persist in their being only by disappearing; and from their disappearance they forge a weapon with many sharp edges. In their perpetual movement of retreat and attack, they are accompanied and sustained by women and children, elders and spirits who participate in their battles; a whole moving diaspora from whence unexpected forms of life spring up" (p. 40). The author's love for the fugue extends to its musical sense of polyphony, the *lyannaj* of matching contrapuntal melodies.

Dénètem Touam Bona stresses the extent to which precarity can contribute to freedom when stability is, by contrast, mortifying, at least in extreme cases. This is how a whole mode of pirate existence came to spread historically in the Americas while the shadow of servitude stretched throughout "civilized" lands. There the tree served as shelter and resource; for the art of sculpted wood developed in the *tembe*. In this art, indiscipline becomes a creative ferment that evades all qualification, and therefore all denigration: it promotes decarceration. This homage to the fugitive appeared in French in 2016. In 2021 the author published a supplement to his panegyric: *Sagesses des lianes* (Fécamp: Post-éditions, 2021). What is the wisdom at stake here?

Between these two books, Dénètem Touam Bona went maroon. After working in the backcountry of Guiana and on the artificially insular Mayotte, the island separated politically from the Comoros archipelago, he left "education" behind, together with the "national" frame, and became deterritorialized. Passing through

Réunion along the way, he trusted the compass of intuition and worked up an exhibition titled *The Wisdom of Lianas* in Vassivières, an international center for landscape art in the heart of the French countryside, where he has a freeform residency. He set himself the task of looking at things from the other side: not only the side of those who seek and find refuge in the forest but also the side of what the vegetal itself teaches and offers to the human animal whom it welcomes. There the liana becomes the paradigm of a baroque practical wisdom in which the sinuous takes the place of the rectilinear. Means and ends become distant and recede from sight. They disappear into the shadows of calculation. The *lyannaj*, like the *lésoté*, is an inspiration to continue living, to exist together, to pursue one's path, if not one's goal. Both are responses to the question of how to work together. The *lyannaj* is a technique for binding sugarcanes together; the *lésoté* is a practice, accompanied by chants and drumming, for clearing the meager land that fugitives wrested from the forest in order to live far from masters or people who see themselves in that light.

The *lésoté* is analogous to the Haitian *konbit*, which is said to be the soul of the small peasantry of the first "black republic." This marronage on a grand scale and of great scope led the landowners, who were "positive" in the sense of "positive law," to flee – not to fugue – from the land and the people of Saint Domingue. It was by lending a hand, each in turn, in setting aside one's own interest that the communal agricultural practices appeared without which sometimes the land cannot be worked at all. *Lyannaj* is a term that, likewise, belongs to Creole languages. It became well known in Guadeloupe in 2009, thanks to the the slogan Lyannaj Kont Pwofitasyon ("Solidaristic Movement against the Profiteering System"). *Lyannaj* has a front side and a back side. On the back, *fouté lyann* means to put someone in a difficult position, to prevent them from doing something, to turn the screw. On the front, *nou an lyannaj* means to be together in struggle, to encircle the adversary, to bind oneself to others. Dénètem Touam Bona's trek through the French overseas territories and his familiarity with matters of encirclement have led him to explore the theme of what it is that augments our power to act from within, above all when it faces repression from the outside. The liana entwines without destroying. A climbing and supple plant, it adheres to the trunk around which it wraps, lifting itself and undertaking a fugue toward the light.

From this living being and its remarkable growth, this clandestine passenger of the forest, the author draws a life lesson. Often equipped with specialized organs (drilling tendrils, roots with suckers, hooks, etc.), a liana can sink, drop, then ascend once more. These perturbations leave phantom traces, stems unfurling in the void, deformed, which form a spectrography of twists and bends; and these are nowhere more intense than in the tropical zone. Cosmo-poetics, an act of rediscovery from without and from within, has nothing in common with geopolitics. It leads to the encounter with a cosmos that vanished into what Europe called "nature," in which "natural intelligences" were no longer recognized as such, or at least not sufficiently. Such a rediscovery entails distancing oneself, radically and for all time, from the flying carpet pasted over the tropics that characterizes the movements of Tarzan, the supposed "lord of the jungle."

For Dénètem Touam Bona, this is a way of showing, or rather indicating, how spirituality dwells in these nomad lines of flight that the lianas and *lyannaj* trace in their wisdom. Here, too, he chooses not to be down to earth, not to be "grounded" or ground down, but to grasp, in each twist, each turn, each crossroads of existence, whatever leads to a gain in lightness and allows the universe of the dream to be pierced; he chooses a narrow escape. Defying subservience, this second work pursues reflection along the vanishing line while converging with the body of a subject. Going beyond Deleuze, it holds that there is nothing more active than a "flight," that one can make a system "leak" or "run away" just as one can puncture a hose. This is no simple task: it is to conceive, at once, of a way of walking and a way of dancing, a style for the body, and thus for the soul as well, assuming and assuring a form for the humanity pushed out into the margins, if not altogether denied, in political spaces of abandonment. A "cosmo-poetics of the refuge" takes its widest meaning from this task.

1

Return of the Maroni
(Forest Secession)

West Indians are frightened and ashamed of the past. They know about Christophe and L'Ouverture in Haiti and the Maroons in Jamaica; but they believe that elsewhere slavery was a settled condition, passively accepted through more than two centuries. It is not widely known that in the eighteenth century slave revolts in the Caribbean were as frequent and violent as hurricanes, and that many were defeated only by the treachery of "faithful" slaves.[1]

It took almost a century of guerrilla warfare against the soldiers of the slave system for the N'djuka and Saramaka, groups of deported Africans, to definitively wrest their freedom from the plantation owners of Surinam, formerly Dutch Guiana. In fact, faced with the threat of a general conflagration in the colony in 1760, the Dutch were forced to sign peace treaties with the *nègres marrons* ("black maroons") who were fugitive slaves. These official accords confirmed the autonomy of the N'djuka and Saramaka territories – vast expanses of the Amazonian forest crisscrossed with rivers and creeks, interrupted by marshes and savannahs, and pierced deep by invisible bogs. Several years later, toward 1770, another group of *nègres marrons*, the rebels of the Cottica, launched a new war of liberation that was more radical than its predecessors: their leader, Boni, had decided not simply to seize independence but also to chase the "white master" from

Surinam altogether. This time William of Orange, Stathouder of the United Provinces,[2] put a significant army on the ground that carried the day thanks to its numerical superiority and weaponry and forced the Boni to retreat to the French banks of the Maroni, Sparouine, and Lawa rivers.

> In 1772, a revolt more terrible than any before broke out on the shores of the Cottica. Its leader was a mulatto named Boni, born in the woods to a runaway slave mother. The colonial militias proved insufficient and the prince of Orange was asked for a corps of regular troops to fight back against the insurrection … [Colonel Fourgaud] stuck to his goal, requiring his troops to manoeuver in all weather and in all seasons, across creeks, bogs, savannahs, and wetlands. He paid the cries and protests of the officers and soldiers no heed, but neither did he give the enemy any chance for rest or mercy. The capture of the village of Gado-Saby, where Boni himself was found, dealt the final blow to the insurrection; but the winners paid dearly for their victory. Of 2,000 men sent from Holland, barely 100 returned to their country, sick and exhausted from the consequences of this disastrous affair … Wounded, pushed beyond the limits of endurance, chased successively from his torched villages, Boni led his soldiers' retreat; he crossed the Tapanoni and took refuge in the upper Maroni with the debris of his scattered nation."[3]

Ever since that moment, the destiny of the Boni – who took their name from their heroic ancestor – has been intimately linked to that of French Guiana, where other groups of *marrons* ("maroons") came to join them over the course of time. Today the Boni, the Paramaka, the N'djuka, and the Saramaka represent more than 20 percent of the Guianese population. However, very few works recounting their existence and their history exist in France. This is hardly surprising, given that the majority of books dealing with slavery present marronage as a secondary phenomenon, a simple systemic reaction. The myth of the docile slave remains difficult to uproot… Because this misrecognition of marronage struck me as a new injustice to the deported Africans and their descendants, I decided to spend some time in French Guiana, on the Maroni river, in the hope of learning from the "revolted Negroes" themselves a little more about their hidden history.[4]

Variations on marronage, slavery, and the memory of resistance movements

My stay in Guiana began in Montreuil, on the grounds of the Parole Errante,[5] one spring evening when friends asked me to review the proofs of an interview that they had just completed with Daniel Maximin. In this interview, responding to questions from high-school students [*lycéens*], the Guadeloupean writer explained the different forms of resistance to slavery known throughout the Americas: sabotage, "suicide," poisonings, acts of arson, and revolts – as well as all the cultural practices, more or less secret, through which the slaves reinvented their humanity.[6] When he got to marronage – the general phenomenon of enslaved persons' escape – he described its two major forms: small marronage and great marronage. The first designated limited flights of several hours or several days: slaves went missing to meet with a friend or family member on another plantation, to escape punishment, or to get a tyrannical overseer removed (in the slaveholding system, strikes took the form of a temporary collective flight). The second designated definitive escapes, whether individual or collective, that the slaves undertook by melting into the anonymity of towns or into the impenetrable tangles of nearby forests, hills, and tropical marshes. Sometimes, Maximin explained, this great marronage gave birth to veritable societies of fugitive slaves, maroon communities capable of introducing cracks into the colonial order itself. As Louis Sala-Molins emphasized, "it was by 'marooning' that the Blacks shook the bases of colonial society in the most efficient way and that they became aware of their capacity for systematic opposition and revolt."[7] One might add that continual raids by bands of *neg mawon* against plantations, roads, and isolated villages caused the colonies to tremble in perpetual insecurity, prefiguring the future liberation movements of colonized peoples (for example in Haiti, Vietnam, or Algeria) as well as their guerilla tactics of immersion in the landscape. Let us recall, with Frantz Fanon, that "decolonization, which sets out to change the order of the world, is clearly an agenda for total disorder."[8]

Certainly, I had already heard talk about *nègres marrons*, but had never pictured them to myself as anything but poor vagabonds forced to be brigands, living from one day to the next, and haunted by the threat of "Negro hunters."[9] Never had I suspected that, in certain places and at certain times, they were able to form significant and lasting communities. My first research into this subject touched on the origin and the meaning of their name. In truth, *marron* has nothing to do with color;[10] rather this noun comes from the Spanish *cimarrón*, a term from the Taïno (one of the peoples "discovered" and immediately subjected to "genocide"...).[11] The word was first used on the island of Hispaniola – the future Saint Domingue – to refer to domestic animals imported from Spain (such as pigs, cattle, or cats) who escaped, and in consequence returned to a wild state. Just as runaway bulls were called *toros cimarrónes*, so too the habit arose of calling blacks who escaped into the woods *negros cimarrónes*. It seemed quite natural to displace the meaning of animal stock onto human stock... Around 1540, the use of the noun *marron* spread throughout the slaveholding colonies of the Americas. In the eyes of planters, a black person who escaped slavery could only be an ungrateful and lazy animal, indeed one badly trained. Before it was revalorized by the writers and artists of the Caribbean (above all, after the abolition of slavery in 1848), the word *mawon* became synonymous in Creole with "vagabond," "delinquent," or "bandit." This reduction of meaning contributed to the redaction of Creole memory.

> It is symptomatic that little by little the colonists and their authorities (assisted by the Church) were able to impose on their population the image of the *nègre marron* as an ordinary bandit or assassin, concerned only with avoiding work, to the point where he was made interchangeable in popular representation with the villainous bogeyman used to frighten children. ... Even more telling is the observation that [in the Antilles] the *nègre marron* eventually became exactly what he was said to be, and that at a certain moment he began actually behaving like an ordinary bandit ... an observation teaching us primarily that a community which is deprived of its "natural" popular heroes and which disowns them under the alien-ating pressure of colonial action has disowned itself.[12]

The use of the term *cimarrón* is revealing in more than one respect. First, it expresses the fact that all slavery, whether that of ancient civilizations, Viking conquerors, or Muslim sultans, happens through domestication – a process of training, and therefore an animalization of human beings. Slavery has always obeyed animal-istic models: "From the very beginning there must have been two distinct types of slave: the single slave, linked to his master as a dog is, and numbers of slaves together, like cattle in a field."[13] But with "modern" slavery this definition of roles began to follow a chromatic logic. Usually only the "lightest" colored slaves – particularly the unrecognized offspring and relatives of the master, his bastards – were admitted "inside," in the master's intimate sphere, and could therefore take pride in having gained his confidence. In the initial division between "house Negro" (domesticated, modeled on the image of the master) and "field Negro" (miserable, but always ready to escape), Malcolm X saw one of the keys needed to understand the divisions and the alienation that plagued African–Americans. Malcolm X's claims should not be taken as gospel, to be sure; they were spoken in a polemical context and their main purpose was to disqualify the "integrationist" path represented at the time by Martin Luther King.

> The house Negroes – they lived in the house with master, they dressed pretty good, they ate good because they ate his food... Whenever the master said "we," [they] said "we." That's how you can tell a house Negro. ... If the master got sick, the house Negro would say, "What's the matter, boss, *we* sick?" *We* sick! He identified himself with his master, more than his master identified with himself. And if you came to the house Negro and said, "Let's run away, let's escape, let's separate," the house Negro would look at you and say, "Man, you crazy. What you mean, separate? Where is there a better house than this? Where can I wear better clothes than this? Where can I eat better food than this? That was that house Negro. In those days he was called a "house nigger." And that's what we call them today, because we've still got some house niggers running around here... The field Negro was beaten from morning to night; he lived in a shack, in a hut; he wore old, castoff clothes. He hated his master... If someone came to the field Negro and said, "Let's separate, let's run," he didn't say, "Where we going?" He'd say, "Any place is better than here." You've got field Negroes in America today. I'm a field Negro."[14]

Because the "house Negroes" were not subject to the same conditions of exploitation as the "field Negroes," they might often be considered privileged, if not outright traitors. But, as *The Infamous Rosalie* makes clear, the historical reality is much more complex: this extremely nuanced novel by Evelyne Trouillot reminds us that, because of their proximity to their masters, domestic slaves were also the first to endure humiliation. This is how the *cocotte* – the mistress's favorite slave, responsible for helping her with her toilette

– came to live in a permanent affective swamp, being caught between the plantation owner's lasciviousness and his wife's jealousy. But this "companion" also knew her masters' intimate secrets, therefore their weak points, and from this fact she drew a certain power to influence or indeed to harm them... In the coordination of flights and uprisings, domestic slaves often played an essential role: as information gatherers, as organizers of networks, and as agents of communication between plantations and groups of *marrons*.

However, it is also true that, in colonies like Saint Domingue, the "people of color" – emancipated slaves and their descendants – constituted a major political and social force (in 1789 there were 30,000 whites and an equal number of people of color to about 500,000 slaves). Now, the majority of these free men of color were "mulattos," who sometimes possessed plantation wealth and hundreds of slaves of their own. Moreover, the colonial administration preferred to recruit from among these mulattos when staffing the Maréchaussée – a police force that specialized in verifying the identity of slaves and tracking runaways in order to discourage any possible alliance between mulattos and *nègres*: dividing to conquer all the better... The mulatto is a profoundly ambiguous colonial figure, indeed the traitor par excellence. To be "mixed" means being condemned to betray at least one of one's parents, either the one from the masters' side or the one from among those enslaved. And there is always this lingering odor of bastardy that attaches to your skin, because in a segregationist society being mixed means that you can be only the accursed fruit of rape or of an illicit love.

Thus, in order to defend the color line, that is, the line of demarcation between whites and blacks, plantation society established a correspondence between the chromatic scale and the social scale. This was done in such a way that access to valorized duties and status (domestic servant, artisan, or cook), access to a semblance of education, and even the possibility of emancipation depended on the degree to which one's skin was white, in other words on the "purity" of one's skin. In the eyes of the newly emergent colonial medicine, the norm of healthy humanity was effectively incarnated in the white male, with respect to whom the woman and the indigenous person (whether black or Native American) could only be unhealthy, impure, pathogenic bodies.[15] Because of the disturbance that it introduces into the social–racial order of the slave system, métissage – being of mixed race – represented a kind of pollution, a formidable political and biological peril that must be contained at all costs.[16] This is what led the colonies to elaborate new kinds of taxonomies, subtle ways of calculating "the mixture of whites with *nègres.*"[17] Thus Moreau de Saint-Méry conceived of each individual as the product of 128 parts of "blood." A mulatto, for example, would have sixty-four "white" parts and sixty-four "black" parts. On the strength of this axiom, people of color could be classified into thirteen categories: quadroon, *mamelouc*, *griffe* ("blend"), and so on. Ubuesque as this mathematics of colors might seem today, it nevertheless offered an efficient technology for identifying and sorting people, since it allowed free persons of color to be kept in a subaltern position through the simple application of a norm. Starting in the 1760s, therefore, thousands of people previously considered white were reclassified by the colonial administration of Saint Domingue as mulattos or as quadroons, which automatically denied them access to official positions, inheritances, education, professions, and even to certain types of clothing. This reflected an obsession with any possible confusion between the "mixed-blood" and the white.

As for the "white," still a unified body, it could have only one name. By contrast with blackness, which shifts as often as a lie, whiteness is as unchanging as the truth. In the end, the color line is diffracted into a vast range of nuanced "black skins": "cashew," "caramel," "raw sugar," "prune," peach," "purple," "chocolate," "syrup," "pistachio," "ripe banana," and so on. This inventory of Prévert's – a sample of the designations employed in Saint Domingue – would be almost mouth-watering if it did not point to a sordid "zoo logic" of evaluating the humanity of human beings by their "lightness." Whiteness is a sign of chosenness, blackness of malediction. To be of mixed race is a movement of ascension toward the light when one is attached to someone more light-skinned than oneself, a descent into the shadows when one is attached to someone more dark-skinned. In this respect, Malcolm X's proposals have lost nothing of their sting: one has only to register the popularity, among Africans and their descendants, of "lightening creams" that, although toxic, continue to be viewed as purifying.

> We declare slaves to be possessions [*meubles*] and to enter the community property as such, not to be mortgaged, and to be divided equally among co-inheritors.[18]

In his pathbreaking analysis in *De l'esclavage au salariat* (1998), Yann Moulier Boutang shows that the prime mover in the history of capitalism is the freezing in place of a constantly fugitive labor force: the ceaselessly renewed effort to capture the landless peasant, the nomad bohemian, the runaway apprentice, the deserting soldier, the escaped slave, the incorrigible vagabond, everyone who resisted the imposition of discipline. Flight – and, more generally, resistance – is therefore primary in relation to power. Moreover, "one of the primary objects of discipline" (of disciplinary power, exercised in European factories as much as on Creole plantations) "is to fix; it is an anti-nomadic technique."[19] Racism is nothing but the chemical agent that fixes the labor capacity of certain human beings when it fixes their color – not only on the surface but also at the greatest depth of their sense of self – as the ultimate truth to which they must submit. Color is fixation, both a shackle and an obsession. As I have already said, all enslavement proceeds from an animalization of human beings. But the reduction of humans to the color of their skin, which is to say their hide, is the properly colonial form of this animalization. Far more than a mere word, *nègre* is the paradigmatic weapon of the chief reducer, the colonist. To every enslaved person tempted by flight, the black codes issue this warning: "you can run, but I will always find you again, no matter where you are... because you wear the mark of the slave, the mark of the beast, the mark of your damnation: a skin as black as your soul, if you even have one... You, my precious, my treasure, my adored 'possession.'"

> Run, nigger, run; de patter-roller catch you
> Run, nigger, run, it's almost day ...
> Dat nigger run, Dat nigger flew, Dat nigger lost his Sunday shoe.
> Dis nigger run, he run his best...[20]

The *cimarrón* is a runaway slave, tearing off a servile skin to take on the striated shadow of foliage in his or her mad sprint. His or her liberation comes about from a process of going wild, from an act of immersion in the forest, the *sylve* (from the Latin noun *silva* "forest," which is at the root of our word "savage") – an act that makes him into a forest creature, a "leaf-being."[21] The Businenge – a generic name for the maroons of Guiana – are nothing but "men of the forest," as the etymology of this name indicates. In fact *busi nenge* comes from an alteration in the English phrase "bush Negroes." But in Busitongo, which is the maroon language, *nenge* means "person," not "slave" (*nègre*). This detour of meaning, which creatively subverts the colonist's language, constitutes a retort to the fixation of a defamatory identity in the soul and body of the enslaved person. In choosing to call themselves "Nenge," the Boni threw the stigma, the insult, right back at the ones who spit on them: from this shameful color, *el negro*, they wove the flag of their liberation and their reconquered humanity.

> Anacaona, who rose up against the Conquistadors before anyone else in the Americas... The Golden Flower [which is what "Anacaona" means] began by chanting the poem of the enslaved miners who worked at the bottom of the gold-digging canyons, and proclaimed the despair of families in the *repartimientos*,[22] the whip of the commanders snapping over the laughter of running water, the epidemics brought by the knights ... the collective suicides after long nights of prayer, finally the interminable baying of the Spanish priests calling the Indians to be converted to the enslavers' god, with their crosses, their hoods and the incense of prayer hovering over the systematic extermination of an entire people... We are all the sons of the Golden Flower."[23]

For anyone who knows how to hear it, the cry of the Taïno still resonates in the word *cimarrón*. The Taïno were the first to be reduced to slavery, and were therefore the first *cimarrónes* of the Americas. The exiled Africans will borrow the same lines of flight as their Amerindian predecessors; and the marronage of each group will be mutually nourished by the others. It was precisely in order to celebrate the memory of these first acts of resistance to colonization that the "black Jacobins" of Saint Domingue called their new nation by one of the original names of the island: Haiti. The first African slaves were introduced to Hispaniola in 1499. As early as 1503, the island's governor, Ovando, complained that blacks were having a pernicious influence on the Taïno: "He opposed as much as he could the sending of Negroes to the Indies, having observed that the earliest of those who came to the Spanish isle ran off among the natives to whom they taught everything bad, of which they were capable and which made them much more difficult to control."[24] In Martinique, one can still pause for reflection at the "gravestone of the Caribbean," a rock from which the last "native" fighters threw themselves, preferring communion in death to the putrefaction of their life as slaves. The Spanish colonists used the expressions *indios cimarrónes* and *indios salvajes* interchangeably, to designate native communities who refused to submit to the Spanish Crown. In the eyes of the sovereign, insubordination always means savagery or barbarism. As everyone knows, laziness is the mother of all vices and work is health; *Arbeit macht frei...* The lazy and lustful nature of the native must therefore be subjected to the moralizing action of labor. These big children – who live only for enjoyment – must submit to the emancipatory yoke of Reason. In short, they must be made into men. Thus slavery refers to a "civilizing mission," however cruel ...

A traveler at the end of the eighteenth century made these observations:

> [The colonists] still much prefer the creole *nègre* to the *nègre* from Africa. In fact, one can hardly count the obstacles that must be surmounted before the latter can be useful. Foreign for a long time in the New World, ignorant of the customary language and the kind of work expected of him, always immersed in longing for his country... On the other hand, what the creole *nègre* sees when his eyes open for the first time is nothing but what he will see for his whole life. Nourished in slavery, his spirit like his body is insensibly molded by small trials and has plenty of time to get used to the crudest work.[25]

The most difficult to govern was the "bossal" [*bossale*], the slave newly arrived from Africa, still "savage," which is to say untamed. This was the category of enslaved persons in which one could find the greatest number of men and women ready to brave the bottomless forests, the swampy deltas, and the filigree of craters in order to re-create their humanity, new brotherhoods, and new lines of ancestry in the space achieved by escape. *Bossale* comes from the Spanish *bozal* and designates a type of bit, bridle, or muzzle. Moreover, among the kinds of shackles imposed on unruly slaves – runaways, saboteurs, dissemblers, those who dared taste the sugar cane, those who defied the "commander" with their speech or fists – there existed "muzzles": iron masks fixed on the head with rivets that allowed their victims to do nothing but see and breathe. To bridle an enslaved person does not stop his or her movement but governs it, submits it to a disciplinary rule and to the sovereign's power, so that nothing remains of it but useful force, exploitable energy, an abstraction fashioned entirely from resistance to its human material. Because the black person's usefulness is proportional to his or her docility and in order for that servitude to seem natural, the slave must be shaped from the most tender years of childhood onward: custom becomes nature through habituation. This is why the colonist preferred the *nègre créole* "possession" cast in the mold of enslavement. For the planter,[26] this "serf-man has lost the memory of his first being" – freedom:

> Custom becomes the first reason for voluntary servitude. Men are like handsome race horses who first bite the bit and later like it, and rearing under the saddle a while soon learn to enjoy displaying their harness and prance proudly beneath their trappings. Similarly men will grow accustomed to the idea that they have always been in subjection, that their fathers lived in the same way; they will think they are obliged to suffer this evil, and will persuade themselves by example and imitation of others, finally investing those who order them around with proprietary rights, based on the idea that it has always been that way.[27]

Slavery does not exclude an aspect of voluntary servitude, because it cannot be reduced to a relation of violence (direct action on bodies: force, bending, breaking, destruction). There is always some room for play, however tiny, in the condition of the enslaved person. If not, how could the outbreak of resistance movements be explained? To enclose the enslaved person – or, in general, the colonized – in the status of a victim is to deny her all capacity for action. Believing that it honors her memory, it perpetuates her dehumanization. As Foucault stresses, "slavery is not a power relationship when a man is in chains (in this case it is a question of the physical relation of constraint), but only when he has some possible mobility, even a chance of escape."[28] From the moment he is no longer chained, the enslaved person can modify the strategic situation. It takes very little to topple the relations of force in that situation, which explains the permanent state of tension, paranoia, and fear among the masters and also sheds light on the extreme violence with which the enslaved person's least infraction was repressed. On the slaving ships, the critical moment always occurs when the black cargo is uncaged. This is because on the ship's deck, where they are allowed to wash themselves and shake out their limbs, the exiles rediscover a small margin of movement. So much so that it takes no more than a second of distraction for a mutiny to explode or for the slaves to fling themselves overboard.

> So that afternoon this young Hausa woman began to dance with her man. ... The whites were laughing. Afraid yet fascinated, they were inventing thousands of fantasies. Then the drumming of our hands

and feet stopped cold. In the same spirit the man and the woman sprung forward and threw themselves into the sea.[29]

If a lesson can then be drawn from all these histories of *nègres marrons*, it is truly one of hope, and not a requiem or a victimology. A situation of domination, whatever it might be, always contains possibilities for resistance, action, creation. For marronage cannot be reduced to a simple refusal of "civilization," a simple reaction against the slavery system, a simple rejection of Babylon (the image embodying every system of predation and exploitation for the Rastafarian movement); marronage is above all an inventive rejoinder that includes attitudes, corporeal techniques, an entire system of in-corporated knowledge. The body is the first theater of operation, the first position to free, the first right to re-establish. The indocile body of the enslaved person – the first complete proletarian – may not be visible as a spectacle and remains imperceptible most of the time, making use of ruses, tactics, and strategies that range from the concerted slowdown of work or negligence to the damage, or even deliberate sabotage, of machines or of production. Thus the stereotype of the "lazy black" reveals one of the thousand forms of micro-resistance against exploitation available to the colonized – a complete art of evasion already implicit in marronage.

Fleeing into the woods makes the maroon into an outlaw, someone who violates the conditions of his own exile and thereby belongs among the social criminals described by Hobsbawm (including figures like Robin Hood or Zapata): "escaped serfs, ruined freemen, runaways from state or seignorial factories, from jail, seminary, army, or navy... formed or joined brigand bands."[30] Like the Waldgänger, the Scandinavian exile of the Middle Ages, the maroon takes back his freedom using the forests. In the Germanic law of the high Middle Ages, the banned individual is defined as a creature excluded from humanity, as a "'wolf-man' (*wargus, werwolf*, the Latin *garulphus,* from which the French *loup garou,* 'werewolf,' is derived)."[31] Thus identified with a dangerous and bloody beast, he may be killed by whoever encounters him. In colonial society, the black rebel also shares this limit condition of the wild man but, by contrast with the medieval exile, he chooses and claims his banishment. The renegade effects a secession, withdrawing from a society that is not one, since it constantly denies the humanity of most of those who compose it. Marronage is a paradoxical process: to escape from the master's power over animals – from the condition of human livestock – presupposes the willingness to enter into a becoming-animal, to proliferate in the form of mobs, hordes, multitudes that are as rebellious as they are imperceptible – to go from being prey to becoming a predator...

> [Colonel Fourgeoud] promised them life, liberty, victuals, drink, and all they wanted. They replied, with a loud laugh, that they wanted nothing from him; characterized him as a half-starved Frenchman, who had run away from his own country; and assured him that if he would venture to pay *them* a visit, he should return unhurt, and not with an empty belly. They told us, that we were to be pitied more than they; that we were *white slaves*, hired to be shot at and starved for fourpence a day; that they scorned to expend much more of their powder upon such scarecrows; but should the planters or overseers dare to enter the woods, not a soul of them should ever return, any more than the perfidious rangers, some of whom might depend upon being massacred that day, or the next; and concluded by declaring that *Bonny* should soon be the governor of the colony.[32]

There is something carnivalesque about this proposal, which reverses positions and dissolves negative presuppositions by employing an acid language in which irony and contempt are wedded. In the maroon arsenal of "voluntary insubordination,"[33] laughter doubtless represents the most diabolical weapon: it brings down the exalted, blackens the white, and throws the seriousness of the dominant order into disarray, along with its supporting dogmas. The *revolted Negroes* hold up a mirror to their hunters: "you track us like wild beasts, but you do not see that you yourselves are slaves, barefoot, collapsing from hunger!" Here the Boni fighters allude to a concrete political and social reality: the great majority of white soldiers were either pressed into service or forced to enlist – forced through misery, debts, or crimes they had committed.[34] Thus, when these rebels offer hospitality to solders of the expeditionary force sent against them, this is not merely a ruse or an irony. They know quite well who the true enemies are: the great proprietors, the merchants, and the "India companies"; in short, those who hold the land and capital – and not their guard dogs (except for the "black rangers" who were considered traitors).

> Having been informed that ... a village of negroes had been discovered by the rangers some time before, [Mr. Lepper] determined with his small party, which was only a detachment from the Patamaca post,

to sally through the woods and attack them. But the rebels being apprized of his intentions by their spies, which they constantly employ, immediately marched out to receive him; in his way they laid themselves in ambush, near the borders of a deep marsh... No sooner had the unfortunate men got into the swamp and up to their armpits, than their black enemies rushed out from under cover, and shot them dead at their leisure in the water, while they were unable to return the fire more than once, their situation preventing them from reloading their musquets. Their gallant commander, being imprudently distinguished by a gold-laced hat, was shot through the head in the first onset. The few that scrambled out of the marsh upon the banks were immediately put to death in the most barbarous manner.[35]

The maroon guerrillas had no hatred toward the whites; for, to hate, one must be afraid, and they were no longer afraid... Fear had disappeared at the same time as the master. For there to be a master, there must be a slave who recognizes him. Now the experience of struggle, the "practice" of violence, the play of hand-to-hand combat laid bare the equal humanity of both the one and the other. A struggle for liberation cannot hesitate too much over the use of violence, but this is not a matter of immemorial human violence (which is always invoked to justify, in advance, the violence of the Leviathan, the sovereign, or the state); rather it is primarily a matter of violence to the self, the slave, the dead who live in us. What must be purged with violence is all these mystifications by which the master paralyzes me and possesses me – the idea that I am only a *nègre* with repulsive features, a talking monkey, a living tool, a beast of burden, a human dead-end – all these mystifications that produce rottenness, rancor, or the zombie in me. To do oneself violence: no longer to lower one's eyes, no longer to tremble, no longer to kneel, no longer to shut up, no longer to obey, and when the occasion presents itself to fight back, "to flee, but in fleeing to seek a weapon."[36] The masters are so great, to paraphrase La Boétie, only because we are on our knees. If Fanon praises combat, it is because there is a kind of jubilation in struggle and, as a result of deploying his desire and joy, the colonized person recovers the power to act: it is only in the very movement of revolt and of turning back against the intolerable that he comes into his own as a subject, as the author of his thoughts and actions.

The colonized subject thus discovers that his life, his breathing and his heartbeats are the same as the colonist's. He discovers that the skin of a colonist is not worth more than the "native's." ... The colonized's revolutionary new assurance stems from this. If, in fact, my life is worth as much as the colonist's, his look can no longer strike fear into me or nail me to the spot and his voice can no longer petrify me. I am no longer uneasy in his presence. In reality, to hell with him. Not only does his presence no longer bother me, but I am already preparing to waylay him in such a way that soon he will have no other solution but to flee.

At the individual level, violence is a cleansing force. It rids the colonized of their inferiority complex, of their passive and despairing attitude. It emboldens them, and restores their self-confidence.[37]

Can one imagine the master liberating the slave simply because the latter asks for it? Quite often, the discourse of peace is a pacifying discourse whose goal is to criminalize in advance any subaltern contestation of the established order: pirates and maroons, witches and heretics, *communards* and *pétroleuses*, the dangerous classes and the Black Panthers... In the eyes of an empire, there is no war in Saint Domingue, there is no war in Algeria, there is no war in Vietnam: just peacekeeping operations. This is because one does not make war on "savages" or "barbarians," one pacifies them. Every Rome, every empire, presupposes a *pax romana*. The colonial order rests on violence – a foundational and conservative violence of the masters' right [*droit*]: the law of the conqueror, the one established at swordpoint and bellowing from the cannon's mouth.[38] This violence derails the counterviolence of the colonizer by bringing its impunity to an end. The violence celebrated by Fanon is therefore not an instrumental violence – according to which the end would justify the means – but violence as praxis, as subjectivation of the self, as a process of giving birth to oneself. It is a matter of bringing about a "self" that would no longer be some master's creature, a docile "Uncle Tom" who identifies with his master more than his master identifies with himself. The violence of Saint Domingue's insurgent slaves simply exemplifies the same right of resistance to oppression that the American and French Revolutions proclaimed throughout the world.

In certain colonies such as Brazil or Colombia, though rarely in Surinam, maroon communities often served as a refuge for deserting soldiers, shipwrecked pirates, Indians escaping the *repartimientos* – the wretched of the earth in every color. What is fascinating in the odyssey of the Boni is that, just like the maroons of São Tomé led by Amador, they fought up to the very end to destroy the enslaving system, thereby endangering their very existence.[39] In 1789, when they had already been forced to take refuge in French Guiana, the Boni made a final effort: "By making an audacious trek through the forest, they reached the Surinam river at the heart of the Dutch colony, setting the great plantation of Clarenbeek and several others on fire. But this movement was not followed by a general slave revolt."[40] It was in the course of this last military expedition that Boni, the maroon chief, met his end. This type of marronage is characterized less by flight than by strategic retreat or furtive secession (from Latin *secessio*, the action of *secedere* – "withdrawing," "pulling away"): a leap outside the space of the plantation that opens the possibility not only of a de-domesticated life but also of undertaking a later offensive. For this reason, the Haitian Revolution could never be considered a simple repetition of the American Revolution or the French: it is inscribed in the continuity of maroon guerrilla struggles, which led to the secession of more or less vast territories throughout the Americas. As we can see from the rhetorical slant of the peace treaties, the autonomy of these territories was recognized by colonial authorities who lacked the power to subdue them (particularly in the case of the terrible colonial wars led against the Quilombolas of Brazil, the Palenqueros of Columbia, and the Maroons of Jamaica).

Everywhere, in the anti-marronage regulations, he is called bandit, savage, or brigand. Now the *marrons* live in an organized way, re-create a familial and religious system, accept the coexistence of Africans from different ethnic groups, cultivate the land. Just as regularly, they organize wholesale expeditions to pillage workshops or plantations. In order to survive the continual hunts that the masters lead against them, they have established a defensive structure for the camps where they settle. Without the support of these camps, many revolts could not have taken place. Similarly, the practices of poisoning that stirred panic among masters throughout the eighteenth century supposed a very close link between domestic slaves and the maroons. But 1750 is the year in which premeditated poisonings, this time with an explicit eye to marronage, will become the formidable weapon of leaders who announce the general liberation of slaves and call them to insurrection.[41]

To be a maroon at war means to be capable of disappearing at any moment in order to reappear on the surface and attack precisely where no one expects you; to know how to melt into the most varied kinds of natural settings and to draw an advantage from their accidental features. Marronage thus becomes a genuine art of the fugue, an art of variation. The site where people live, more of a camp than a village, represents only one variable in a great game of hide-and-seek played at the level of enormous regions: dense forests, arid and aggressive *caatinga*, mountains with abrupt slopes. Marronage always supposes a form of nomadism. Even when a maroon community remains in the same place for a long time, it remains nomadic, in other words stealthy, because of its capacity to escape the gaze and the grasp of external forces. Cultivating invisibility is a question of life or death when one is faced with far more numerous and much better armed enemies. Protected by devouring swamps mined with deadly traps, Boucou, one of Boni's strongholds, was accessible only via paths submerged in water.

> I have called this settlement strong, because, like an island, it was entirely surrounded by a broad unfordable marsh or swamp, which prevented all communication, except by private paths under water, known only to the rebels... it was moreover fenced and inclosed [*sic*] on every side by several thousand strong pallisadoes [*sic*], and was on the whole no contemptible fortification.[42]

To camouflage the community, to remove it from watchful eyes, is to extend the forest's cover, to prolong the shadow of its foliage, to call down the fog of the marshes on oneself.

> The great geographical adventures of history are lines of flight, that is, long expeditions on foot, on horseback or by boat: that of the Hebrews in the desert, that of Genseric the Vandal crossing the Mediterranean, that of nomads across the steppe, the long march of the Chinese.[43]

Each maroon line of flight is the unforeseeable resultant of many variables: natural settings (such as mountains and rocky craters, boggy deltas, dense forests); the respective importance of different categories of population (big landowners, "small whites," Amerindians, freshly arrived Africans, "Creole" blacks, mulattos – among others); geopolitical configurations (conflicts between rival colonial powers, for example); and types of productive operations (mines, plantations, fisheries, transportation for commodities, domesticity, etc.).

The classic distinction between "small" and "great" marronage originates in the discourse of the slavery system: it served to establish the gravity of escape and the level of punishment risked by fugitives. Rather than revisit this heritage, I will therefore sketch a new typology:

- occasional marronage: individual temporary acts of flight; a form of absenteeism or strike by the enslaved;
- "clandestine" marronage: "For the slaves who lived in the environs of Cap or Port-au-Prince, the populous quarters, the markets located at city gates, and the faceless crowds of the ports offered the possibility for moving about rather freely among the deck hands, carters, slaves on commission... ."[44] In order to ward off eventual surveillance by the Maréchaussée, fugitive slaves had recourse to the services of educated free people of color who would counterfeit travel authorizations and letters of emancipation. At this moment, the outlawed maroon merges with the contemporary figure of the *sans papiers*, the undocumented;
- marronage of "secession" (withdrawal): movement of collective retreat that sets the growth of an underground community in motion: quilombos and mocambos in Brazil; palenques, cumbes, patucos of the Spanish Americas, and so on. What opens the possibility of a liberated zone, of a "heterotopia," is the fold back into the forest.

If my approach to marronage gives pride of place to what I call "secession," this is because the creative dimension of maroon resistance is best illustrated by the secretive communities to which it gives birth. In fact these are the cases in which marronage appears fully as the seedbed for new forms of life, as the creator of novel values diametrically opposed to those of the plantation society. In the collective epics of maroon peoples we find an affirmative force that arises independently of any dialectic between master and slave.

> Europeans tend to believe that he [the great man or maroon chief] commands the tribe in the same way in which a colonel commands a regiment ... The great man possesses hardly any temporal power ... For everything that concerns material life, each has the absolute right, one might even say the duty, to act as seems best for himself,

so long as he does not harm anyone... Among the Refugee Blacks there exists no privileged class and all face life on a footing of rigorous equality... None of them practiced any form of commerce, this activity being manifestly linked in their minds to the idea of exploiting others...The villages do not even have markets. Each one produces, or finds among the people of the same lineage, whatever he or she needs to eat.[45]

Leadership among the Boni comes close to the Amerindian chieftainship described by Clastres: the chief has no instituted power apart from his prestige.[46] His domain of competence is limited to the relation with sacred powers and to the mediation of disputes. The Boni have therefore laid bare a series of mechanisms that prevent the accumulation of power and wealth. The maroon community strives to ward off [conjurer] the risk of allowing a separate power to form within its own body, the risk of the master's return, or the perpetuation of domination. The experience of resistance to enslavement shaped Businenge culture through and through, which explains the traditional prohibitions weighing on commerce or on employing others (prohibitions that have lost their force today) and the central place accorded to the individual's autonomy. Maroon societies are not miniature reproductions of Africa but, much like Creole societies, composite cultures: the unforeseeable resultant of an encounter between heterogenous cultures. As "bare migrants,"[47] the common ancestors of the Businenge and Creoles knew how to draw on elements from European, Amerindian, and African societies in order to reinvent a culture. Certainly, the Businenge are not Creoles, but the genesis of their culture testifies to what Édouard Glissant calls a process of "Creolization."[48]

One of the things that struck me most forcefully during my time in Guiana was the ignorance, the indifference, and indeed the scorn that many Guianese Creoles affected toward the history and the culture of their Businenge compatriots. It is not so much physical appearance as the way each group relates to its respective history that distinguishes the Creoles from the maroons. Many Caribbean writers (including Naipaul, Chamoiseau, and Damas) have stressed this point: Creoles, marked as they are by enslavement and the self-loathing that this institution inculcates, have difficulty relating to their own past without shame or rancor, when they do not repress it plain and simple. Their mixed status, this "caramel" tone whose beauty is celebrated by tourist agencies and creamy Créola desserts, hides a *différend*: "Abena, my mother, was raped by an English sailor on the deck of *Christ the King* one day in the year 16** while the ship was sailing for Barbados. I was born from this act of aggression. From this act of hatred and contempt."[49] Male domination and racial domination went hand in hand, on the slaving ship as well as on plantations: rape was one of the chief instruments of the slave system's violence, a theme that returns elsewhere in the literature of the West Indies. Here there is a striking contrast with the Businenge – a community proud of its history, even if it is just as filled with betrayals, acts of cowardice, and compromises as all other histories.[50] This is not about judging or knowing whether it is the Creoles or the Businenge who are right or wrong, but about understanding the consequences of both sides' divergent forms of historical consciousness [*conscience*]. For example, inasmuch as they descend from the enslaved, Creoles will tend to feel themselves damaged by "history," to consider themselves victims, to demand reparation. "Creole" history is a wound, a trauma, a rape. As descendants of "revolted Negroes," on the other hand, the Businenge will tend to consider themselves the actors of their own history. If they have struggles to carry out, these will be in continuity with older struggles – in such a way that they will consider history a reserve of forces and not a source of complexes. Their memory of past battles is in fact always ready to be reactivated, as is illustrated by the conflict in Surinam that lasted until 1992:

> In 1986, a civil war pitting the Maroons against the national army brought back to life many of the horrors of the eighteenth-century colonial struggles. African medicine bundles that had lain buried for two hundred years were unearthed and carried into battle... Ndjuka and Saramaka warriors, often armed with shotguns, confronted the army's automatic weapons, tanks, and helicopter gunships dropping napalm.[51]

The ancestors of the Creoles undoubtedly showed as much combativeness as the fugitives who were their contemporaries, but their more subterranean style of resistance has been papered over, little by little, by an official history implicitly resting on the myth of the docile slave. The grand narrative of abolition functions as the privileged instrument of a "French" history that excludes Creoles from their own "liberation." Every street, every square, every school, every monument that, in the former French slaveholding colonies (Antilles, Réunion, Guiana), celebrates Victor Schoelcher's memory[52] simultaneously rejects, throws into silence, and overshadows each of the emancipated, each of the enslaved, each of the maroons who contributed actively to the end of slavery. The slaves never expected that someone would deign to liberate them; and the evidence is the general and constant phenomenon of marronage. Resulting from the conjoint action of free people of color, rebellious slaves, and maroons, the Haitian Revolution of 1804 likewise attests to the determining role that the *nègres* played in their own liberation. These were *nègres* who knew how to appropriate the ideals of the French Revolution – the soldiers of the "indigenous army"[53] sang the Marseillaise or other French revolutionary songs as they went into battle – and how to turn them against their own authors, thereby contributing to the active elaboration of a true universalism: human rights extended to the whole of humanity and not simply reserved for the "white man," as in the American or in the French Revolution. Thus struggles against slavery – insurrections, marronages, juridical and political combats, and so on – were pioneering struggles of political modernity.

> This victory of 1804 is a beautiful accident of history, something that at the time was inconceivable, unimaginable, running against the current of history. The present shipwreck in no way diminishes the splendor of this event. In a region where slavery was the rule, in a century when the European powers divided the world among themselves in the name of white racial superiority, Haiti, this black republic, could only be an anomaly, an act of defiance.[54]

For those descended from Africans, the reconstruction of self-esteem passes necessarily through the revalorization of their ancestors' modes of resistance: this is one way for them to reappropriate, for their own ends, a history largely written from the point of view of the "conquerors."[55] How can the resistance struggles of "black" peoples be taken seriously without at the same time falling into folklore or mythology? The turn to historical research appears indispensable: the problem is that, even today, such research is focused on the organization of the plantation, on the mechanics of the "triangular trade," on acts of "abolition" – in short, on the visible surface of the history of slavery. Only rarely does it explore the obscure domain of "resistances" for its own sake. We must admit that the multiple, local, punctual, and most often anonymous

acts of resistance to which the slave system gave rise benefited from
no official chroniclers.

> Women are rediscovered in the course of writing women's history, the
> mechanisms of their domination are revealed, and their oppression,
> their silence, their revolt, their obstructive force are understood. The
> idea that women have always been passive is completely false; they
> have always tried to escape. Doing women's history means rediscov-
> ering forms of domination but also forms of cultural expression and
> resistance.[56]

The recently published works on women's history, that other
forgotten zone, can serve as a model for a history of anti-slavery
resistance movements.[57] Indeed, they show that in the absence of
written traces we must know how to rely on oral and material
memory and combine complementary disciplines if we want to
dissipate the shadow that surrounds actions, "micro-actions," and
the whole palette of the modes of expression and resistance used by
those who are dominated. From this point of view, the Businenge
communities, among which resistance to enslavement shaped not
only the collective memory but also interpersonal relations and
society as a whole, are exceptionally interesting. "First-Time"
knowledge, the vast historical corpus of the maroons, constitutes a
counter-history in its own right, a history whose first historians were
the actors themselves, a history whose principal theme is the fight for
freedom.[58] To treat acts of resistance to slavery as historical in their
own right, to begin inquiries starting from African–American oral
traditions and the infinite richness of their musical forms, dances,
and syncretic cults, to bend an ear to the sounds of past struggles
that have survived in maroon cultures: this means decoding as many
traces for a different reading of the history of slavery, a reading that
finally does justice to the enslaved and their descendants.

> The Peruvian Indians... demonstrated fierce fidelity to their old
> traditions because, of course, no other form of revolt was available
> to them (except in the imagination). From the start of his rebellion
> Manco Inca indicated the form this fidelity to tradition should take:
> resistance to the Spaniards. Passive resistance, certainly, by the force
> of inertia; but that force was deliberate and cultivated, the inertia
> ferociously defended. Here tradition provided the means of refusal;
> silent, obstinate refusal, repeated with each new generation. And
> to the extent that fragments of the former Inca civilization have

persisted down through the centuries to the present day, one may even say that this type of revolt, this impossible praxis has, in a way emerged triumphant. The vanquished Indians have, in defeat, won a moving victory.[59]

I wanted to use an investigation into the maroon community as a way of paying homage to popular forms of resistance, particularly those of the Amerindians and the descendants of Africans. A revolt can never be reduced to a simple, instinctive reaction, as the classic – animalistic and Pavlovian – interpretation of indigenous insurrections would have it. In the very gesture of refusing European domination, Native Americans and Africans expressed positive attachment to the culture by which they defined themselves. But acts of indigenous resistance did not truly take the form of violent revolts; they were defined first and foremost by cultural practices. They always presupposed the maintenance and the reinvention of a tradition on the basis of its tiniest traces, in opposition to the amnesia that all colonial power attempts to impose – whence the importance of dances, rhythms, religious rituals in the genesis of black and Native American insurrections. Neither can the relationship between resistance and memory be seen as one of conservation. Even as they provide an anchoring point for acts of resistance, memories are transformed by the very action that would save them: they are taken back up in an original, absolutely new sense, that of revolt against the order of colonization. Those who were long perceived as "savages" and thereby denied any form of political action and life have their own concrete utopias, their own liberation theologies, their own political spiritualities. And it may be that in our future struggles – struggles for a world that would no longer be governed by the fear of the other, by predation and generalized commodification – we will have to learn some subterfuges from them…

On the verge of a line of flight: a tale of experience

Travel diary:
A little after my arrival in Cayenne in September 2002, I managed to obtain a teaching job on the Maroni River, in Apatou. This village was approximately two hours by canoe from Saint-Laurent,

the second largest city of Guiana. In a packed dirt parking lot near "Chicago," one of the troubled neighborhoods of Cayenne, minibuses were waiting on standby. This is the only "bus depot" in the prefecture of Guiana. It costs €30 to make the 250-kilometer ride along the paved road that separates Cayenne from Saint-Laurent-du-Maroni, the former capital of the penal colony. No need to try to find a timetable; the "taxicos" do not hit the road until all seats are taken, and therefore departures are random. A little past Iracoubo, on the road linking Cayenne to Saint-Laurent, the countryside visibly changes. The forest becomes more persistent; the littoral plateau, its grasslands, its farming and grazing zones are progressively left behind, and one is gradually buried in the land's interior. The asphalt ribbon of National 1 weaves between modest undulations and their subtle shades of green, whose range varies depending on the nature of the vegetation and the sky's animation. The Creole communes give way to small maroon and Amerindian villages: a succession of open dwellings on stilts and small houses, simple constructions made of unfinished wood planks, woven palm leaves, sheet-metal roofs with nuances of aluminum plating and orangey rust. We pass a black woman carrying on her head a bowl filled with manioc and yams, short Amerindians pushing a cart through a field with cut logs (slash and burn farming), a young Saramaka aiming his slingshot in the direction of the treetops: as Saint-Laurent approached, another Guiana came into view, very different from that of the coastal regions of Cayenne, Kourou, or Sinnamary.

At Saint-Laurent, the Maroni River forms a large, long lake whose brown or gilded waters bathe vast expanses of earth – islands covered with a bushy vegetation – depending on the angle of the sun's rays and the density of the clouds. We are in the estuary of the largest river in Guiana. The currents and tides are strong, the winds cause shivers in the palm trees' chiseled foliage. From this place called La Glacière, which is very close to the Charbonnière neighborhood (the "maroon" quarter of Saint-Laurent), canoe taxis depart for the upstream villages. The Maroni River takes its name from the maroon populations that populate its shores. The entire life of the maroon blacks centers around the river and the infinite tangle formed by creeks in the land's interior. "Liba" refers to the river as much as to the territory. The territory of the maroons of Guiana is a flux – a smooth space with variations of intensity, leaps, and ruptures. Boni, N'djuka, and Saramaka define themselves as *businenge*, "men of the forest" – but also as masters of the river.

The pier of La Glacière consists of a simple beach of dark sand, humid and heavy, a beach strewn with tin cans, shards of glass bottles, plastic bags, and other refuse of our modernity. Every morning, between 9 and 11 o'clock, a half-dozen canoes park there directly on the sand, ready to load passengers and merchandise. To convince travelers to choose their company, so that they can then pocket the €12 of the Saint-Laurent–Apatou trip (50 km as the bird flies), each canoe driver claims to have the best boat and the most powerful motor. It is not easy to choose; the taxis of the Maroni are all equally flamboyant, their sides and their seats covered in vivid colors, some ornamented with *tembe* (traditional motifs), others with symbols or Rastafarian characters, or even with enticing pinups. Conceived of both for speed and for transporting freight in fairly shallow waters, dotted with rapids, these canoes and their perfectly sharp lines are without doubt the most beautiful skiffs in all Amazonia.

Once the departure time arrives, the pilot pulls off the first sputters from his motor (generally 75 hp). Then, slightly unbalanced by the wake, the canoe picks up its prow and launches toward the other bank of the Maroni, toward Albina, the Surinamian neighbor of Saint-Laurent. This is a small makeshift port where the *botoman* ("boatman") comes regularly to load up on fuel and various kinds of merchandise. From a distance, the famous scallop of the Shell company can be made out on the side of three huge aluminum-plated cisterns. Albina's pier is just as rudimentary as that of La Glacière, but the riverbank is better kept up and much more animated. All along its length and in the adjoining side paths, one finds a series of large groceries where everything can be found for sale: sacks of potatoes, rice, onions, Morello cartridges, packs of Parbo beer, canned vegetables, baby food, hardware supplies, and so on. The advertisements are painted directly on the walls; most of them portray glasses, bottles of alcohol, and packets of cigarettes. A little further back, minibuses park near a dilapidated music kiosk. The drivers chat with one another or hail potential clients, while waiting to go back on the road – a battered path – in the direction of the Surinamian capital, Paramaribo.

When the canoe finally leaves Albina and the pair of Indians carved into the stone that silently preserve its banks, an hour and a half to two hours of navigation still remain before we will reach

Apatou. The maroon pilots take invisible roads; for a while they travel on the Surinamian bank, then come back to the Guianese side, and finally commit themselves to the middle of the river; they endlessly explore new paths through the water. This tacking back and forth never happens by chance; moreover, the waters of the Maroni are treacherous (particularly at low tide and during the dry season), the currents are powerful in certain places, and sandbanks and rocks are always a worry. Quite precise itineraries must therefore be followed, to draw maximum advantage from the currents and avoid foundering, running aground on sand, or colliding with submerged rocks. This explains the importance of the "takarist," the pilot stationed on the vessel's prow where, as we go along, he can decipher the surface of the river in order to thwart its caprices. When confronted with rapids, this tightrope walker mobilizes the whole of his body atop the waters' thread: he manoevers using a *pali* ("oar") or a *takari*, a long wooden pole, and by enigmatic pantomimes, shows the *botoman* the path that must be followed through the difficult parts. Officially the Maroni is not navigable, but no law regulates its navigation. To navigate there is already to be an outlaw. And what could be more natural, since we are among the descendants of the "revolted Negroes"...

As soon as Albina and Saint-Laurent disappear behind the stern of the canoe and the silvery backwash of the waters, the murky green of the Amazonian forest extends as far as the eye can see. The banks of the river are the only place where one discerns, from time to time, a human presence. Bastien, New Campo, Sparouine, La Forestière, Patience, Maïman; the hamlets [*kampu*] follow one after the other, syncopating and enlivening the Maroni's embankments. All travel takes place by canoe, since the maroon villages are always located on the edge of a river or tributary. They sit on flat land, raised sufficiently above the water to avoid flooding. Each village opens onto the river through a *dégrad*, that is, a spot on the bank where a gentle slope allows for access regardless of the water's level. Each time the canoe passes before a hamlet, one notices children making a racket in the water, women washing their laundry, men cleaning their fishing nets. The life of the Businenge of the Maroni is organized entirely around the river.

The first thing to be seen of Apatou is the triangle of its National Gendarmerie. Inspired by traditional Businenge houses, which are characterized by sloping roofs that descend almost to the level of the soil, this building dominates the principal *dégrad* of the commune.

Beyond the Gendarmerie, a cement promenade stretches along the riverbanks for 100 meters; it serves a preschool, a dispensary on stilts, and a fish market. From this promenade one can access the upper levels of the village – the slope being very gentle – through a multitude of small paths in the dirt that pass through the inhabitants' plots of land. The center of the commune is organized around the Faka Tiki – the ritual site dedicated to the ancestors – the city hall and the church: the foliage is very dense and the disposition of houses, which are mostly quite small, is rather anarchic, at least to the untutored eye.

Apart from the "town" proper, Apatou continues through recent neighborhoods with evocative names: Colombia, China, Jamaica... The houses of cinder block and corrugated iron outnumber the traditional ones made from angelica wood, with wai [*wäi*] roofs. Apatou also includes several orchards and timber farms, which lead the visitor imperceptibly from the village to the forest. In the course of such a walk, one often passes bulldozers, trucks, mechanical shovels, and drilling machines, a whole slew of engine-driven machinery; one also notices panels announcing the improvement of a public square, the installation of a water treatment plant, the extension of the electrical grid, and still other work sites. Apatou is no longer a small traditional village but a commune in transformation. Apatou is also a huge educational establishment: it has in fact four elementary schools and a junior *collège* undergoing expansion for only three thousand inhabitants. In the morning, through the fog and the floods, canoes arrive from all the hamlets. The heads of schoolchildren and older students are barely visible beneath their overstuffed yellow and orange life jackets. When the children from the hamlets disembark and mix with those from the town of Apatou, the streets and packed dirt roads are decked out in yellow, green, blue, and white, the colors of the different school uniforms. In these moments, just before the start of classes or when they let out, Apatou belongs to the children.

"The *nègre* is not. No more than the white man."[60]

On the day after my arrival, I presented myself at the Collège d'Apatou where, throughout the course of the year, I was going to serve as librarian. With the exception of one Amerindian pupil, a

Wayana, all the students were Businenge. Given that the majority of teachers came straight from the Guyanese seaboard, metropolitan France, or the Antilles, this was a completely unprecedented situation for most of us: with no prior training, we found ourselves abruptly facing students who, for the most part, hardly spoke any French and had a culture and a lifestyle completely different from our own. We were in maroon land, smack in the middle of a society that until recently functioned in an entirely customary manner.[61] More than half of our pupils lived in the hamlets, in little wooden houses with neither running water nor electricity; outside school, many of them went to the timber farms, fishing, or hunting to help out their families or, quite simply, to rediscover the Maroni River's complicity with the forest. Of course, essential domestic tasks fell on the girls' shoulders: housework inside, laundry and cooking clean-up in the river; and then, regularly, the long and fastidious preparation of *couac*, grilled manioc flour, the basis of the local diet. To these constraints, some have the added responsibility of a child.

On the shores of the Maroni, French pedagogic methods and educational programs seemed somewhat detached from reality. In the *collège*, after each class, a nagging question returned: what did the students remember, what part of our pantomimes and gesticulations did they understand? For many of the children, coming to school is like participating in a huge collective game. "Occupation," "work," "professional future": rare are the students who grasp what these terms mean. It must be stressed that the majority of their parents never had what we call "wage work"; they live from their gardening, their fishing, their hunting, small trade, or various kinds of sales and, for those who have French nationality, social assistance. The chief difficulty of teaching on the Maroni, whether among the maroons or among the Amerindians, is not the "extreme weakness of academic achievement" – a meaningless expression in the context of a non-francophone traditional community – but rather the cultural difference that exists between teachers and students. Inasmuch as our national education fails even to register this difference, the schools and *collèges* established in these communities will produce nothing but deculturation and mass educational failure. The problem is not so much that formal schooling is substituted for the transmission of forms of knowledge and traditional practices of the "elders," but rather that this schooling is carried out on the basis of a rejection of Businenge culture (for example, the use of maroon languages is often forbidden, the Businenge and other maroon peoples are absent from the history textbooks, etc.). This really leads to the devalorization of maroon students who, graded according to restrictive academic criteria, cannot but appear as "dummies" to the instructors.

The Businenge have not been required to submit to French "republican" education for very long. The oldest public school in Apatou is only ten years old, and the Collège itself opened its doors in the fall of 2001. Why, then, should we be astonished that the maroon students react so badly to academic "discipline"? Throughout the year, one must fight to keep their shoes on their feet, to keep them seated in their chairs, to stop them from suddenly breaking out in song, to keep them focused for more than ten minutes... None of this is self-evident. Normally these things require a long period of preparation that, in our society, begins at birth and is transmitted from generation to generation. It is therefore understandable that the teachers on the Maroni River find their well-being entirely disrupted; they are often young and inexperienced or working on short-term contracts, when they find themselves in isolated communes (sometimes several hours, or even days, away from Saint-Laurent by canoe), without the support of institutions, without books of their own, and armed with training and pedagogical methods that are completely unsuited to their new situation. To the lack of funds, the difficulties of transportation, and the communication obstacles, we can often add the shortage of personnel. The Collège d'Apatou, for example, had access to a school infirmary and to a social assistant only once a month. We never had a school doctor or an orientation counselor. How are we supposed to deal with *baklu*, the possession crisis of an older adolescent? How can you open a dialogue with parents who understand neither your language nor how your school system functions? Given that the families you are dealing with are matrilineal and matrilocal, whom do you contact when a problem arises with a student? In general, the Teacher Training Institute (IUFM) is not the place where one learns how to handle this kind of situation.

The Businenge children brim with all sorts of knowledge and competence. The whole problem is to mobilize them successfully and get them to make their knowledge useful in the framework of a French educational establishment. Once outside the school walls, the students are, undeniably, the teachers. In one-to-one interaction, they have taught me the basis of their language, have initiated me into the art of fishing through intoxicating plants [*à la nivrée*], have told me *matos*, "maroon tales," have showed me how certain plants are used, and much else. Being a librarian at Apatou granted me the richest experience that I ever had. For this reason, I would have preferred to speak only about my privileged relationship with the students, and about the projects we successfully completed with associations or with colleagues – for instance an exhibit on Captain Apatou (the founder of the village), the school newspaper, the welcome of a visiting Haitian writer in connection with the *salon du livre* in Cayenne, and so on. But over the course of this academic year, which was filled with events, discoveries, and encounters, pupils also reported to me some situations that involved academic mistreatment. I myself can testify to the psychological and physical abuse inflicted on students by members of the teaching body. I include these facts not to present prosecutorial evidence but to interrogate what is still unexamined in an educational system whose characterization as "Creole" allows the authors of these abuses to justify their actions.

> So many things in these West Indian territories, I now began to see, speak of slavery. There is slavery. … Slavery in the absence of family life, in the laughter in the cinema at films of German concentration camps, in the fondness for terms of racial abuse, in the physical brutality of strong to weak: nowhere in the world are children beaten as savagely as in the West Indies.[62]

In relating these "anodyne" forms of behavior, these aspects of Creole social life that he bites off into a few words, Naipaul hears the distant echo of the time of the slavery system. If the trauma – exile, rape, the condition of human livestock – that inaugurates Creole becoming never truly ends, it is because the iron of enslavement was conceived in order to mark not only minds and bodies but also a "color" and a "race": the "black." Tocqueville gives a perfect analysis of what makes "modern" slavery distinctive, namely the racialization of stigma: "among the moderns the immaterial and fugitive fact of slavery is combined in the most fatal manner with the material and permanent fact of difference in race. The remembrance of slavery dishonors the race, and race perpetuates the remembrance of slavery."[63] From the outset, in the Americas, the privileged instrument of the slaveholding enterprise was the self-referential "denigration" (from the Latin *denigrare* "to blacken") of the "black" person. There is evidence for this in the way the church theorized the affliction laid on Ham, Noah's cursed son, as the source of black people's corruption and moral inferiority: "this nation bears a temporal affliction on its face and is heir to Ham, from whom it is descended; thus it is born to slavery from father to son, and to eternal servitude."[64] The pseudo-scientific theory of the black people's racial inferiority presents the same schema. Humiliation and inferiorization were the preferred training techniques legitimating a system whose goal was the production of "humble" slaves. This humiliation still resonates in the terms used even today to identify different degrees of "black–white" mixed ancestry. "*Chabin*, in old Norman, was the name for a variety of sheep with red hair. *Mulâtre* comes from mule. *Capre* or *capresse* is derived from goat (*chèvre*). The white masters wanted to animalize their offspring so that the latter would not have the audacity to claim any rights over their fathers' wealth."[65]

What struck me the most in the acts of mistreatment that I witnessed or that were reported to me is not the "physical" violence they might have involved but precisely the character of humiliation that rose from them like a stench. I will mention only three cases, the most revealing and the least contestable, without entering into the details (for obvious reasons):

- stripping two pupils naked in an office, behind closed doors (testimony of victims before the Gendarmerie);
- forcing a student to kneel for around a half hour (an incident I witnessed and for which I submitted a written report to the academic inspector of Guiana and gave oral testimony to the Gendarmerie of Apatou);
- "sending into the sun": regularly, a member of the teaching staff would punish students by making them stand in blazing sun in the courtyard, where everyone could see them, for an amount of time that lasted from thirty minutes to one hour.

To people in metropolitan France, this obviously sounds unbelievable. But, once on the scene, if I or any other colleague were to express opposition to these kinds of disciplinary measures, the authors of the tactics in question and their defenders would promptly retort that it was "like this" in Creole education and that, as *métros* (Frenchmen and women from the metropole) we had nothing to say in the matter. The principal, himself a Creole, implicitly backed such practices, which is why we had such difficulty contesting them. Moreover, the fact that I got myself involved in something that, according to the principal, was none of my business – the "pedagogical practices" of my colleagues – earned me a report to the hierarchy from his office. The report translated into a "severe warning" from the academic inspector: "If I should learn of such events again, I would not hesitate to set a termination process in motion." If I linger over these details, it is in order to make clear that certain teachers were opposed to mistreatment in the Collège, but our status as *métros* and newcomers limited our range of possible action.

The education of children is often very harsh among the maroons, but it does not have this dimension of self-hatred (contempt for the *nègre* in oneself) that one still finds frequently among Creoles. I have, on occasion, heard Creole mothers call their own children "dirty *nègres*" (*sales nègres*), which is what Naipaul is talking about when he speaks of the "fondness" for racial insults. I have never heard a black African woman call her child a "*sale nègre*," or a "white" European mother call her son or daughter a "dirty white." Frantz Fanon analyzes very well the kind of schizophrenia that haunts the descendants of enslaved people even today. The centuries of slavery and racist representations of the black person still mark Creole minds and bodies; this phenomenon expresses itself in strategies of "lactification" or "whitening":

> In a word, the race must be whitened; every woman in Martinique knows this, says this, and reiterates it... The number of phrases, proverbs, and pickup lines a lover in the Antilles chooses is extraordinary. The crux of the problem is not to slip back among the "nigger" rabble, and any Antillean woman in her flirtations and her liaisons will prefer the lighter-skinned man."[66]

This "epidermization" of racial inferiority, which Fanon diagnosed at the start of the 1950s, is still current, if one is to believe Biringanine Ndagano, who wrote in 2000:

> We hear *I gen lapo clè* ("he has light skin"), *I gen bon chivé* ("he has soft hair"), *Lapo chapé* ("a skin saved from blackness") ... No, the mentality has not disappeared. Perhaps it is more diffuse, like the domination to which it gave rise. ... A black person with dark skin and frizzy hair is the object of scorn. Expressions like *Nègre-gros-sirop* ("cane-syrup *nègre*"), *nèg nwè* ("black *nèg*"), *nèg Kongo* ("Kongo *nèg*"), *ti samaka* ("little Saramaka"), or *ti boni* ("little Boni") sometimes ring out as insults.[67]

"New Negro movement," "Négritude," "Black Power"... To revalorize this color, which was for too long denigrated, as much by the Arabs as by the Europeans, constituted an important moment in the liberation struggles of those scattered by the African diaspora. But can one continue to define oneself as "black" today without risking the perpetuation of a "colonial mentality" (as the great Nigerian artist Fela Kuti puts it)? When Fanon explains that "[t]he *nègre* is not. No more than the white," what he means is that this chromatic dualism is only a colonial construction and is, moreover, as reductive for the Europeans as it is for the Africans. Europeans did not invent slavery, but Europeans were the ones who "racialized" it for the first time in human history by associating the status of enslaved person with the black color of sub-Saharan peoples (in the dictionaries of the seventeenth and eighteenth century, *nègre* is defined as "slave.")

> Am I going to ask today's white men to answer for the slave traders of the seventeenth century?
> Am I going to try by every means available to cause guilt to burgeon in their souls?...
> But I have not the right to put down roots... I have not the right to become mired by the determinations of the past.
> I am not a slave to [the] slavery that dehumanized my ancestors...
> The black man is not. No more than the white man.[68]

Even in recent times, the "one-drop rule" was still applied in Louisiana: one drop of black blood puts you in the ranks of the blacks. No matter how white you might be, if you discovered the smallest trace of black heritage among your distant ancestors, your civil status was modified: you were downgraded to the category "black." This is how it came about that, at the start of the 1980s, the Louisiana administration informed a respectable woman who until then had been "blond and white" that she would henceforth be reclassified as "African–American," on the grounds that someone had discovered a distant black "great-great... grand-mother" in her family tree.[69] Black is indelible! Thus it is difficult not to feel "dirtied" when "black blood" runs in your veins. The challenge is to break free of the shame of being "black" and of scorn for those who are "blacker" than you without at the same time letting yourself be locked in the same color that, for centuries, was stuck on our skin: *el negro*! ... As an "Afropean" or "Eurafrican" myself, and therefore Creole in a certain sense, I feel the *différend* of my "origins" on a daily basis, as a micro-war in black and white. It is a strange paradox that, to call someone a "person of color" one says "black person," when modern optics defines black as absence, as the absorption of color, as a "black hole."[70] Little Richard's astonishment is therefore justified:

> "What has Papa got in him?" I asked.
> "Some white and some red and some black," she said.
> "Indian, white, and Negro?"
> "Yes."
> "Then what am I?"
> "They'll call you a colored man when you grow up..."[71]

The mixed person is not. No more than the black. No more than the white. Let's play hooky then, let's make race, gender, class, nation run away...

2

The Art of the Fugue

From Fugitive Slaves to Refugees

When Israel was in Egypt land,
Let my people go
Oppressed so hard they could not stand,
Let my people go
Go down, Moses, way down in Egypt land,
Tell old Pharaoh
To let my people go...[1]

As early as the sixteenth century, societies of runaway slaves were appearing on the edges of the New World colonies: palenques and cumbes in Spanish America, quilombos and mocambos in Brazil, maroon communities in Jamaica and Florida, *kampu* in Guiana and Surinam. What these "truant" communities shared in spite of their differences was a common art of the fugue: in fact retreating into the forest gave birth to their cultures. Whether those who flee are slaves, refugees, vagabonds, or deserters, the act of running away is always composed as a counterpoint to apparatuses of capture. Although the historical experience of marronage is its most obvious manifestation, the fugue is nevertheless a universal form of resistance, identifiable in other places and other times, including times still to come...

In essence, two ideas are implicit in the notion of flight: (1) the idea of cowardice, a refusal to act; (2) the idea of a simple reaction, an "animal" instinct of survival when one is in imminent danger or endures violence. In both cases, however, flight appears to be a passive and secondary phenomenon. With its musical allusions, the notion of "fugue" gives us a better sense of the creative dimension of "lines of flight": "the fugue (Latin *fuga*, 'flight') is a form of musical composition whose theme, or subject, seems to run away endlessly by passing successively through all its voices and diverse tonalities."[2] "To fugue" is not to be sent running but, on the contrary, to make reality flee, to put it through endless variations so as to evade its grasp in every way. The fugue is creative ardor.[3] Having appeared in the French language during the fourteenth century to designate certain kinds of polyphony, the term "fugue" draws our attention to the voice that is followed and evokes, by analogy, the flight of game before the hunter. But, before the name "fugue" took hold in the Middle Ages, this kind of composition was called *chace* ("hunt"), which put the accent on the voice that engaged in pursuit.[4] The transition from one term to the other consequently expresses a change in perspective as well as the fact that the prey and the hunter can exchange roles (see Figure 1).

Once the target of a manhunt, the runaway black man can also become a predator. Thus we find that, in Honduras, the *wanaragua* dance foregrounds a military tactic of the Garifunas[5] – young men dress up as women in order to entice the colonial settlers and subsequently capture them. "To hide, to camouflage oneself, is a warrior function... the man of war is inseparable from the Amazons," as Gilles Deleuze and Félix Guattari remind us.[6] The rebel *nègres* do not flee, they fugue. Masters of subterfuge, they evade pursuit, beat around the bush, vanish into a cloud of tricks: false paths, lures, stratagems, ruses of every kind. As they escape, the runaway warriors persist in their being only by disappearing; and from their disappearance they forge a weapon that can cut in many ways. In their perpetual movement of retreat and attack, they are accompanied and sustained by women and children, elders and spirits who participate in their battles; a whole moving diaspora, from which unexpected forms of life spring up. Despite its fragility, this common existence of men and women, Kongo and Ashanti, living and dead, is the source of community. And in this context what we mean by "community" is a religious and political organization with agricultural and construction technologies, bodies of art and medical knowledge, in short, a complete culture. Thus, in the space opened by a fugue, in the folds and retreats of dense and muggy woods, runaway countercultures appeared and spread out,

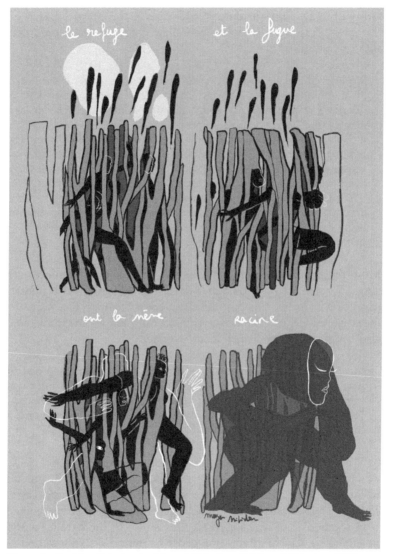

Figure 1. *Fugitive*. Painting by Maya Mihindou. © Maya Mihindou, 2022.

cultures whose organization and values were diametrically opposed to those of slaveholding societies. If marronage traces the line of flight away from colonial space, that very same creative movement also generates new, unheard of forms of space: the living spaces of surreptitious villages, the carnal spaces of scarified bodies, mystical forms of space–time in dances and rituals, the plastic spaces of crafted objects (boat paddles, container gourds, houses on stilts, etc.).

> We arrived in the most beautiful field of ripe rice, in the form of an oblong square, from which the *rebel town* appeared at a distance, in the form of an ampitheatre…. Inconceivable are the many expedients which these people employ in the woods, where in a state of tranquillity they seemed, as they boasted, to want for nothing … *game* and *fish* they catch in great abundance, by artificial traps and springs, and preserve them by barbacuing [*sic*]; while their fields are even overstocked with rice, cassava, yams, plantains, &c. … They might breed hogs and poultry, and keep dogs for hunting and watching them, but this they decline, from the apprehension of being discovered by their noise, as even the crowing of a cock may be heard in the forest at a considerable distance.[7]

Most of the names of these rebel camps contained some ironic allusion, some provocation aimed at the colonial troops that hunted them down. In his expedition log, Captain Stedman lists some of these names for us: *Gado saby*: "God only knows me, and none else"; *Mele me:* "Do disturb me, if you dare":[8]

> Mechanical Hound *never* fails… Tonight, this network is proud to have the opportunity to follow the Hound by camera helicopter as it starts on its way to the target… [a] nose so sensitive the Mechanical Hound can remember and identify ten thousand odor indexes on ten thousand men without resetting![9]

With spidery feet, thunderous velocity, and an infallible sense of smell, a colossal cybernetic attack dog throws itself in pursuit of Montag, the rebel firefighter of the famous futuristic novel *Fahrenheit 451*. This man's crime: to have knowingly preserved and read the books he was supposed to destroy. In the parallel world imagined by Ray Bradbury, the order of things is reversed: houses being fireproof, the firefighters become arsonists. Fahrenheit 451 is the exact temperature at which books are reduced to ashes. The soldiers of fire are henceforth the new inquisitors of a totalitarian power that has banished everything capable of promoting reflection, passion, sedition: books are dealt with by flamethrowers, and their readers are shut away in psychiatric wards. In the generalized amusement park, in the obligatory Disneyland, in the permanent reality show that the United States and its empire have become, the "screen walls" of dwellings pour forth apathy and amnesia around the clock, in the form of televised programs: zombification by cathode rays.

> A magnificent machine was invented to track down and destroy escaped Indians and runaway slaves: the killer bloodhound. Its fame spread throughout the territory and very soon many were exported to the United States' southern regions, where they were known as Cuban hounds.[10]

We can hear the echo of old stories about escaped slaves and manhunts in Bradbury's futuristic fable. Montag's getaway is inscribed in the even older tradition of the maroon. The fugitive slave and the attack dog form an inseparable couple, in the imaginary of slavery as much as in its reality. Like the maroon, the hero of *Fahrenheit 451* escapes the apparatus of capture by plunging under cover of a timber forest. A domestic animal's return to life in the woods (whence the Spanish *cimarrón*), the maroon's line of flight is a line that returns to the wild. The runaway shares the practice of creative indocility with the Caribbean pirate, with the social bandit, with the "celestial bum" of the Beat Generation, with all those who refuse the subjection of minds and bodies. It is surely not accidental that, in Mark Twain's *The Adventures of Huckleberry Finn*, which is one of the foundational books of American literature, the flight of the child and that of the slave merge into a single liberatory odyssey: Jim, the black slave who refused to let himself be sold, and Huck, the young orphan who refused the good manners of "sivilization," drift together on a makeshift raft down the majestic waters of the Mississippi.

> I went to the woods because I wished to live deliberately, to front only the essential facts of life, and see if I could not learn what it had to teach, and not, when I came to die, discover that I had not lived. I did not wish to live what was not life, living is so dear; nor did I wish to practise resignation, unless it was quite necessary. I wanted to live deep and suck out all the marrow of life, to live so sturdily and Spartan-like as to put to rout all that was not life.[11]

With Henry David Thoreau, the pursuit of the wild life took the form of a philosophical retreat into the forest: a form of marronage carried out by thought and involving the capture of prejudices, conformism, stultifying routines. We often envision flight from the perspective of defeat and, quite rightly, as a matter of "undoing" [*défaire*] the gregarious element in us, the irrepressible bleating that overcomes us when we find ourselves stuck together with others, in an undifferentiated and malleable mass. Running to the woods is a way of putting that narrow little life to flight, losing everything superfluous whose acquisition condemns us to work and to be endlessly busy. In a society ruled by the tyranny of the majority, it is by melting into the woodlands, by becoming wild, by practicing the language of plants and animals that Thoreau finds his voice again: a voice whose singularity means that it cannot help being dissident, a voice that can do nothing but declare its independence and break away.

In the dark future of *Fahrenheit 451*, thousands of dissident readers escape from the cities by following abandoned railroad tracks: "The track that came out of the city and rusted across the land, through forests and woods, deserted now, by the river. Here was the path to wherever he was going."[12] Thanks to the shadows and the solitude of the forests they traverse, these readers form unprecedented "literary" communities linked to one another by rusted rail lines. These utopian microcosms whose portrait Bradbury sketches can give us an idea of what the maroon communities might have represented during the era of slavery. The resistance of *Fahrenheit 451*'s fugitives is initially cultural: what binds them together is a vision of the world, a shared culture – in this case, world literature. "*We're* book burners, too. We read the books and burnt them, afraid they'd be found... We are all bits and pieces of history and literature and international law, Byron, Tom Paine, Machiavelli, or Christ, it's here."[13] Thus each of the fighters has memorized chapters, indeed complete books: one guerilla incarnates *Don Quixote*, the other *Gulliver's Travels*, and they are relying on all of them to reinvent the world. "Bums on the outside, libraries inside,"[14] their action space is a utopia from the outset. Just like these living libraries, the fugitive Africans who began the first maroon communities had committed to memory complete paragraphs of their birth cultures (Ashanti, Yoruba, Kongo, etc.).[15] They did this in such a way that each new community of rebel blacks corresponded to a unique anthology. Of course, this is only an image: the maroon communities are not miniature models of Africa, but original societies in their own right, urgently cobbled together from fragments of African cultures and borrowings from European and Amerindian cultures.

Beyond the use of violence, the things that enabled enslaved people to conquer spaces of freedom even within the plantation were cultural practices such as the mystical and festive communions of the *macumbas*, the rhythmic scansions of work songs (the seedbed of the blues), the verbal jousting of storytelling evenings, the creative variations of Creole tongues and "Negro speech" (a "minor" usage of major languages). The maroon community is just the final culmination of these processes of subjectification, these arts of the self by means of which – through improvisation, the continuous variation of rhythms, corporeal and vocal phrasing – the slave once again becomes, for him- or herself and others, the subject of his or her actions and creations. Because they reactivate memories of the body and of orality, because they nourish a new spirituality,[16] the "rhythms of resistance" – which make themselves known in dance, in music, in the "awakening" of spirituals – offer the best antidote to the zombification imposed by the slave system. The spirit of "black" forms of dissidence always manifests itself through rhythmic dissonances.

A creative utopia coincided with the birth of fugitive slave societies. Rather than going to meet the "land of the ancestors" by committing suicide, the maroons will choose to re-create this "beyond" right where they stand, *hic et nunc*, in the interstices of the enslaving system. Benjamin Péret's brilliant study of the Brazilian quilombo ("community") of Palmares has grasped the universal implications of maroon dissidence quite well:

> Here we have Blacks from every part of Africa who have almost nothing in common: neither language nor religious beliefs, and not even customs or culture. After their escape, these men, so dissimilar, found themselves in a particularly isolated area of the virgin forest. Moreover, they shared a common aspiration: freedom.[17]

Thus the "maroon communes" have nothing to do with any "ethnic" community: they will serve as safe havens not only for escaped slaves but also, in certain circumstances, for deserting soldiers, for peasants chased off their land, for Native Americans fleeing the "missions," and for outlaws of all "colors." Certain maroon groups such as the Congos of Panama or the Garifunas of central America will even venture to weave stable alliances with pirate gangs in order to raid Spanish ports and ships transporting gold. None of this is in itself surprising, given that marronage regularly produced forms of banditism (black cowboys in the Far West, *cangaceiros* in Brazil, etc.) and that piracy itself was partly nourished by marronages that were both black and white (e.g. those of "indentured" servants[18] and sailors).

> Decimated by epidemics and accidents, whipped until bloody on the least pretext, weakened by a monotonous diet, the sailor's life was nothing but a long nightmare. With no exit: badly paid, always behind schedule, lacking family ties, incapable of reentering the society of landsmen, these unhappy sorts found themselves very quickly in the gears of a diabolical mechanism – from which they could escape only by death, illness ... or piracy[19]

Just as the quilombos represented "a constant appeal, an incitement, a flag for black slaves,"[20] "the appearance of a black flag on the horizon was a promise of deliverance"[21] for mariners kept in miserable living conditions. True political communities in which deliberation played a primordial role, the pirate and maroon countersocieties were permeated by a visceral rejection of relations of domination. On the other hand, the historical reality of these rebel groups was often a far cry from the ideal that they incarnated: many pirates were implicated in the slave trade and, thanks to agreements made with colonial authorities, many maroons returned other runaway slaves to their masters.

For Gregor H., the fugitive in a novel by Alain Fleischer, the "forest was a free zone, like extraterritorial waters where one could sail far offshore while avoiding the watchtowers of the coast guard and the navy's outposts":[22] the path par excellence of escape, migration, disappearance, border crossing. There we find vertical lines of trees, reeds, ferns, stalks, and entanglements of roots, vines, branches, leaves. The forest is everywhere a striated space, but its striations are those of the zebra or of camouflage gear. For a long time, European forests sheltered those who had been condemned, brigands, outlaws (such as the character Robin Hood), gangs, and minorities who resisted banishment. For this reason, the fight against illegalisms and popular uprisings in the West often took the form of deforestation. The case of Ireland's colonization is particularly revealing: in the seventeenth century, the British dealt a decisive blow to the Irish rebellion by connecting a policy of deforestation (clearing the ground, destroying the underbrush, distributing land to English and Scottish colonists) with a policy of deporting insurgents and their families to the other side of the Atlantic in massive numbers, where they were then treated as "white Negroes."[23] As European penetration advanced, the wooded surface area of the New World retreated and gave way to vast agricultural farms linked by a network of roads to cities, to forts, and above all to colonial ports.

> *Heterotopias*: sorts of actually realized utopias in which the real emplacements, all the other real emplacements that can be found within the culture are, at the same time, represented, contested, and reversed, sorts of places that are outside all places, although they are actually localizable. ... the ship is a piece of floating space, a placeless place. ... The sailing vessel is the heterotopia par excellence.[24]

Foucault's words regarding "hetero-topia" ("other space") apply perfectly to pirate and maroon communities. If the pirate's hetero-topia is intimately linked to the ship, the maroon's heterotopia is, by contrast, a manifest product of the forest. A liberated zone (the "outside") was subtracted from the space of slavery by the fugitives' retreat and their entrenchment in the woods: an "other space," which in turn subverted that space (the "inside"). This first act of folding back meant that the maroon community was a secessionist community. However, far from inaugurating the official birth of a new state, the maroon secession consecrated the rebel community in its "becoming surreptitious." In fact the borders of the maroon territory could be maintained only to the extent that they were effaced or permanently blurred the apparatuses of capture. As a collective form of the fugue, secession constitutes a metamorphic process: the fold back into the forest that sets it going is the "un-fold" of a continuous variation, applied to the living space as much as to the fugitives' own way of appearing.

The striped space of the forests envelops, enfolds, and covers the actions of animals and humans in a perpetual shadow. It is a place where one disappears, whether in search of shelter or in becoming lost. If, as Deleuze and Guattari teach us, the nomads invented speed, the maroons and the invisible peoples of the forests (Amazonians, Papuans, Pygmies, and so on) invent stealth. Marronage is a war machine only to the extent that it is a machine for disappearance ... and the forest is the privileged scene for this disappearance. The forest demands that prey and predators mimic each other. Melting into the most varied kinds of "nature" – the vegetal arabesques of the Amazon basin, the *caatingas* (spiny shrubs) of Brazil, the craters and craggy mountains of the Caribbean islands, the marshes and labyrinthic mangroves of Louisiana – and taking advantage even of their smallest obstacles, the maroon community is also a phantom community. The theme of the runaway's stealth returns again and again in most of the colonial reports of military forays: "as the Blacks are the masters of these forests and know them perfectly ... they inflict heavy losses on us that we cannot avenge, because they are hidden by the forest and protected by the trunks; we escape after having been beaten down."[25] The fugue always initiates a cycle of metamorphoses: it is by modifying his or her form and appearance, by generating decoys, by becoming a downright simulacrum that the fleeing slave comes to escape and, indeed, to defeat his or her adversaries. Escaping one's enemies is a matter of producing one's own disappearance: lying in ambush, blurring the traces, playing dead, vanishing in order to spring forth immediately again. The thousand and one maroon variations provide the framework for a genuine art of the fugue, which has found its most beautiful plastic expression in the sculpture of the Businenge.

"Transformation for flight, that is, in order to escape an enemy, is universal, being found in myths and fairy stories all over the world." The most common of these "flight transformations" is the linear mode of the hunt:

> One creature is pursuing another, the distance between them diminishing all the time until, at the very moment when the quarry is about to be seized, it escapes by transforming itself into something different. The hunt continues, or, rather, starts afresh. The danger to the quarry mounts again and its pursuer may even succeed in getting hold of it, but, at the very last moment, it transforms itself into yet another shape and thus escapes again.[26]

It is in Surinam and on the Guianese banks of the Maroni that the most complex maroon cultures appeared, those of the N'djuka, Saramaka, Aluku, Matawaï, Kwinti, and Paramaka. The first examples of a specifically maroon sculptural style date from the start of the nineteenth century: combs, paddles, benches, everyday objects. *Tembe*,[27] the art of the maroon peoples of French Guiana and Surinam, spreads before the viewer's gaze one of the most beautiful fugue spaces imaginable: even today, the pursuit of marronage continues in its interlacings of sculpted wood. First and foremost, this is an art of relief; relief which is released from wood that has been marked, hollowed out, smoothed, and sculpted. The term *tembe* is an alteration of the English word "timber" – namely wood for construction. There is nothing "primitive" or "early" about maroon art; from the outset, it belongs to western modernity, from which it unhesitatingly appropriates the latest available techniques for its own ends: motors built into the boats, chainsaws used for sculpting, modern textiles reincorporated into patchwork arts, and so on. When they appeared in the twentieth century, *tembe* paintings bore the style of their initial source: sculpture on wood. In fact the same interlaced forms and the same geometric variations can be found in these paintings.

But how did the western tool – an instrument of slavery, of alienation – become, in the hands of maroons, an instrument of creation, of self-reconstruction? In the middle of the eighteenth century, faced with the prospect of a widespread insurgency throughout Surinam, the Dutch were forced to sign peace treaties with the "bush Negroes." In exchange for ending the hostilities, these accords required that the rebels be sent an annual shipment of tribute in the form of tools, weapons, and various goods and, by way of compensation, that the rebels seize any newly arrived fugitive slaves and return them to the colonists from whom they had fled. The *tembe* was born from nothing less than creative appropriation of the colonists' own tools. It was born when their meaning and function were derailed and put to new purposes. The *tembe* is the reinvention, in the hollows of trees, of the body, of the family, of the *nègre* community dismantled by slavery. This reinvention can be read in the lexicon used by maroons to identify the elements of their sculptures. Thus we find that the "eyes" refer to the small folds in the intertwining, the "neck" to the intermediary parts, which make the sculpted ribbons communicate with one another (tying the head to the rest of the body, the neck is a binding); the "navel" is the central space of the composition and the "hands" the struts that support the composition, while the "mama" is the most important figure and the "children" the secondary figures. The reference to the body here must not be taken in a symbolic or metaphorical sense. *Tembe* sculptures do not represent the body, they function *like* bodies: fugitive bodies.

We must insist that, contrary to some interpretations of so-called primitive art, there is no "metaphysical" sense to decipher beyond the beauty of a *tembe*'s forms. The moment a grid of symbolic interpretation is applied to a piece of art, the personal creativity of the artist tends to be overshadowed, and he or she tends to be reduced to someone simply carrying out a supposed "collective mentality." Thus we reject the prejudice according to which only the modern artist can demonstrate creative freedom, while the "traditional artisan" contents him- or herself with reproducing models handed down by tradition. The *tembe* is from the outset an act of love, a presence, a gift offered to the woman one desires, to the uncle who initiated us into the hunt, to the grandmother who nourished us with tales and lullabies. *Tembes* circulate between individuals, and their circulation contributes to the weaving of social bonds, to the maintenance and renewal of the maroon community. The intertwining ribbons of wood act out the intertwining of desires, the enlacing of the *libi na wan* (this is a communal expression in Busitongo, meaning "to live as one"). *Tembe* is an erotic art, if by Eros one means this power that unites human beings through bonds of love, esteem, fraternity, and hope and makes a heterogeneous multitude into a unity. *Tembe* belongs to a set of countermeasures that restless black people invented to free themselves from the reign of Thanatos – the slaveholding regime that transforms humans into commodities, into beasts of burden, into the living dead.

At the aesthetic and technical level, the *tembe*'s reliance on the medium of wood corresponds directly to reliance on the forests as a medium of action proper to marronage in general. As a rhythmic principle of encoding and variation, the fugue is inscribed directly into the structure of *tembe*. Each work is built around a system of ribbons: complex figures, intertwined, carved into the wood like so many lines of flight and false tracks. The ribbons turn, plunge, rebound above and below one another, thus presenting a vertiginous challenge to the eye. The *tembe* figures are read by following, with the tips of one's fingers, the itineraries inscribed in the hollows of a winnowing tray, on the head of an oar, or on the seat of a bench. These trajectories are pursued the way one would follow a trail in the forest. The artist's virtuosity is gauged by the ability to blur the evidence of his or her passage. This means that the work is composed by halves or quarters, in such a way that its governing principles remain ungraspable. To read a *tembe* is to throw oneself into a labyrinth, in pursuit of a fictitious runaway. In maroon sculpture, which uses the compass almost systematically, most of the figures and motifs are inscribed in circles. Now the circle circumscribes. The artist's entire effort will be concentrated on escaping from this self-consciously imposed constraint. The *tembe* is the circle's jailbreak: a bolt into the woods materialized in the engraving of sculpted wood. The maroon aesthetics is an aesthetics of disappearance.

This aesthetics of the fugue can also be found in the most contemporary works of African–American culture: "Come on feet, do your thing, we all know whitey's game, come on legs, come on run…" chants the chorus of *Sweet Sweetback's Baadasssss Song*, the funky manifesto of Melvin Van Peebles.[28] In this experimental film of 1971, the hero's jubilant forward motion is mixed up with the motion of modulated musical and visual patterns (e.g. riffs and bluesy phrases, images of flight, and the superimposition of overexposed legs), repeated indefinitely at varying speeds and in varying registers and planes. Here the excess of special effects and rhythmic effects gives a mythological aura to the runaway slave. Whether we are dealing with the formal plane or the plane of the (semi-underground) conditions under which it is being filmed,[29] Van Peebles' political diatribe presents all the ingredients of a creative marronage (for the first time in American cinema, a black man rises up against the established order and kills white police officers).

When the Sun comes back
And the first quail calls
Follow the Drinking Gourd.
For the old man is a-waiting for you to carry you to freedom
If you follow the Drinking Gourd.
The riverbank makes a very good road.
The dead trees will show you the way.
Left foot, peg foot, travelling on
Follow the Drinking Gourd.
                    (Excerpt from "Follow the Drinking Gourd")

"Follow the Drinking Gourd" is one of the best-known songlines – that is, coded songs that explained the path runaway slaves from Alabama and Mississippi would have to follow in order to reach Illinois or other abolitionist states. The "gourd" refers to the pole star of the Big Dipper (also known as the Plough or the Great Bear), an essential landmark for those who were trying to orient themselves toward the north.[30]

During the deadly era of slavery in the southern United States, music acquired a profoundly emancipatory dimension among "black" people: during a religious service punctuated by the refrains of the sermon, the clapping of hands and feet, and the trances of various participants, enslaved people escaped from their miserable condition – collectively, they raised themselves toward God. And this spiritual ascension took shape and was magnified through song: the Negro spiritual, the gospel, the "Go Down Moses" of Israel's black children. The slaves in fact recognized themselves in the Exodus of the Jewish people and in the heroic figure of Moses. This "communion" in song that sent shivers through the black churches – sometimes no more than simple plank shelters – played an essential role in the genesis of what, after many battles, would one day become the "African–American" community. An undeniable spiritual escape, the song of black slaves occasionally functioned as a vehicle for escapes that were quite concrete. In the sugar factories and mills, in the cane and cotton fields, unknown to planters and commanders, runaway itineraries circulated from one slave to the next, in the form of encoded songs: the songlines or sung roadmaps. The melody from a songline was the prelude to a line of flight whose subtle branchings covered a vast territory, from the tropical Mississippi delta all the way to the icy banks of Lake Ontario at the Canadian border. This escape route was affectionately called "the Underground Railroad" by abolitionists, by the enslaved, and by free people. To be sure, this was no actual railroad but a fugitive network: a secret organization of smugglers and safe houses dedicated to advancing the passage of escaped slaves toward the North. From 1830 to 1860, more than 30,000 black people fled the slaveholding South by taking the "freedom train" to reach the Union states in the north and to reach Canada. This gigantic marronage began in 1780, but did not take on the singular name and distinctive form of the Underground Railroad until around 1830, at the moment when the development of rail lines accelerated. By the end of the Civil War in 1865, over the course of 80 years, more than 100,000 black fugitives fled the plantations of the deep South by means of the different escape mechanisms known from North American history.

> I guided [them] toward the North Star, in violation of the state codes of Virginia and Kentucky. I piloted them through the forests, mostly by night – girls, fair and white, dressed as ladies; men and boys, as gentlemen, or servants – men in women's clothes, and women in men's clothes... on foot or on horseback, in buggies, carriages, common wagons, in and under loads of hay, straw, old furniture, boxes, and bags; crossed the Jordan of the slave, swimming, or

wading chin deep, or in boats, or skiffs, on rafts, and often on a pine log.[31]

Committed to fighting the slaveholding system through a concrete program of sabotage that consisted in provoking a massive and continuous flight of slaves, black and white abolitionists consciously diverted the technological model of the railway network to their own advantage. With its detailed simulation of departure times and routes, its tangle of alternative pathways and emergency rails, and the interplay of its connections and signals, the web of rail lines (prefiguring those of the World Wide Web) truly incarnated the ideal network of flight. The complexity and the extent of its links made the Underground Railroad a totally decentralized organization, which rendered it all the more effective and all the less easily destroyed. In *Cloudsplitter* – a vast literary fresco centered on John Brown's band and the guerrilla struggle that they led against slave owners – Russell Banks portrays this aspect of things very well: "It was real, this Subterranean Passway. … The slaveholders had not been able to sever it or to block it permanently anywhere along its length. If they attacked it in one place, it appeared the next night in another."[32] One must thus understand the Underground Railroad as a sort of ghost train, a locomotive simulacrum, a sublime subterfuge (in Latin *subterfugere* meant to flee underneath or secretly, *subter*). Every element of this enormous escape network was described and conceived of in terms of rail transport: the families welcoming runaways were "stations," the guides were "conductors" or "station masters" responsible for carrying "goods" (the fugitives). The most famous "conductor" would turn out to be Harriet Tubman (herself a runaway): she completed almost twenty trips between the southern United States and Canada. More than three hundred enslaved people owed their liberty to her. The entire nascent African–American community recognized itself in her and baptized her "the black Moses." Moreover, the spiritual "Go Down Moses" was composed to announce her approach on the plantations and in the workshops.

Little by little, a community built up around the tracks of the "freedom train" – a mobile and surreptitious resistance front, which propagated through "transfers." But, unlike traditional maroon communities, the community of refugees of the Underground Railroad formalized itself and became self-conscious by creating a space for writing: a centrifugal circulation of letters, political tracts, "railway" maps, songlines, and, above all, newspapers. For the first time in North American history, by taking up the orator's lectern and the pen, fugitive slaves burst onto the political scene. With the support of abolitionists, they fought for the general emancipation of their brothers and sisters, still enslaved in the southern United States. Indeed, Canadian society and, to a lesser extent, the society of northern American states offered these fugitives the possibility of appealing to the law, to the press, and to political action in order to assert their rights. And this is what the African–American writer and journalist Mary Ann Shadd (1823–1893) strove to accomplish: in 1852 she published *A Plea for Emigration*, to encourage the emigration of American blacks to Canada. Although she was considered a voice for the refugees, she also edited and directed a newspaper during this period (she was one of the first woman editors): the *Provincial Freeman*. Nor was this the only newspaper of the new Afro-Canadian community; for there were also the *Voice of the Fugitive*, the *Voice of the Bondsman*, and others.

By retreating to Canada, the fugitive slaves ceased to be *marrons nègres*, black runaways. This is because, in proclaiming themselves "refugees," they had made the choice to live openly at the heart of a white society and to place themselves under the protection of the civil laws of a modern state. By provoking a genuine migratory movement, the Underground Railroad introduced into the young American nations the difficult question of the status of minorities, as well as that of the right to asylum. These questions are still very much with us at a moment when, in Europe and particularly in France, it has become almost impossible to obtain refugee status. Confronted by the stigmatization, the criminalization, and the growing repression of "migrants" and given that checks and profiling practices (by administrations, marketers, police, etc.) are continually proliferating, it might be necessary for us to reinvent marronage, to reinvent the underground railroad, to reinvent the ruses that forced a society obsessed with containment, immunity, and security to burst out through the cracks in its own pipes. What is fascinating about the movement around the Underground Railroad – and worth pondering, too – is the way in which the old figure of the runaway slave has become so closely intertwined with the more recent one of the refugee: the one illuminates the other, and vice versa.

3

Manhunt

Spectral Analysis of Slavery

Anyone who wants to rule men first tries to humiliate them, to trick them out of their rights and their capacity for resistance, until they are as powerless before him as animals. ... His ultimate aim is to incorporate them into himself and to suck the substance out of them.[1]

When it comes to power, we usually grasp only the superficial features: the ceremony, the rituals, and the acts of consecration that bring it onstage: its monuments, its palaces, its immortalizing chronicles. Meanwhile, we must not forget that an act of predation lies at the origin of all power, whether it be human or animal. Even when they employ the language of love, the powerful are always predators; seduction is the most terrible weapon. What is pursued via the tender euphemism of "integration" is always the foreign body's assimilation. Thus it is not without reason that Deleuze and Guattari see an apparatus of capture in the state. But slavery, whether or not it is tied to a state, is what reveals the inner workings of power's metabolism: seizure, absorption, digestion. In the lines that follow, I will try to carry out a spectral analysis of the slavery system, an analysis of the shadows that it projects into the social imaginary. From this "spectrography" will emerge the figure of the *nègre marron*: the fugitive par excellence.

Although they are overflowing with the living dead, American horror films never invoke the birthplace of the zombie: the slave-labor plantation.[2] "At the least awakening of insubordination on a zombie's part, slash his skin, crush his flesh, break his bones, smash his head, to the point of complete pulverization. Then drink your fill of his blood."[3] Here, in the form of a parable, the Haitian poet Frankétienne presents us with the pedagogy of enslavement – a pedagogy of cruelty. If the master's power belongs among practices for the taming of wild animals, this is because it appears first as the power to make blood (Latin *cruor*) flow. The zombie is the spectral double of the slave, the shadow haunting crime scenes: it is born from the human being's depersonalization, animalization, and negation.

Slavery's fundamental language is that of the whip. To properly "season a *nègre*," every blow must cut or deepen a furrow in the latter's flesh. Usually this is followed by binding the victim to "four stakes" or a "ladder." But one can also choose the "hammock" method – suspension from the four limbs – or the "lurch" – suspension from the hands. One can choose to employ vines that cut the skin, the *rigoise* (a leather whip made from the nerves of cattle), hemp ropes, and every imaginable and possible variety of vegetal and organic fibers. Among the tortures foreseeable in cases of flight, sabotage, sucking sugar cane, revolt, or even poisoning (slashed mouth, enucleation, cut Achilles tendon, etc.), the iron cage could evoke the refinements of a Marquis de Sade:

> An iron latticework cage of seven to eight square feet is exposed on a scaffolding. The condemned man is closed inside, straddling a sharp blade, his feet in stirrups. Sooner or later the lack of food and rest, and the strain on his legs, is too much; he falls onto the blade. Then, depending on the seriousness of his wound and the energy left to him, the condemned man may lift himself up, to fall again.[4]

Cruelty plays an essential role in every taming process. Nietzsche has described it as a terrible "mnemotechnics": "If something is to stay in the memory it must be burned in: only that which never ceases to *hurt* stays in the memory."[5] This is a constant; every power tries to imprint its mark on the bodies it subjugates. Certainly, one could object that today one no longer educates, trains, or punishes by recourse to physical violence, much less to torture. But this novel kindness in the government of humans contains forms of subjection that are all the more efficacious the less painful they are. Henceforth one will be followed, accompanied, and cared for rather than punished or imposed upon. For this, we have the evidence of certain medico-political projects such as the "tracking" of deviant behavior from the earliest childhood. Thus the normalizing control of conduct follows on the heels of the disciplinary taming of bodies.

In our control society, a central role is played by the technology of "traceability": in fact it represents the most sophisticated form of marking the body. Whether they know it or not, the "urban nomads" of the twenty-first century circulate in a vast electromagnetic field (doubled by the "net" of the World Wide Web), their bodies outfitted with a growing number of trackers: radio frequency identification (RFID) and GPS devices, credit cards, cell phones, subcutaneous implants, and so on.[6] These virtual markers not only identify their users but also allow their location and the history of their movement to be recorded in real time. Because it is virtual (immaterial and dynamic), this cybernetic marking process has universal scope: it is applied equally to merchandise moving through logistical chains, wild animals moving freely in nature preserves (e.g. Argos tags), and humans who use the urban mass transit network (e.g. Navigo passes in Paris). The futuristic film *Gattaca* explores the social and political consequences of the current biometric monitoring of identities (the appearance of a new form of eugenics) and draws the following conclusion: "We have made discrimination into a science."[7] In fact the acts of discrimination and social control that we can expect to see in coming years will rely more and more on stealth technologies (detectors, scanners, drones, camera networks, etc.) that activate individual identifiers and imperceptible spatial demarcations of which we have no personal knowledge.

But let us come back to the fabrication of the slave and to the way in which enslaving power marks bodies in order to make them submit. The mark of the enslaved person is initially the stigmata (from the ancient Greek *stigmata*, *stigma* in the singular), those corporeal marks through which the Greeks displayed the infamy, degradation, or impurity of the person who carried them (slave, traitor, criminal). The stigmata establish an unbridgeable distance between the master and his slave – one that separates the human from the livestock that bears the mark. It was in carving his initials into the shoulder of the *nègre* with a hot iron that the master took ritual "possession" of him, thereby becoming his official owner: the skin is thus a kind of parchment. In the plantation setting, the first function of cruelty is to imprint on the body the law of inequality, the law that establishes the master's domination over the slave, and to make it permanently visible. Depending on the intensity with which it was applied and on the circumstances under which this happened, dominical cruelty (from the Latin *dominus*, "master") oscillates between "orthopedic" violence and "exceptional" violence. Violence is orthopedic when, through the corrective and systematic use of the whip, cruelty keeps the individual within social and spatial bounds, within the sequence of operations, within the rhythm of production. Violence is exceptional when, through excess of torture, it reactivates the master's power, which has been momentarily damaged by the "criminal" slave. The kind of torture that constituted an exceptional penal practice in Europe (one related to royal or inquisitorial justice) became an ordinary practice wherever the slave system reigned. The greater the number of enslaved people on a plantation or in a region, the more frequently the minority of enslavers used terror to maintain their domination.

Even beyond the body, the machinery of slavery mutilated the soul. From the soul of the *nègre*, the enslaver tried to subtract the mind, the memory, the personality – what the Haitians call the *ti bon ange*, that is, the principle of individuality in Vodou religion. It was a matter of making the *nègre* brainless the better to reduce him to a beast of the field. On either side of the Atlantic, from the shores of Angola to those of Haiti, the zombie incarnated the ideal slave: a living being without consciousness, a "living dead" who no longer offered any resistance to the enslaver's will. Laënnec Hurbon tells us that, indeed, among

> the Douala [Cameroon], one still talks about those who were sold after seeming to be dead, who work night and day for their owners in the mountain regions. The description of these false-dead slaves perfectly matches that of the zombies of Haiti. An individual is separated from his shadow or his double; he falls ill and appears to be a cadaver; he is buried; a sorcerer comes to reawaken him so that he can be put to work as a slave on plantations.[8]

No doubt the enduring element in stories of zombification is the memory of the slave trade. In the social imaginary of African and Creole societies, sorcery is presented as capturing and devouring the soul in such a way that the order of the slave system is confused with the order of sorcery itself. The zombie is the bewitched being: it is therefore inseparable from the inverse figure of the witch. The notion of being bewitched translates a concrete situation of alienation onto the symbolic plane: to be a slave is to be "possessed" by a foreign power, to be dispossessed of one's selfhood so that a master to whom one becomes a piece of property may benefit. That which is most intimately ours – our body, our very life – will henceforth constitute a possession for someone else. If the films of George Romero (e.g. *Night of the Living Dead*, *Dawn of the Dead*, *Day of the Dead*) have a political and social message, this is precisely because the revolt of slaves, of the exploited, of the wretched of the earth looms behind the zombie rebellion.

While zombies appear as sub-humans who move in flocks, creatures roaming between life and death, shadows with neither memories nor hopes, the vampire on the other hand represents the overhuman, the solitary and super-lucid predator, the master par excellence, who feeds on the blood of those he stalks. The vampire is an aristocrat who, like all members of his caste, is dedicated to the sacred ritual of the hunt. In the medieval West (and even long after the Middle Ages), it was in the context of the hunt that the lord's sovereignty over nature and over his subjects was replayed and reactivated. For the nobility, the finding and tracking of big game represented schooling in courage and character formation. But the supernatural aristocracy of vampires preferred human game over animal game. What the vampire chases is a person. And it is in this respect that the enslaver is related to him.

The Most Dangerous Game, a 1932 film directed by Irving Pichel and Ernest Schoedsack that takes place on a Caribbean island, speaks to us unwittingly of this old practice of the manhunt: a decadent aristocrat obsessed with hunting provokes shipwrecks in order to ensure a supply of fresh human prey – future decorations for his trophy room. In the slaveholding societies of the Americas and the Indian Ocean, the manhunt was a full-fledged institution. "Wanted" signs were posted and search parties were organized on a regular basis, to track escaped slaves – those referred to as *nègres marrons*. The fugitive slave and the attack dog form an inseparable couple in the imaginary as well as in the reality of slavery. The Spanish in Cuba, experienced breeders, furnished the entire Caribbean with powerful bloodhounds [*limiers*]. The attack dog was the privileged instrument of the slave system's apparatus of capture: it traced the fugitive's steps, pursued, and seized him.

Three days ago two hundred dogs were brought here. ... we expect another 400 tomorrow. ...

They [Spanish specialists hired to train dogs] train them, turn them loose on live Negroes whom the dogs ferociously tear apart and devour.[9]

The success of the maroon's escape, his physical integrity, and his very survival depend on his capacity to vanish and become not just invisible but imperceptible. In *Slave Old Man*, Patrick Chamoiseau depicts the maroon as a master of camouflage:

I took care, during my run, to baffle its sense of smell ... I smeared myself with the *fourmis-santi* stink ants that populate the *liane douce* – a wild potato vine – as well as big termite mounds, living on dead roots. I used vetiver leaves, *manicou*-possum nests, warm muds that smelled mysterious ... I was hoping to dissolve into this forestine soul.[10]

A fugue always inaugurates a cycle of metamorphoses. To gain his freedom, the slave must wed himself to the feline pace of the jaguar, the fluid undulation of the serpent, the mimetic disappearance of the chameleon. The Spanish, as Victor Schoelcher explains, originally applied the term *marron* to "once-domestic animals who returned to the wild... and this is undoubtedly the reason why they extended the term to their blacks. Since one speaks of a wild pig [*cochon marron*], why not speak of a *nègre marron*?"[11] Marronage, the return of a domestic animal (the enslaved person) to life in the wild, is a process of "de-domestication," a sort of creative indocility. The slave's flight presupposes the reappropriation of his body, his "unchaining," his "enwilding." And this liberation of the body is nothing but the affirmation of a mind, its reinvention on the other side of servitude. In their very names, cultural forms such as "soul music" or the "Negro spiritual" clearly allow the claim of a "black" spirituality to shine through. Marronage is the conjuration of the zombie.[12]

When the European migrants set sail for the Americas, they brought along their clothes, their tools, their Bibles, their icons, their religions, their languages. When they crossed the Atlantic, the English, the German, and the French all had the possibility of speaking and living with their compatriots. In the first large American cities, they reconstituted their communities of origin, for example Italian, Greek, or Irish neighborhoods. To the contrary, enslaved Africans left for the New World separated from their own people (those who spoke their language) and deprived of everything, including their humanity: in fact their Atlantic crossing began when they were stripped bare and branded. The captives were no longer anyone; they no longer had a name, only a scar – the one left on their skin by the incandescent red of their ship's initials. The *nègres* are – in Glissant's words – "stripped migrants": men, women, children denuded and reduced to "bare life" – strictly biological life – in the belly of the slaving ship. The slave trade is a one-way migration, away from Africa and away from humanity, a deportation. The slaving ship did not transport people; it lined up, chained, and juxtaposed bodies, which it allowed to rot in their own fluids. Those who could not hold up against hunger, those who could not stave off madness, those who could not ward off illness were, over the course of the crossing, thrown into the sea. The European got off the boat in America as a pioneer, the *nègre* who ran aground on its shores as a survivor.

In western eyes, the nudity of African, Oceanic, or Amerindian peoples constituted the first sign of their savagery: "See, they are still living in the state of nature!" But how could tattooed, scarified, scored, painted, oiled, or pierced bodies, adorned with feathers, be naked? In societies said to be "primitive," marking is primarily an act of self-stylization that, by means of a collective "corporeal language" (from scarification to sculpture, one finds the same aesthetic codes), testifies to cultural membership. For the "savages," a body becomes human only at the moment when it is modified by another human: a body that is not sculpted is a meaningless body, lacking identity and lacking in status. From this point of view, it is the Christian who seems "nude": the Christian with nothing but the nakedness of a blank page under his prudish clothing. "And you will make no cuts in your bodies for the dead, and you will mark no tattoos," commands the Bible (*Leviticus* 19: 28).

"Congo, with pointed teeth and bearing the signs of their country in the form of a cross on each breast":[13] by "signs of the country" the colonists meant these permanent motifs visible on the bodies of Africans when they arrived in the Caribbean. These scarifications are the only visible traces of their birthplace that the "bossals" (enslaved persons born in Africa) carried with them. The body is a surface for writing: culture works over its bodies to better incorporate them. A scarified body immediately constitutes a recording body [*corps-mémoire*]:[14] a surface on which the writing of a given people (e.g. Kongo, Hausa, Yoruba), the singular tale of a life (e.g. the first hunt, admission to the ironworkers' caste), or the genealogy of a clan can be laid out. Thus scarifications represent the first obstacle to the stripping or dispossession imposed by the slavery system. In the furrows, the cuts, the incised cartography of their flesh, enslaved Africans will always find some assurance as to their humanity, where they come from and what their history is. Slaves are humble only because they feel humiliated. From dawn to dusk they are surrounded by the word *nègre*, a word that denigrates, dirties, brings down everything it touches. To remember that one is named "Kunta Kinté" (like the character in Alex Haley's novel *Roots*) is already to resist "denigration," the erasure of name and memory. Self-esteem is the first moment of resistance.

From the Caribbean to Louisiana and passing by way of Peru, the *nègres marrons* incarnate the rejection of servitude, an absolute thirst for freedom. The cost of this freedom was terrible retribution for the fugitives who were recaptured and, for the others, a dangerous existence in a hostile environment. To flee demanded a great deal of courage and a great art, the art of the fugue. By their fugue under cover of the forest, the runaway blacks never stopped making slaveholding society "leak away," bringing in their wake ever more rebellious and insurgent slaves.[15] In many regions of the Americas they were able to re-create societies, reinvent cultures that are still vibrant today: those of the Businenge in Guyana and Surinam, the Maroons of Jamaica, the Garifunas of central America, the Quilombolas of Brazil, or yet again the Palenqueros of Columbia. But marronage was already dawning in the night-time escapes of slaves, when, taking advantage of the darkness, they slipped off the plantations to commune with one another in dances, in oral battles of storytelling, in mystical cults and secret oaths to the rhythm of drums. In this way the Creole cultures of the Americas were born, cultures that continually subverted the enslaving order by creating spaces of freedom at its very heart. From whispers a world can be born, a safe place, a utopia. It is always by whispering that we foment our escape plans. To whisper is to address words to an acolyte in such a way that they cannot be intercepted: a stealthy word that encodes the secret of a community to come. Truant words, whispers encrypt, distort, and make language rustle. The fugue is always born from a creative variation...

4
"Heroic Land"
Spectrography of the "Border"

In South Africa too, a phobia about foreigners, above all from elsewhere in Africa … has congealed into an active antipathy to what is perceived as a shadowy alien-nation of "*illegal* immigrants."[1]

In the following philosophical dialogue, I experiment with a spectral analysis of the borders that diffract our territories and our lives. More precisely, I propose a paradoxical genealogy of contemporary borders, one emerging from a timeframe that stretches from the dystopic ruins of the "Jungle" of Calais – once a camp on the northern edge of France inhabited by exiles who were trying to cross into the United Kingdom – to the sub-Saharan borders from which the first "shadows" – the first "illegal" forms of humanity – were deported in order to feed the slave regimes of the Americas and to underwrite the first wave of capitalist globalization.[2] The origin of this speculative fiction was an entirely "real" plan to build an amusement park near the former site of the Jungle with the intended name "Heroic Land," whose goal, in the words of the Calais City Hall, would have been to "redress the city's notoriety throughout France and in neighboring European countries."[3] If Calais' image needs to be burnished, this is because the presence of the immigrant is always considered a misplaced presence, a presence that dirties, a presence that contaminates just like the *nègre* body, against which the color line must always hold fast.

Heroic Land was thus, first and foremost, a "whitening" operation. It was a matter of simultaneously effacing the trace and the memory of lives unworthy of being lived and producing a blank, transparent space – a space in which there would no longer be any resistance to the fantasmagorias and simulacra of commodities. Heroic Land was also an exemplary case of cynicism of the powerful, because this amusement park was supposed to celebrate heroism, to offer every citizen-consumer the possibility of living a hero's life. But what could have been more heroic than the fact of having crossed deserts, mountains, overflowing seas, and fields of barbed wire and having undergone periods of imprisonment and even torture, in order to arrive at an abandoned moor and, there, to reinvent a world, a refuge bustling with all the languages and habits of the South? As a result of the withdrawal of Chinese investors, the project was abandoned in 2019. However, its proposal still testifies to the violence of a neoliberal racial order where the "control society" and the "society of the spectacle" are perfectly combined.

*

A desert beach. Far offshore, the incessant back-and-forth of ferries, container ships and supertankers. Directly above the scrubland and the harbor zone, the furtive and random trajectory of ovoid drones indifferent to the wind. Filtered by a double fence, white and immaculate, the rumble of semi-trucks destined for England gives a sepulchral tone to the backwash of the North Sea. In the background, beyond the ring road, one of the two chemical factories of Calais. And, further inland still, the crystalline belfry of Heroic Land – a new amusement park that sprang up not long after the destruction of the Jungle – a park whose "New Worlds" celebrating manga characters, video games, and sci-fi films enchant visitors from around the world. Under the oblique rays of the setting sun, a silhouette sets fire even to the wet blanket of the beach. The runner, his visage hidden beneath a hood, draws closer, in great steps toward the blockhouses entrenched in the bush-spotted dunes, where his path ends by crossing that of another exile: an ageless man seated cross-legged near a fire, his gaze lost somewhere between the two banks of the channel. The first day of the year 2030 comes to an end.

Still breathing heavily, after a shake of his head, the runner slowly crouches and extends his hands above the flames. Without a word, the seated man offers him a cigarette. A match crackles in the crook of a palm; soft whistles come through a halo of vapor and smoke.

THE SEATED MAN: What good is running? If you look at images of the Earth lit up at night, if you observe the phosphorescent synapses that trouble its surface and envelop us without our knowledge, you will understand that we live under an invisible dome. No matter how hard you try, you will not escape them...

THE RUNNING MAN: You can't understand, that's where my heart is, under this skin of white sand. And each time I hammer the ground, which my weakening steps have made brittle, its pulse revives. *Harraga!* I am a burner of borders: I have burned my documents, I burned my dinars, my CFAs,* my shillings, my *nairas*, I burned up my past life, I even burned my fingers so as to leave no more fingerprints, all to throw myself into it body and soul. And, if I must make myself understood, it would be with a sewn-up mouth, because a shadow has no voice.

THE SEATED MAN: But who is going to hear you, then? As if an illegal's mental states could interest anyone! As for the heart, you should know that it always betrays us. Come back to earth for a little, don't be afraid, the soil is quite hard under your feet. Let's not talk a lot but let's talk seriously: engineers have developed detectors for the heartbeat, and the breath as well, not to speak of infrared sensors. The surest way to get through the border is to fall into a coma... which, my faith, is much more restful than a sleep populated with desires and crazy fears. Nothing complicated; you take a product, tetrodotoxine, and you wake up on the other side. The TTX that I sell is a quality product, organic and not synthetic, extracted only from fugu, the puffer fish.

THE RUNNING MAN: You're making fun of me, that's your solution, to become a walking cadaver? Not for anything in the world, not even a ticket to Eldorado, would I renounce the beating of this bag of blood, this fire that animates me and consumes me. An old Chinese cook told me one day that writing was born from the steps sowed in the earth by a sparrow. They were harvested by a mandarin who passed by and their combination hatched the first alphabet. Often I wonder who will know how to read my path...

THE SEATED MAN: *Wake up brother, Jungle finished!* ... After all you have lived through, you can't give up so close to your goal. I've

---

* The CFA franc is the currency of the Communauté Financière Africaine.

been waiting for you, from the moment I first laid eyes on you. I slip you the "substance" and you can get on the "dead ship," in one of the places reserved for bare migrants in the refrigeration compartments of secured containers. Between the use of a cryogenic gel, breath and cardiac rhythm suppression, and all these beef carcasses that function like a screen, the zombies – that's what we call those who attempt the crossing, my brother – the zombies pass through human detectors with no problem. The only side effect is a slight change in memory. A negligible detail – we are already living a dead life here, so it's just a matter of taking it to the end.

The runner leaps up, as if he were waking from a bad dream, and nervously throws some twigs into the fire without for a moment taking his eyes off his host.

THE SEATED MAN: Why are you making such big eyes at me? I am only a smuggler, I'm just providing a service; certainly a paid service, but all the same a service: if it weren't me, it would be someone else. I do not claim to be an angel, just to play the role that has been given to me and to take my fee in the course of things. Nothing diabolical in itself, I won't ask you to sign a piece of parchment with your blood – that stuff is in the films – a fistful is good enough. Look at me rather as a pioneer, I'm just following the slogan of our time: "push back the limits," including those of life or death...

THE RUNNING MAN: You think that I haven't recognized you? I should never have accepted this dubious water that you offered me in the desert. You save your debtors only to lose them all the more surely. People call you by a thousand names: smuggler, coyote, counterfeiter, ferryman, stalker. The truth is that you are the master of crossroads. I am not blaming you; you are just a mediator. And a sacred trickster! Your travel agency is a racket; you work for the faceless slave traders.

THE SEATED MAN: Yes, yes, I already know your fable about the trafficking of human beings! It makes me sick, all these *nègres* who spend their time fretting about their lot. And they are supposed to be different, innocent because they were victims. But all they want, in the end, is to make good money off the dead, to convert them into cold hard cash, that's what you call "reparations." You make history into a tribunal, and justice into vengeance.

THE RUNNING MAN: No need to get off on it; I don't care about your
guilt. You talk about *nègres* as if such a thing really existed. A
nègre is an invisible man! A few years ago, in 2017 I believe, I
came across a video where I saw a dark point emerging from
a wave, several fathoms from a Venetian taxi boat. I had to
rewatch the scene several times before I understood, before I
realized what was happening. "African!" "Let him die!" "Go
back home!" To the tune of the locals' laughs and insults, a
young man with dark skin was swallowed by the waters. Later I
learned that he was a refugee from Gambia named Pateh Sabally,
and that he was only 22 years old. That's a really young age to
see Venice and die. That day I recognized the indelible atrocity of
a waking nightmare in the setting of the Venetian dream. Now
this has become so common that one no longer even gets angry
in the face of all these cops, all these coastguards, all these right-
thinking people who split their sides laughing when they see
bicots and *bamboulas* perish under the waves.

*The running man stops all of a sudden, overtaken with convul-
sions. His eyes bulging, his voice hoarse, he seems to be addressing
a crowd:*

THE RUNNING MAN: Don't just go on your way, open your eyes to
the trash that's watching us… To those who laugh at drowning
humanity, I would like to say this: the black man who suffers
agony before your eyes and whom you insult, this fantasized
African, this imaginary *nègre* born from the decomposition of the
blanc, this *nègre* does not exist! Quite simply because he doesn't
live anywhere but in the depths of you yourselves. But what do
you believe? One doesn't get free from one's shadow so easily!
Yes, I know, you didn't say "nigger," you settled with treating
Pateh Sabally *as* a *nègre*, a waste of a man, a life unworthy to
be lived. You didn't say it because "nigger" is not a word but a
barking, which dehumanizes the master as well as the slave! But
there, where you see a *nègre*, I for my part see a young man, I
see the promise, the desire, the breath, the dreams, the courage,
the humanity that has burned out in you – and that you secretly
envy.

You have to remember, *nègre* is not a word but the common
ancestor of all the illegals. *Nègre* is not a word but an evil spell:
the sorcery of capital, which turns human beings into spare

parts. Do you know that it was in the bowels of the slaving ship that this farce of political biology – which is attached to sorting, selecting, and managing bare lives – was perfected? This is how our humanity was first warehoused: a humanity managed according to a floating currency, convertible into sugar, cotton, indigo, stock prices, algorithms.

The *nègre*, I guarantee you, is the quintessence of the flexible workforce, the integral proletarian, thoroughly scanned by capital: his price was evaluated over the whole of his life; the cost of his reproduction was calculated by including the price of rearing to adulthood, and, although one is guaranteed a copyright on that, in general it is preferred to wear them down completely when they are in their prime and then import new batches – which is in fact much more financially sound than to raise them and let them grow old. Oh yes, you can put on your fine airs, but in the meantime you aren't worth much more than a slave! Who cares about your names and your lineages? In the eyes of the universal market, you are nothing but "human resources," which is to say, much less than bodies. Bodies liquidated and liquified: a flow one feeds from, even while pretending to close it off.

Dark star succumbing to its own density, the fugitive collapses in a spiraling movement in the wet, cold sand. The seated man places his hands on the feverish temples of his companion, after having covered them with cinders. One, two, three minutes pass before the latter comes back to his senses in a leap, as if returning to the surface from a breathless dive.

THE RUNNING MAN: That happens to me a lot lately, I say and do things that I immediately forget, when I come back to myself.

He rubs his face and scalp.

THE RUNNING MAN: Who is that there? … Can one say "I" when nothing assures us that there is any "we" in play? How say "we" when "I" is another?

One day, after one of these fits, I saw myself on the screen of a friend's smartphone: I danced, I leaped, I stabbed at the air with an imaginary sword, spinning around myself, a dervish drunk on the breath of the dunes.

THE SEATED MAN: Ah ah ah! … Breath of the dunes or breath of the djinns? Rest assured, you are in their favor; I know this, I have my sources. Whatever happens to you is a blessing. Above all when one comes from your background…

THE RUNNING MAN: My background!?

THE SEATED MAN: Yes, your background, and don't try to play dumb. You went to school didn't you. From Islamabad to Paris, I have met a whole stack of people like you, who know how to "talk," who have never worked the earth, sold from a cart, dug in the trash; "well-born" citizens, produced and certified within the standards of clinics where everything is white and purified. You have always had women or descendants of slaves to serve you, but among the "whites," I know not by what black magic, you suddenly become the "oppressed," indeed the "community" spokesman. But what does that mean, to be "Ethiopian" when one is "Omorro," what does it mean to be "Mauritanian" when one is "Harratine," what does it mean to be "Burmese" when one is "Rohingya"?!

THE RUNNING MAN: My brother, you're hiding your game well, that's a nice rage that keeps its cool, and I admit that I prefer to see you sharpen words rather than knives… yes, I know, I'm a bourgeois asshole, and I would never have been able to manage in all that hell. I had the future before me, I was a favored son, a *peau noire, masque nègre* who glorified the pharaohs and the apostles of negritude all day long while spitting on the black rabble who populate the African shantytowns.

But since I have seen the world through the eyes of the damned, I'm sick when I think about the future I was supposed to have: I can no longer live in a gilded bunker, I can no longer put up with the access codes, the control screens, the bodyguards, the striptease of success on the Afropolitan social scene.

In my journey across the continent I have known interminable shakedowns and degradation, I have shared my bed with rats in nauseating, overpacked cells, I have been a trophy for Saharan militaries on the payroll of a Europe as arrogant as it is hypocritical. But for the first time I have also experienced a limitless fraternity.

THE SEATED MAN: Stop your blah blah blah, you're wearing me out. Things are simple: there is a border, there is someone who can get you through, there is a candidate to get through. So if you do not want to make the attempt, tell me why the fuck are you here?

THE RUNNING MAN: You really take me for a fool, I just want to save my skin… "We didn't cross the border, the border crossed us!"

What's the use of crossing borders, if they already cross us, since they follow us with their tracking devices, since they are registered in our very flesh? Like these electronic bracelets that one puts on the ankles of outlaws, like these chips that people put under the skin of children that they love too much, like this iris that opens the door of a secured home in the blink of an eye. What's the point of crossing borders, if we always remain on the threshold, if these walls, these enclosures, these armored barriers that you propose I cross are only the crudest of their forms? The borders have become "smart," real microprocessors in their own right that never stop spilling over the edges of nations, proliferating at the very heart of their domestic territory, to the point of transforming the tiniest point of access to a public or private space into a checkpoint and every human element of a flow into some kind of suspect.

What is the use of crossing borders, if they pass through our very interiority like a scalpel, dividing the autochthone from the foreigner, the man from the woman, the white from the black, the secular from the Muslim, the hetero from the homo, the healthy from the pathological, thereby handing us over to the metastases of schizophrenia? To sort the wheat from the chaff, we have finished by extending to humanity as a whole procedures that previously were applied only to migratory bipeds: the recording of fingerprints, biometric inquisition, the detection of "at-risk individuals."

THE SEATED MAN: You are right at least on one point: from here on in nothing counts but our thousand and one profiles, the digital shadow that doubles each of our steps and acts, the "ghost," as the Japanese say. It is this hemorrhage of data flowing from our daily lives that the swarm of algorithms captures and permanently reconfigures; and this they do primarily to profit the occult powers of capital, for which governments and security agencies are only transmission belts.

THE RUNNING MAN: All praise to transparency, you know well that it's for our common security! In these dark times, citizens have the duty to be as clear as spring water. Because an endless war is being waged against an enemy that is inside as much as it is outside, an enemy that is all the more pernicious as it can hide in the smallest corners of cities, countryside areas, bodies and is always ready to talk back.

Although the fear of the alien – the viral migrant – may have become second nature, we don't even have goosebumps anymore. Our skin is no longer anything but a control interface. Who has not felt those little terrors at the moment when the fractal geometry of their iris or the spirals of their fingertips are scanned? To be authenticated is to be admitted among the "elect," at least until the next scan. To be preoccupied with the fate of the "reject" – the ones who were not born in the right neighborhood or on the right side of the river, or even those who dare join in dissidence – is to be guilty even before having been judged. Look how anesthesia is the price of immunity!

The silhouette of the runner freezes abruptly in the waning light. With a few quick and effective gestures, he covers up the embers with sand and enters a biomimetic combination, which leaves visible only his eyes.

THE SEATED MAN: You have keen senses, I hardly noticed the buzzing of the cyberhounds. One might say, my brother, that your skin is getting less valuable from moment to moment.

THE RUNNING MAN: Rest assured, there are still a couple of trips in my bag. Why do you think that only a small number of migrants are finally sent back, given how many are tracked, captured, imprisoned?

From the port of Calais to the Cape of Good Hope, this is the debacle of nations, and so citizens are reassured in the only possible way: to ward off this fate, walls are put on display like so many fetishes and protective divinities – get thee behind me, Satan! But their repulsive effect on the migratory bipeds is just a diversion.

The border is less a wall than a filter, it captures and manages human resources, it is a sorting machine: a matrix in which the fugitives are secretly encoded as a shadow workforce, all the more docile as it is spectral. It's obvious that employing "living beings," by which I mean "autochthones," has become too expensive.

You know very well that Babylon needs us: we are its house servants, its hardhats on the construction sites, its football stars, its sex workers, its programmers of algorithms, its emergency doctors, and of course the foundation and the prime matter of its new war of capture: the business of incarceration. The great hunt that we are running aims only to keep us in the beyond, always on the edge of life and the law, in a bare life stripped of the right to have rights, in an indefinitely deferred death.

Spare the rod and spoil the child! – you will say to me. The clatter of the whip, the charge of the riot police, the dog's bite, the burning of tear gas, the laceration of barbed wire, the sum of this old pedagogy of cruelty has always had the goal of saving the damned from their own lack of dignity. "The first thing that the native learns is to stay in his place, to not go beyond the limits," said some philosopher whose name I have forgotten.

THE SEATED MAN: Then you admit that the limits are there to be violated. So why wait to seize your chance? You're on the side of the hero in this great reality show. You survived torture in the Saharan camps, overflowing seas, the disinfecting power hoses of Lampedusa, the dissection of the organ traffickers in Tripoli. With your knack, you could become whatever you wanted on the other side. I don't really understand what's keeping you here. The Jungle was only a camp, one mega-squat among others…

THE RUNNING MAN: Schools, restaurants with movies, hammams, an Ethiopian church, mosques, a theater, bakeries, soup stands… you call this "one squat among others"? They did everything possible to make it into a factory for selective sorting, a decontamination chamber for dehumanization, and still the border can always be subverted. It is the very possibility of transgression that led the Jungle to emerge. Don't you remember the words of Zimako, the one who created the secular school of the Dunes: "this isn't a jungle here, it's a forum!" he so often exclaimed. That was his way of reminding us that the first forum – the public place where the communal business of Rome was deliberated – was constructed outside the city, at its gates and on its borders.

In short, that which is peripheral may someday become central. The Jungle had to be a place of exile, far from the city, for it to finally (and pretty quickly) become one of the city's hubs: a space where people who had no prospects at the start (Afghans, Sudanese, city planners, artists, legal experts, and volunteers from all over Europe) enter into relationships with one another, experiment with other forms of organization, put their expertise at the disposal of others, forge new alliances, elaborate a new common language – everything necessary to sabotage the humanitarian and police order of controlled assistance.

A cosmopolis surging from the mud through its insolent freedom, the Jungle escaped the imaginary of waste that people stick on camps and shantytowns these days. The Jungle was not this shameful place deprived of laws, populated with former natives and the human refuse that the experts dissected on television news programs. Yes, it was a forest, but certainly not Tarzan's forest; it was rather the forest of *nègres marrons*! Do you see, the forestine refuge can be born in the heart of cities as well as in the interzones of transit: it is born from our deviations, our acts of poaching, our contraband, our lost and unmanageable steps.

I still feel the fires of the Jungle under the dunes. The other side will not give up its fight, because there is no longer any inside or outside; it will continue in the chaotic vortex of the interworlds. The refuge is neither outside us nor inside us; it is found at the infolding between the world and the self, the self and the other, in a suspended relation that is deployed only in the very movement of the fugue – this force of flight that makes our bodies into graphic and utopian waves. The real question today is not how to cross the border but how to inhabit it, how to make it into a new fault line from which the magma of a future humanity can erupt. I know that in the word "border" one always hears the clash of arms, the grappling of combatants, the clamor of armies confronting each other. But before it is the trace left by confrontation, the border is a contact zone and makes distinctions only in order to bring them back together. Before they are lines, borders are places of life where human beings have always reinvented themselves by feeding off the strangeness of their neighbors. Like coral reefs, borders only breathe and live using their pores, their rough patches, the openwork of their surfaces, where the reciprocal fertilization of incommensurable worlds takes place.

With the gentle pace of sprouting plants, shadows emerge from the surrounding dunes, androgynous silhouettes bearing a portable flamethrower in one hand and a waterpik in the other. After hovering for a moment, they reach the running man in several catlike leaps.

THE SEATED MAN: So then, where are you going with this fire and this water, and what is this gang of X-Men?

He points to the translucid spire of the Heroic Land belfry with his finger.

THE RUNNING MAN: Vine women, Mami Watas, alligator men, panther men... south of the Sahara, nobody needed Hollywood to develop secret societies.[4] We are going to burn paradise and to put out the fires of hell!

Suddenly, a riot of cyberhounds and a swarm of drones spring from behind the blockhouse. The chimeras intone a Nyabinghi song whose pulsations blur and disrupt the navigation devices of the robots.[5] In just a few minutes, collisions multiply and the machines destroy one another. He rests his hand on the bare forearm of the seated man.

THE RUNNING MAN: This skin I touch you with, which never stops molting, in the end there is nothing deeper than this. So let's celebrate our ashes together...

5

Mayotte, the Impossibility of an Island

The island is not an isolated location, every island is part of an archipelago.

Édouard Glissant

"Seven undocumented migrants were drowned in the wreckage of the fishing vessel which carried them just as they were arriving in the lagoon of Mayotte, announced the prefecture today."[1] One news item among others, squeezed between the burglary of a house and the derailment of a truck. We get used to everything, including the cyclical return of the dead at breakfast. "Inch Allah!" … we continue to listen absent-mindedly to the radio while swallowing all this with our cups of coffee. As if seven dead did not count, any more than all those, numbered in the thousands, who preceded them into the waters.[2] Today Mayotte remains in France's blind spot: a territory missing from its library shelves, its cinema and television screens, its preoccupations, and its imaginary. Out of sight, out of mind… Meanwhile this island is the laboratory par excellence for republican "postcoloniality." The colonial mechanism in Mayotte censors its own history like an implacably advancing tectonic plate that divides, partitions, and finally erases the landscape of an archipelago – that of the Comoros – before becoming embedded in the psyche of the "neocolonized" and making them into their own enemies.

Republican postcoloniality

According to Françoise Vergès, republican postcoloniality means "the choices and policies of governments of the French Republic that, since 1945, has worked to reconfigure its territory in the face of increasing calls for decolonization, the universal condemnation of racism."[3] It is a matter of transforming a republic that has long been the world's second colonial power into a "world power" respectful of human rights and scrubbed free of the crimes of colonization and their aftereffects.

For this reason there has been a change in the vocabulary: the remaining colonial possessions became the Outre-mer – "Overseas Territories" – and since then play a key role in the preservation of France's economic and geostrategic interests. Thanks to the Outre-mer and the 11 million square kilometers of its exclusive economic zone, France has the second largest maritime space in the world at its disposal, being surpassed only by the United States. And thanks to the fact of its sovereignty over Mayotte and the "scattered islands," France controls the greatest part of the Mozambique Channel, whose deep waters overlay hydrocarbon deposits and polymetallic nodes.[4]

"Give in to the temptation of Mayotte…"

If Mayotte is so little known in France, this is doubtless because the Mahorans, as human specimens distinct from the Comorians, do not yet exist: they are in the process of being fabricated on the basis of images, tales, and a rewriting of history whose goal is to set the stage for a "Mahoran people" and to bring them into existence in the eyes of the world. This allows the Comoros archipelago to be partitioned for France's benefit. In the international offices of tourist agencies, Mahoran hostesses wish *karibu* to tour operators and their potential clients.[5] Their pamphlets are invitations to exoticism:

> Give in to the temptation of Mayotte, the perfumed isle, the isle of makis… Its lagoon offers an atmosphere in which dolphins, whales and sea turtles happily show off. Come also to meet the original people: the Mahorans have a joyful soul, everything here is still authentic.[6]

The "authochtone" of the tourist guides is the new version of noble savage: a gentle and spontaneous being who has barely entered into history. The Mahorans' accession to the status of a French overseas department (DOM), takes place via their "naturification," their reduction to nature.[7] Thus the Mahoran dies as a Comorian but is reborn as a "Frenchman of Mayotte."[8] In the advertising agencies and the design offices of Mamoudzou or Paris, *métros* are busy reworking the image, the design, and the packaging of Mayotte.[9] It is a matter of defining this island not from a culture that extends in fact throughout the archipelago,[10] but from a natural environment presented as edenic. This is a nature outside time, because it has been detached from the thousand-year history of a civilization of the *dhow* – a traditional Arab sailing boat adapted to the archipelago by its residents. The promotion of a "Lagoon Island of Mayotte" contributes to the erasure and outlawing of the remaining archipelago. From this point of view, the logo chosen for the new Mahoran airline company Ewa, a stylization of the "S path" (a long sinuous corridor through the coral reef), is completely revealing: this reef is the preferred spot for the *wazungu*, the *métro* divers who will henceforth represent the entire island. This "S" is not a symbol but a brand aimed at assuring a French copyright over a space that has been purged of its own history and culture, a label supposed to guarantee the quality of a product of global tourism.

The picture would be idyllic if not for the unfortunate presence of all these exogenous creatures in the lagoon ecosystem: the *kwasa kwasa*, or typical Comorian boats. They are considered akin to the ten plagues that brought Egypt low, so that Pharaoh would be forced to liberate Moses' people: the invasions of frogs, locusts, and flies and, above all, the river waters changed to blood. No matter how often the French navy may have inspected these boatloads of "migrants" coming from Anjouan, ever new waves of *kwasa* continually revive and renew the assault on Eldorado, only to sink into the depths, to wander blindly in the Mozambique Channel, and to redden the lagoon's waters with their uproar. To escape the motorboats of the Air and Border Police (PAF), the gendarmerie, and the customs inspectors, to evade the patrols, the helicopters, and the state-of-the-art radar stations of the national navy, indeed this entire armada, one must take risks – navigate by night without lights, sometimes cutting the motors, or brave the gusts of wind and the fog. Inch Allah! One plays Russian roulette with one's fate.

"The canoe overturned on a reef, near to the Kani-Keli coast. – Nine people died there, including five infants." So the news bulletins tumble, on one another's heels, all alike, always further undermining the dream of a virgin and innocent Mayotte.

> The *kwasa* comes to Mayotte. He is the one who trembles even more than the "illegals." His canoe gets tangled in the corals and overturns. Screams are overheard, and the police fish them out with a net. (Djorane, Terminale Littéraire, Lycée du Nord (Mayotte)[11]

The Arab pilots baptized this island *al mawt*, "death," because of the countless shipwrecks caused by the formidable coral belt that protects its shores. Today these sharp reefs are doubled by an invisible border, all the more effective for being virtual. A control zone in real time – which can be extended at will thanks to the coupling of naval forces and positioning technologies (such as radar and satellite imagery) – makes Mayotte into a high-tech nature reserve dedicated to the protection of indigenous nonhuman species. The protection of the "right to life" for some (the nationals) exposes others (the foreigners) to death.

Mayotte Channel Gateway

On Mayotte, the port of Longoni is tucked against a wide, majestic bay set off by interwoven mangroves, the lush hills of the northern tip and an invisible girdle of coral reefs. The bay of Longoni has long offered shelter to passing ships. *Ulingoni* is a Bantu root meaning "port of call," and thus reminds us of Mayotte's precolonial history, this millennial circulation of *dhows* and outrigger canoes from which not only the archipelagic society of the Comoros was born but also what one calls the "Swahili" civilization (from the Arab *swahil*, "coasts"): a chain of city-states – Lamu, Zanzibar, Mogadishu, and so on – that punctuate the shores of Eastern Africa and constitute so many steps along routes that lead away from the Arab Peninsula, from India, from China, or even from Malaysia. It was into Swahili Africa, the epicenter of the first commercial and cultural globalization of the Indian Ocean – the Afro-Asiatic world system of which Europe was merely the periphery at that time – that the ports of the Comoros archipelago and the north-west of Madagascar were integrated. Much like the societies of the Caribbean, Swahili worlds

were born from unforeseeable events, from the reciprocal fertilization of cultural elements and infinitely diverse peoples: Somalis,
Bantus, Persians, Yemenites, Austronesians, Portuguese, refugees of
all kinds – all actors in a creative archipelization.

In 2013 Longoni was renamed Mayotte Channel Gateway – no
longer to be considered a port but a "hub," a logistical platform.
This mechanism completes the process of "containerization" of
Mahoran life: let a container ship or a supertanker arrive late and
it's panic, the specter of scarcity: interminable single-file lines form
before these altars of modernity, the gas station and the super-
market. The transformation of Mayotte into a French department
and the exponential growth in imports that this presupposes now
add the deafening murmur of merchandise to the wall of the
Balladur visa: consumption is the only way I still relate to the world.
The creation of a tiny island of fictitious prosperity on Mayotte
necessarily leads to the reinforcement of the archipelago's partition,
the hardening of the border, the hemorrhage of vital forces from the
other islands to the profit of the Mahoran Eldorado, and therefore
the growing rejection of all those – the "Comorians" – who threaten
our privileges as French consumers. One of the first indications
that the former geography of the archipelago is being censored
is this geopolitical separation of the 101st department from its
surrounding landscape, like a tectonic fault line that grows wider
the further it is integrated into French mercantile circuits. "The
world here is accounted for in containers, nothing else, and this is
perhaps the best possible way to filter it."[12] The four-by-four trucks,
the sedans, the plasma screens, the cases of beer... all arrive by way
of Longoni; the magical umbilical cord which binds Mayotte to the
metropole while at the same time cutting it off from all the familial,
cultural, and historical bonds that attached it to the other islands
from time immemorial. Its inclusion as a DOM always presupposes
a shrinking of its horizon and a "mutilated cartography": "To
reinforce dependency on France, the state hindered relationships
between the overseas territories and their neighbors."[13]

Under the DOM[14]

Is it reasonable to imagine that one part of the archipelago might
remain independent and that one island... might hold a different
status? ... When a territory becomes independent, we need not

propose to dissolve the unity of what has always been the Comoros as a single archipelago.

This declaration was made by Valéry Giscard d'Estaing, then president of the republic, during an interview with *Le Monde* on October 26, 1974.[15] Two months later, in an initial referendum, 93 percent of the population of the overseas territory of the Comoros – including the islands of Ngazidja, Mohéli, Anjouan, and Mayotte – declared itself in favor of independence. But in June 1975, under the pressure of various lobby groups such as Mahoran elites and Action Française and under American pressure linked to the Cold War, the French government effected a radical about-face and decided to hold a second electoral consultation – island by island, in violation of international law – which in February 1976 gave Mayotte's reattachment to France a semblance of legitimacy. The United Nations and the African Union have never recognized French sovereignty over this island. Since 1960, the United Nations has in fact imposed a juridical obligation on former colonial powers to respect the territorial integrity of onetime possessions during any process of decolonization.

As the partition of the archipelago hardened over the course of time,[16] the term "Mayotte" became an empty but divisive shell: an abstraction in the strong sense, because today the only thing that this word suggests is the division itself, an abstraction of the territory from its hinterland – namely the other islands and Madagascar. Thus the island of Maore is no longer anything but sky and lagoon; it no longer has an archipelago or a continent. How many times does one hear a Mahoran or a *métro* say, "Mayotte isn't Africa, it's France!"? It must be said that

> the Mahorans do not know their history; what one learns here is always "our ancestors, the Gauls." Nor do they have any grasp of history, they do not know what binds them to the other Comorians, to the Malagasy, to Africa. How can you expect these people to be moved by the fate of their neighbors? This is a population whose horizon has been amputated, from which all vision has been taken away, whether in time or in space. *Just look at your plate, vote and shut up!*[17]

"That's what their politicians teach them," explains Ali Hafidou, a member of the Mahoran collective Suluhu ("Reconciliation"). We are thus dealing with a floating island, an offshore platform, and an autarchic biosphere that people would prefer to be perfectly water-tight, with neither cracks nor infiltrations.

Given the size of the "migratory flux," there were a deplorable number of deaths in the waters of Mayotte, explains a TV presenter. But a migratory flux has no face, it does not die, so why should I be moved by it? Using this kind of expression is the best way to suppress our emotions toward our neighbors, because it turns human beings into abstractions. The euphemisms, the compound words, the litany of figures and statistics, a whole series of discursive elements permit the construction of social reality according to the interests of dominant parties, while concealing everything that could lead us to question the simulated reality that they are trying to impose on us. The way a photo is framed shapes our perception of what has been photographed; the terms "foreigner," "Mayotte French," "Comorian," "migrant," "French department," and the like form a supple and adaptable web that imposes a pernicious frame on our gaze. By assigning a defamatory identity to the other – that of the "illegal," *clandestin*, who necessarily lives in the shadow of crime – this perceptual grid closes us up into our own fantasmatic autochthony. Such closure is all the more outrageous in these islands, where the first meaning of the word used to designate the foreigner, *mdjeni*, refers to the hospitality offered to the refugee; it means "the invited one." And in fact, as the author Soeuf Elbadawi and the anthropologist Damir Ben Ali remind us, this basalt and sulfur land was first populated by successive waves of refugees from the most varied horizons – Bantus, Persians, Yemenites, Malays, Portuguese, and others – who had been forced to weave their lines of flight together around a dinner table: they formed the circle of the *shungu* (the word comes from a Bantu root meaning "steamed rice").

> The Comorians of Mayotte have acquired the habit of thinking "Mayotte and the Comoros" and indeed of seeing Réunion as their "sister island" ... In allowing themselves in this way to be defined by an external gaze and categories, the Comorians make themselves the accomplices and the consenting victims of their own annihilation.[18]

Under the invisible dome of Mayotte, one still hears the call of muezzins and the chants of the *fundi wa madjinni* (masters of djinns), but what is celebrated first and foremost is the cargo cult, rituals through which the Melanesians tried to capture western wealth by doing their best to imitate the gestures and attitudes

of radio operators, long-haul ship captains, "white sorcerers."
Comorian skin, French masks; from now on, the "Mahorans"
believe themselves to be "old stock," not like those foreigners
who set off as *kwasa* from the distant island of Anjouan...
70 kilometers away. In *Le Discours antillais*, Glissant gave an
exemplary analysis of the mechanics of the DOM, that is, of
"domization" [*domisation*]: it is a matter of converting public funds
– subventions, endowments, bureaucratic salaries and bonuses, and
so on – into private benefits for the advantage of big French groups
(e.g. Total, Bouygues, Casino), which form oligopolies and therefore
collude on prices – hence the problem of the rising cost of living.
Direct descendants of the colonial exclusivity established by Colbert
in the seventeenth century, the DOMs are therefore captive markets
in disguise. The entire ideological power of the system resides in the
fact that it is presented as a gift from France, and thus transforms
the "domisized" residents into eternal debtors of a fictitious and
perverted development.

Tropical micro-fascism

Mayotte is possessed by a specific kind of bad djinn, a desire for
apartheid – the pathological dream of a homogeneous community.
It is an island asphyxiated by its own border, a space where schizophrenia and paranoia go hand in hand; here the stranger – down
to his or her deepest self – is chased out in village after village.
Not even schools were spared in the manhunt that unfolded from
January to July 2016, when students disappeared overnight without
warning. Sometimes they were found in the Place de la République
of Mamoudzou, sleeping right on the ground with their families,
without even a scrap of tent to protect them from the inclement
weather and the eyes clustered around the bars of this nameless
camp. These were not refugees but rejects of the Republic: people
banished from communal living [*vivre-ensemble*]. Among children, a
new game appeared, rehearsing events outside the schoolyard walls:
"gendarmes and Anjouanais"... More than ever, cries of *Mdzuani!*
("Anjouanais!") stung the air like insults and left indelible traces
in the vulnerable souls and hearts of the children of Mayotte, who
were perceived as outsiders, the "cursed children." "Comorian" had
already become a carcinogenic word, a synonym for "foreigner,"
and thus for "delinquent" – it had been that for a long time. Now

the word was no longer pronounced but spit, above all in the media. How could anyone be astonished, then, to see pseudo-citizen militias roaming the streets one day in search of Comorian dwellings to destroy or pillage?...

On the other side of the mirror, beyond the mirages of the migrant's and the *mzungu*'s (or *métro*'s) thirst for the exotic, the luxurious hills of Mayotte enclose a vast warren, in which a permanent manhunt unfolds under the open sky. The human being pursued is the brother, the cousin, the grandmother of the Mahoran: he or she comes from the other islands of the Comoros archipelago. "In fact," declares a certain lieutenant-colonel Guillemot,

> what I am trying to do is put foreigners in an irregular situation in the midst of a climate of insecurity. They have to know that they can be questioned at any moment. They have to be afraid of this. ... It is right for people in an irregular situation to feel endangered. This insecurity is necessary.[19]

In place of the common opinion, endlessly repeated by the media and politicians, that immigration is a source of general danger, the gendarmerie officer substitutes the idea that keeping the peace demands a pedagogy of terror vis-à-vis "illegals." From here on, this will be the goal of "hunting teams" (as they call themselves), which regularly carry out searches followed by raids and roundups in villages or on the roads. The permanent tracking, of which so-called migrants are the object and which stops them even at the doors of schools or hospitals, leads them to develop maroon tactics: evasions, lookout networks, hidden pathways, and refuges in the *malavoune* ("wooded hillsides"). Sometimes solidarities are forged between Mahorans who accept the risks of showing hospitality to their relatives from the other islands. Unfortunately, the growing power of a police state on the island and the banalization of these extraordinary measures, which it presupposes, drip the poison of denunciation into the veins of the population: cowardice is elevated to the rank of civic action, while solidarity, in other words humanity toward the neighbor "without papers," is criminalized.

What is new today is that the police share with resident groups their monopoly on the legitimate right to track people, and these groups are as anonymous as the nauseating pamphlets they propagate on the social media and on the walls of the 101st department. "Mayotte asphyxiated": this is the title of a downloadable tract that appeared on April 28, 2016, on the website Kwezi. It announced that "a demonstration and a peaceful removal action against illegal immigration will take place Sunday May 15, 2016. Starting point at the Boueni plateau at 6 o'clock, to make the rounds of the town. To be followed by a big barbeque [*voulé*]."[20] That an operation of this kind could have taken place despite three weeks of advance notice says a lot about the banalization of a certain xenophobia and about the complicity of media, elected leaders, and local authorities in the proliferation, across much of the island, of abuses committed against the Comorians: harassment, insults, racist attacks, instances of looting and arson of dwellings, threats and break-ins at the homes of people who sheltered those "removed" (*décasés*), and so on.

Each time, these "removal" actions took the form of sinister street parties where the beating of cooking pots clashed noisily with songs and with the vengeful shouts of *bouenis* (local women). At Tsimkoura, where everything began in January, more than 100 residents advanced to a hunting expedition through their munici-pality, dressed "in red, to recognize one another,"[21] when they were prevented from pinning a yellow star on the chest of a Comorian invader – an inner enemy, all the more perfidious as he was indistin-guishable from the rest of them. But the hunt for Comorians would not have grown to such proportions without the climate of impunity that reigned in Mayotte at that time, a phenomenon that Maître Ghaem, a lawyer for organizations that defend migrants, continually denounced with reference to "municipalities that openly welcome 'collectives' of villagers into their bosom, photocopying their tracts for them and organizing festive *voulés* around 'removals.'"[22] As the human rights organization La Cimade analyses it, the lack of any reaction from the Gendarmerie and from the Préfecture "guarantees the impunity of these collectives and gives them an opportunity to generate these kind of illegal and xenophobic operations."[23] More troubling still is that, according to a consultant who preferred to remain anonymous, some members of these militias emerged from "citizen councils," originally structures of local administration designed to ensure feedback from local residents. Supposedly "civic" work has thus been divided up: one radicalized fraction of the population takes care of flushing out and cornering suspects, the Gendarmerie isolates the victims (under the pretext of trying to control the activities of the militias), the PAF examines their papers and clears them out. Given its apparent efficiency, the tropical micro-fascism that is being experimented with in Mayotte – this communion between a small fringe of "citizens" and the forces of order, set on tracking and tracing the "foreigner" – may yet show up in metropolitan France someday...

Unease in the lagoon

> I was born in Mayotte, with an Anjouanais mother and a Mahoran father... Because the villagers of my town do not like foreigners, particularly Anjouanais, I was ashamed of my mother for a long time. I was ashamed to tell my friends that I am Anjouanais on my mother's side. I hid this truth from them, I did not want to be rejected on account of this origin. I told myself to be happy with this truth hidden at the bottom of my heart, but I felt very much alone. I did not dare go out in public with my mother. When she spoke to me in front of people, I ignored it, as if she were an unknown person, a stranger. (Student)

It was in reading this text, written by one of my students, whom we can call Amina, that I really came to grips with this fact: borders divide souls as well as territories, often rendering them strangers to themselves. Fanon's claim is confirmed: alienation cannot be understood only from the side of the individual psyche, because it is generated by the entire (post)colonial situation.

But I already hear voices shouting: "Stop with your colonial history, all that is in the past!..." There is no more forced labor or *code de l'indigénat*, of course. What is exploited today in the DOM is consumption,[24] the subsidized assistance of the "autochthones": populations that have become superfluous and whose landscape is little by little being transformed into an ecological reserve. Moreover, the asphyxia mentioned in the pamphlets that call for Comorians to be hunted down is in fact only the asphyxia of a social, cultural, and economic life that is less and less capable of doing without respiratory assistance from the French motherland–fatherland. The effect of "domization" is therefore not limited to the sterilization of initiatives, production, and local economy but extends to the hollowing out of the *domisés* themselves, who over the course of time lose their ability to function independently and find themselves obliged to take refuge in ceremony and folklore if they are to maintain a minimum of self-esteem. This is the last phase of assimilation, a perfect colonization because it is not recognized as such and because the neocolonized desire it themselves. In this complete subjection to dependency – a guardianship as insidious as it is invisible and comfortable – it becomes ever more difficult to express differences of opinion [*différends*] with respect to the metropole and its representatives. Thus, fed by the nursling's primal fear, a process of permanent self-censorship is instituted: "the Mahoran officials are afraid of the prefects who treat them like beggars."[25] Indeed, we could hardly bite the hand that feeds us: we are too afraid of losing that which already led us so far astray.

Mayotte's malaise is partly rooted in its inhabitants' more or less conscious feeling that they have been dispossessed of their own image, their own history, and its becoming. This malaise goes much deeper than the thousand and one economic and social difficulties that face this territory (bottomless unemployment, medical and educational systems on the brink of implosion, exponential growth of burglaries and assaults, 85 percent of the population below the poverty line). An incredible malaise, touching on the very feeling of existence, as if to say: "Even if I renounce my brothers, spit on their shitty independence, hang up the French flag and sing the Marseillaise, it doesn't matter; I am still invisible in the eyes of the motherland–fatherland, to the point that I sometimes start to doubt my own reality." Mayotte suffers from not being recognized by the faraway metropole, even though it does not want to be recognized among its sister islands.

The first source of the malaise in Mayotte thus stems from the growing repression of this island's Comorian and African character [*comorianité, africanité*]. This repression does not come uniquely from the psyche of individuals but is first produced through police tactics such as the home raid, internment, or expulsion. Today more than ever, the expulsion of "foreign bodies" is presented as a remedy against all the evils of Mahoran society. The problem with the repressed is that it never stops returning, and in the form of a violence that is internal to the individual who engages in repression: instances of somatization, behavioral disturbances, psychoses. In the case of Mayotte, this return of the repressed is expressed most notably in the ever more numerous population of "unaccompanied minors": children living on the streets and in the woods, rejected children who grow up with rage between their teeth, far from their repressed parents – children given over to an impossible citizenship.

Swahilization: the archipelagic power of coastlines

Last night they announced that one of mine was dead
my cousin snatched by the wave crushed by the swells...
We have not wailed not screamed not even cast a tear
into the family's closed backyard...
The muteness of a mother emerging from her spellbound state
Face ripped by the weight of official self-congratulation
over the waves of a neighborhood radio... A newscaster counting
    off the long rosary of victims...
Where are the fathers of this newly germinating nation buried? ...
the news is harsh ninety-eight names overboard Perished in the
    swells...
Grappling with suspended destinies on two frail skiffs of bric
    and brac Coming from Domoni They went out at the end of a
    ghastly voyage between the frenetic radars of the north point and
    the agitated fleet of the Soroda...

I said that I am burning and that I will be carried to the shadow of
    the womb as a dead cinder, defeated Like these human remains
    that drown in the lagoon by the thousands at the dawn of a
    morning with no mist...
The denial of what we once were lives forever within us.

Soeuf Elbadawi[26]

Testifying to the intolerable is the first act of a resistance that is political because it is poetic: the first revolution is that of the word. To this "fable written in the master's hand" – "this story of wild migration on one's own land" – the artist Soeuf Elbadawi crafts riposte by means of a poetic counter-spell from beyond the grave: *A Dhikri for /o/ur Dead: Rage between the Teeth*. His text breaks open the unsaid regarding all these unhappily departed who haunt Mayotte and the other islands of the archipelago. This is the story of a shattered man enraged by his inability to bury his dead, contemplating the archipelago's slow shipwreck. "How long are we going to look at those who bury themselves under the waters... without giving the Unthinkable any opposition?" he asks himself. This man then decides to organize a *dahira* – a Sufi funeral ceremony – not only for his cousin but also for these thousands of dead whom no one names. When the dead are suppressed and abandoned to their fate, when they are no longer anything but numbers in statistical charts or curves on graphs, what comes into question is our own humanity – our capacity to recognize ourselves in the other, death being the other par excellence, since it is "beyond." To the dehumanizing rhetoric of the "migratory flow," Elbadawi opposes the creative word, which offers a face and a voice to the wretched of the sea, thereby testifying to their humanity and... to our own. Faced with the banality of evil, the most terrible form of silencing, he rediscovers the poetic capacity to be astonished, he rediscovers the meaning of the intolerable. He brings into light the scandal that is smothered again and again...

Before being lines, borders are places of life where humans have always reinvented themselves by drawing sustenance from the strangeness of their neighbors. Like coral reefs, borders breathe and live only through their own pores, their rough patches, the lacy surfaces on which a continual intertwining of incommensurable worlds is produced: a creative hybridization. Fertilized by the trade winds and monsoons,[27] the *swahil* ("coasts") incarnate the border as the paradigmatic place of life, as a pulsing space of creative symbiosis. Whether it involves the politics of assimilation to a DOM or the establishment of a security dome (the networking and resonance of detector devices), "domization" is the negation of the shorelines and of their archipelagic power. Let us therefore call for new swahilizations, for unexpected and stealthy drifts!

6
Cosmo-Poetics of the Refuge

The horizon is a bow
but also the arch eyebrow
of a pharaoh.
Woe to the one
who is content with merely
curling up beneath the blade
of his enemy.

Call me dead ash
I will draw you a flaming circle
from my tongue.[1]

"At São Tomé, the Angolan slaves are revolting, taking refuge in the mountains, from where they undertake outright raids on the plantations several years after the establishment of this agricultural regime."[2] The year is 1455 and we are at sea, off the African coast, in one of the many Portuguese archipelagos of the Atlantic Ocean, during one of the first significant maroon insurrections. From this point on marronage will be indissociable from the proto-industrial system of the plantation, for which the island of São Tomé served as the principal African laboratory before it was transferred and perfected in Brazil. Just like colonial slavery, marronage begins on African soil: it is transatlantic from the start. But it is of course in the Americas – the heart of the slave labor system later on – that this form of life and resistance will experience its greatest growth, up to the point of becoming the seedbed of genuine maroon societies. Counterplantation practices and cultures were born from marronage from the outset. If there is indeed an ecological dimension to the experience of "maroon secession," it cannot be separated from the other dimensions of existence. Marronage is not a "decolonial ecology" but rather the abolition of ecology, inasmuch as it integrates concern for the living and an (ethical and political) reconstruction of the self in a single movement of regeneration twining together [*enlianant*] bodies and territories. Hence, when I use the notion of "ecology," my goal is simply to give the reader some reference points and to bring her to question this notion without necessarily rejecting it.

Afro-diasporic subversion and anarchism

Marronage – the general phenomenon of slave flight – may be episodic or definitive, individual or collective, discreet or violent: it may lend itself to banditism – examples are the black cowboys of the far West, the *cangaceiros* ("social bandits") of Brazil, and the black pirates of the Caribbean – or accelerate a revolution (Haiti, Cuba); it can appeal to the anonymity of cities or to the shadowy character of forests. There is thus no need to find a precise definition; profoundly polyphonic, the notion of marronage refers to a multitude of social and political experiences, deployed over almost four centuries, in territories as vast and varied as those of the Americas or the archipelagos of the Indian Ocean. The essential thing is to understand that throughout these territories the memory of the *neg mawons* in the Francophone Antilles, of the Quilombolas in Brazil, and of the Palenqueros in Latin America continues to irrigate contemporary struggles through cultural practices (such as *maloya*, capoeira, or Afro-diasporic religions), which subvert the dominant order because they reactivate the vision of the damned – their version of history, and therefore of "reality." If I privilege maroon secession – and by "secession" I mean here the tactical retreat of subaltern peoples, whoever they may be, into underground communities – it is because this is where marronage appears most fully as the matrix for astonishing forms of life.

Situated in tropical zones, the plantations were often surrounded by dense and impenetrable woods, labyrinthic marshes and mangroves, craggy *mornes* (hills) with dense vegetation, arid and aggressive *caatingas* (spiny shrubs); and all these expanses hostile to the penetration of civilization constituted so many spaces of disappearance. The forest – the ensemble of lines and elements that humanity draws out from a vegetal meshwork – thus offered maroons a refuge, a citadel, a privileged living place that cannot be reduced to a physical space: it projects them immediately toward the "land of the ancestors" beyond the seas. This is how it happened that in the mambos, the ritual songs of those who practice Palo Monte (an Afro-cuban religion), the forest, *nfinda*, is synonymous with Africa. In African cosmologies, the forest is in fact the dwelling place par excellence for spirits of the dead, protective divinities, and elementary cosmic forces. So many memory sparks and dreams are tucked even into the folds of the living world. It is because it assures the vertiginous coupling of vegetal and human memories – of which Alfred Hitchcock's *Vertigo* offers us a gripping view[3] – that the forest constitutes a spiritual refuge: more precisely, a virtual portal that secures the connection between heterogenous spaces and times (putting the Americas as a land of exile in resonance with the ancestral land of Africa), a place from which a negated humanity – that of the slave, the indigenous person, the sorcerer, the prole-tarian, or the mad – can draw resources.

> In the context of slave escapes and the creation of quilombos, the *nfinda* takes on a new connotation: in the Americas, it comes to evoke the forests of Africa or Africa plain and simple. In their ritual theater and their songs, the Cuban *paleros* [workmen], spiritual descendants of Bantu slaves, suggest even today the equation between *nfinda* and Africa. The space of ritual is "Africa"... in our time, the will to preserve or to re-create the discourse and certain practices of enslaved ancestors is primarily guided by the need to respond, through the affirmation of an old martial culture, to the sociocultural discrimination and marginal-ization that still weighs on communities of African descent, particularly in the Americas.[4]

In 1988, an aboriginal militant turned up at Dover, planted the aboriginal flag and declared: "I, Burnum Burnum, being a nobleman of ancient Australia, do hereby take possession of England on behalf of the Aboriginal People... we are here to bring you good manners, refinement and an opportunity to make a *Koompartoo*, 'a fresh start'.... For the more advanced, we bring the complex language of

Pitjantjajara; we will teach you how to have a spiritual relationship with the Earth and show you how to get bush tucker [food]."[5] Let's then follow the teaching of this noble aboriginal, and let us invoke the spirits of the *silva* ["forest" in Latin], "savage" spirits, in order to chase away the ghosts of Columbus and of El Dorado, which continually reappear in the form of successive waves of mining or agro-industrial projects devastating lands and modes of life throughout the globe.

> A centuries-old exclusion is revealed by the expression "land outside" [*pays en dehors*], used to refer to the rural world of Haiti. The entire peasantry, the majority of the Haitian population, is organized into pockets of resistance in the face of a vampire state; it is thus organized with its religion, its culture, its own mode of life... Society is *marron* because, ever since its founding, the Haitian state has incarnated the new figure of the master.[6]

It would take far too long to review the fine points and the stakes of the Haitian Revolution, which gave birth to the first black republic in 1804. To be sure, this revolution was in principle opposed to the slave system, but the reality is more complex because, for many reasons, the official leaders of this insurrection had from the outset a tendency to reproduce the model they were supposed to be bringing down. The Haitian Revolution reversed the slavery system, only to establish a black republic that behaved like a colonial state toward its own population: to the mass of bossal farmers (those born in Africa), the *grandons* (large landholders) and the army constituted so many forces of occupation and exploitation. To understand this, remember that at the moment of the Revolution two thirds of the island's population were *nègres bossales* perceived by the "free men of color" (Creole *nègres* and mulattos born in Haiti) as "African savages." Now the new Creole elite that took the reins of power after independence aspired only to reproduce "civilization," the western mode of life and of development. One interesting thing about this paradoxical territoriality of the "land outside" is the reminder it sends that marronage is a kind of resistance that can be thought and activated even outside the context of the slavery system. Maroon secession is the first form of Afro-diasporic anarchism:[7] it evades the grip of capital as much as that of the state.

> Europeans tend to believe that he [the great man or maroon chief] commands the tribe in the same way in which a colonel commands

a regiment... In reality he possesses almost no temporal power... For anything that concerns material life, each has the absolute right, one might even say the duty, to act as seems best for himself, so long as he does not harm anyone... None of them practiced any form of commerce, this activity being manifestly linked in their minds to the idea of exploiting others.[8]

As Jean Hurault stresses, the Boni (one of the Businenge peoples of Guiana) have developed a series of mechanisms preventing the accumulation of power and wealth. For the maroon community it was a matter of warding off the risk that a separate power might form within it: the domination of a state apparatus. The experience of marronage shaped the totality of Businenge culture, which explains its traditional prohibitions on commerce or on employing others (even if this is no longer the case) and the sacred character, as in Rastafarianism, of personal autonomy.

When, in 1940, Leonard Percival Howell founded the first Rastafarian community, which he baptized "the Pinnacle," at the peak of a wooded mountain in Jamaica, he was in fact renewing the gesture of the first maroons. By searching for self-sufficiency in matters of food and for the common management of lands and means of production, Howell replayed the maroon quest for something "outside" colonial society. "Babylon system is the vampire," chants Bob Marley. The Negro spirituals staged the exodus, captivity, and servitude of the Jewish people, with which the descendants of Africans identified, thereby converting their enslaved condition into a sign of divine election. In the "maroon," Marxist, libertarian, and pan-African reading of the Bible created by Rastafarianism, Babylon is the image that allows for reflective engagement with the system of predation, exploitation, and alienation to which blacks and peoples in general are subjected: empire and the grip of capital over lives and bodies, the thorough commodification of the living being – for which *nègres* were the first guinea pigs. Since colonial slavery represents only one modality of capitalism and of the state, Babylon perpetuates itself under new forms such as the multinationals, consumerism, the star system, and so on. Why this reference to the vampire? Because what the vampire hunts is humanity. Now the enslaving system is a system based on the manhunt. And the master – which is to say, capital (whose first servant is the state) – is related to the "vampire" which "lives only by sucking living labour, and lives the more, the more labour it sucks."[9]

Vodou cosmopolitics

In the hills of Haiti, it was through rhythm that the tradition of African work societies was transmitted and reinvented. Former slaves gradually appropriated patches of land in order to shore up a freedom that had been conquered in pitched battle against Napoleon's troops but that they also had to defend, after the revolution, against the attempts of new Creole elites to reestablish the disciplinary regime of the great plantations (i.e. to implement forced labor via laws that criminalized "vagabondage," like laws elsewhere in the West). Reclaiming for their own needs the practices of alliance developed within maroon communities, these peasant associations rely on the principles of reciprocity and of equality: you cultivate the land of your neighbor, who in turn will cultivate yours. Work is not paid but exchanged. In the case of the Haitian "squad," eight farmers work together the whole year on the respective lands of each member, each comrade [*compère*] benefiting from the work of all the others one day of the week. It is an extremely egalitarian system: the squad is commanded by the owner of the

Figure 2. 'Caligula', 2019, a 'voodoo' and futuristic interpretation of Albert Camus' play, conceptualized by Dénètem Touam Bona. Staging Patrice Le Namouric, Compagnie TRACK (Martinique). Image: Legba vèvè (symbol), the invocation of which allows the ceremony to commence. Source: the author.

field. The rotation of fields brings with it therefore the rotation of "command."

"Line up!" the squadron chiefs would yell.
Then Simidor Antoine would throw the strap of his drum over his shoulder. Bienaimé would take his commanding position in front of his men. Simidor would beat a brief prelude, and the rhythm would crackle under his fingers. In a single movement, they would lift their hoes high in the air. A beam of light would strike each blade. For a second they would be holding a rainbow.
Simidor's voice rose, husky and strong:
Stroke it in!
The hoes fell with a single dull thud, attacking the rough hide of the earth....
The men went forward in a straight line. They felt Antoine's song in their arms and, like blood hotter than their own, the rapid beat of his drum...
There sprang up a rhythmic circulation between the beating heart of the drum and the movements of the men. The rhythm became a powerful flux penetrating deep into their arteries and nourishing their muscles with a new vigor.[10]

In assuring the synchrony of gestures, cadence regularizes efforts, the choreographic alignment of bodies; the rhythm produces the fraternal community of the comrades [*paysans*, *paysannes*, *compères*]. In the southern United States, this tradition of danced and sung labor took the form of work songs, the seedbed of the blues. To work together is to espouse a collective pulsation, to vibrate in unison, to commune in a single song. In the rural Haitian world, rhythm represented a principle of social organization in its own right that, through practices such as the *coumbite* – the work society or community of work – set itself against every hierarchy.

This society refuses social structures as soon as they might lead to structures of power... It has found in rhythm the ideal instrument for causing spontaneous and immediate modes of organization to emerge, permitting it to master material production as well as the sacred.[11]

Even today, the powerful hooting of the queen conch [*lambi*] – the maroons' old rallying cry – sometimes resounds from one valley to the next on the sharp slopes of Haiti's mountains. With the rhapsody of work songs, the palpitation of tambours, the hammering of hoes, the peasant world is made musical and mystical. With nightfall, the work societies of the "day before" are sometimes transformed into Vodou brotherhoods; daytime labor is then followed by nighttime trance. From *coumbites* to mystical ceremonies, it is the same rhythm that is propagated and, with it, one and the same Afro-diasporic cosmovision: a conception of the world that stands point by point against the values of the capitalist system (private property, search for profit, etc.). The unplanned scattering of the habitat, the farmers' extreme mobility, the cosmic relation to the land, a whole series of elements makes Haitian peasant culture a formidable response to the system of the plantation. Far from being reducible to practices of "black magic" or to superstitions, Vodou enacts a spirituality and a singular relationship with the world, the seedbed of a cosmic agriculture: to inherit a field is in fact to inherit the *lwas* (Vodou spirits) that inhabit it, the only true possessors of the earth. Vodou constitutes a cosmopolitics because, via dialogue with the plants and elements, it institutes a relationship of alliance between farming communities and the living environment for which they have a duty to care.

> The *nanm* [soul, cosmic force] of plants is understood in a more personal sense than the *nanm* of other things. When the herb doctors go to gather plants, they choose a time when they think of them as being overwhelmed with sleep, and then go up to them gently so as not to aggravate the *nanm*. As they pull them up, they murmur: "Get up, get up, go and cure someone who is sick. I know you're asleep but I need you." They are careful to put a few pennies beside the main stem – to pay the soul for the effort that will be required of it. ... A woodcutter about to chop down a tree will give the trunk a few taps with the reverse of his axe, so as to warn the resident soul and give it time to get out... In addition to the "great soul of the earth" (*gâ nâm tè*), every field has its own spirit which assures it fertility, through action on all that grows there. The soul of the earth is not un-material. A worker in the fields, under the midday sun, can feel its presence in the form of a breeze stroking his face, and can see its shadow outlined behind him.[12]

In Haiti, the institutions of the *lakou* (cluster of homes) or *demanbré* (former plantation land on which a family's enslaved ancestors were buried)[13] are among the most powerful expressions of a maroon cosmopolitics. It concerns a portion of the family land that one cannot sell, divide, break up, or transform into property because it is linked to the *lwa heritaj* – the ancestors and tutelary divinities of the family. In Haiti, anchoring the peasant family in an ancestral territoriality constitutes the most powerful tool of self-defense against processes of enclosure, privatization, or capitalist monopoly over lands. The built-in ecology of Vodou is equally apparent in the contemporary struggles of certain Haitian collectives, which aim to create or to reactivate "sacred forests" – to rearm "nature" by reenchanting it... in *Masters of the Dew* (1944), the communist Haitian writer Jacques Roumain sheds light on the utopian import of Haitian work societies that he once dreamed of generalizing into a political and social model for the whole of his country.

> We [the peasants] don't know yet what a force we are, what a single force... Some day, when we get wise to that, we'll rise up from one end of the country to the other. Then we'll call a General Assembly of the Masters of the Dew, a great big *coumbite* of farmers, and we'll clear out poverty and plant a new life.[14]

The "master of the dew" is the "watering master" (*mèt lawouze*), the one charged with distributing water and dividing the work of irrigation among the farmers of the peasant community. This character embodies an ideal of justice, equity, solidarity, and life in harmony with nature. Because it presupposes an autonomous and egalitarian organization, in contrast with the disciplinary regime of the plantation, the rhythmic mystique of the *coumbite* will have contributed to the genesis of a maroon Haiti: the *péyi an déyo*.[15]

Rhythm of unchained fury

The *nègres* are "bare migrants," as the Martinican thinker Édouard Glissant reminds us: men, women, children stripped and reduced to a strictly biological "bare life" in the belly of the slave traders' ship. Meanwhile it seems that, from the moment of setting out to sea, a sort of bodily inscription resisted the stripping and the scratching out of memory, the zombification, all this enslaving sorcery that strives to transform humans into plantation livestock. In fact, what the documents of the era describe is not bare bodies but hieroglyphic bodies, bodies traversed by indelible patterns. Here is one inscription among many: "Congo ... bearing the signs of their country in the

form of a cross on each breast."¹⁶ These scarifications are the only
visible traces that the sub-Saharan deportees preserve from the land
of their birth: an existential cartography graven on the skin itself.
The scarified body is a memory body: the surface on which the
writing of a people, the singular story of a life, the genealogy of a
clan are deployed. In the furrows, the crevasses, the uneven relief of
his or her flesh, the *nègre* will always find assurance of her humanity,
of where she comes from, and of what her history is.

But an invisible, more intimate system of marking is juxtaposed
with this visceral writing, a system active at the joint between mind
and body: the rhythmic tattooing of Afro-diasporic bodies. The
body's memory is not static: it is passionate, dynamic, actualized
only in gestures, in attitudes, in a whole series of corporeal
practices such as dance or music. The rhythms of the black Atlantic
are often confused with the very repetition of myth: its ritual
actualization. This is evident in ceremonies of Candomblé, Vodou,
or of Santeria in which "each divinity has its patterns played
by the drums, repeated indefinitely, which constitute a sort of
Wagnerian leitmotif ... in this African mysticism."¹⁷ Roger Bastide
sees in rhythm the source of a genuine African mysticism. To this
Afro-mysticism, which is rooted in the resonances of the body, he
opposes Christian mysticism, which, on the contrary, presupposes
the body's extinction. Through the rhythmic tattooing of their
bodies, the migrants in the hold of the slave-trading ship brought
a whole cosmovision with them. And the forms of black resistance
were deployed precisely on the basis of this memory's creative
reactivation, starting from the incarnate thought that rhythm
constitutes. The slave's liberation demands the reappropriation of
his or her body, its explosive "un-chaining"...

At first, every rhythm is the rhythm of a race: a hammering
of feet on the ground, a hammering of the heart in the breast, a
hammering of the hands on taut skin. It is through rhythm that the
nègre first traces a line of flight. Rhythmic phrasing, the propeller
of dreams, effects distortions even in bodies and in space–time. In
trance, the possessed person is the horse ridden by gods. In the land
of slavery, this theater of the invisible can be only subversive: for
as long as the ceremony lasts, the condition of being enslaved is
suspended, negated, reversed, "abolished." Traversing the cycle of
mystical metamorphoses, the *nègre* thus passes from enslavement
to a divine epiphany. Now what would a divinity have to be
afraid of?

What they first did was to enter the hearts and heads of their sons, bringing to their throats their ancestors' battle cries, each one a stunning Oshosse, each one an irresistible Shango, not one of them feeling any fear, not one feeling pain, all fighting like the wind bending back tall grass.[18]

Trance is a technology for the intensification of flows: the body is no longer a collection of organs but a vibratory wave. Metamorphosis takes place via the rhythmic pulsations of a sacred eroticism. The possessed body is a carnivalesque and utopic body in which identity, civil status, or the binary machine of gender are subverted. From the metamorphoses of trance to carnivalesque transformations, the same phenomena of role inversion can be found, along with the reversal of hierarchies and the parody of conformisms and of powers. Trance implies a kind of transsexuality from the outset, because the *lwas* ride the *ounsi* (the initiates) regardless of their gender.

Ridden by Ogun, the Yoruba god of war, the most fragile girl brandishes a machete in the air like a sword, swears like a mercenary, demands more rum at the top of her voice and chases whatever young women are present. Mounted by Erzulie Freda, the Vodou equivalent of Venus, the most athletic man does his makeup carefully, strips off his pants to pull on a dress, and, swaying his hips or tossing around a languorous eye, strolls among the men in search of a kiss or caress. Because they transgress the heteronormative social structure "consecrated" by the church (one of the sources of the colonial order) on a daily basis, because their very way of life already presupposes a kind of metamorphosis, cross-dressers and homosexuals occupy a privileged place in Vodou.

But the repeated challenge to gender dualism and sexual norms is not limited to the time of the ceremony. Whether in Haiti, in Brazil, or in Cuba, "Afro" religious sites constitute veritable refuges for queer people confronted with the masculinism of their societies as well as with the rising tide of religious intolerance – particularly that of evangelical churches. Thus in 2016 Erica Malhunguinho, a queer Afro-Brazilian artist and activist, opened in São Paolo an urban quilombo dedicated to the arts and to black cultures, and baptized it Aparelha Luzia. In Brazil, *aparelho* refers to the secret places where Brazilian dissidents gathered to fight the dictatorship, and "Luzia" to the oldest human skeleton found in the Americas 11,000 years ago, whose skull manifests rather sub-Saharan traits...

The fact that many of the spaces of creativity and resistance were conceived of by the Afro-Brazilians as quilombos attests to the persistent relevance of maroon secession. In this way, the contemporary reactivation of quilombos and mocambos is not limited to struggles for the defense of rights and territories of "communities of descent" (recognized as inheritors of maroon communities or of peasant communities struggling for autonomy). Such institutions actually redraft the form of struggles, of creativity, and of popular organization in the most varied domains, even beyond the confines of communities descended from Africans: from the formation of autonomous urban zones that link permaculture and centers for musical education such as the Casa for Taina Culture in São Paolo to the institution of a network of quilombos and subaltern communities, for example the Rota dos Baobás project.

Dissidences and distortions of space–time

> The Commission, informed that dangerous assemblies known as Vaudou, are continuing despite the prohibitions levied by the constituted authorities; whereas the object of this dance seems to be the incitement of ideas inimical to a republican government... the commission has decreed and does hereby decree the following: Art. 1. Vaudou Dance gatherings are strictly forbidden.[19]

It is from their appeal to the gods of "Guinea" – from this mobilization of a composite African memory – that popular Afro-American forms of resistance draw their ardor and their power. As a spiritual experience in which the body becomes the place of initiation and of "knowing," *konesans*,[20] trance furnishes a general model for the explosive release of the enslaved person. The trigger of revolts always corresponds to the unleashing of cosmic powers. For this we have evidence from the foundational event of the Haitian Revolution, the Bois-Caïman gathering, the Vodou ceremony at which the magical plot [*conjuration*] between the enslaved and insurgent maroons was sealed in blood.[21] The abolitionism of the black Jacobins was both a revolutionary movement and the culmination of the French Revolution in its full radicality; and it appeared well before Victor Schoelcher's abolition decree of 1848, whose celebration tends to exclude the descendants of Africans from the story of their own liberation. There are similarities between the history of Amerindian revolts and that of Afro-American revolts. In autochthonous societies, the Spanish conquest provoked inconceivable collective trauma: the death of gods, the sun's fall and fracture. In addition, the great Amerindian revolts always began with the resurrection of divinities and the abjuration of Christian faith. Thus in 1541 one of the most terrible indigenous rebellions the Spanish empire had ever known broke out in the north of Mexico, in the land of the Chichimecas: the Mixtón War. Its leaders were "savage" sorcerers who "announced the coming of 'Tlatol,' accompanied by all his resurrected ancestors."[22] In the same way, the descendants of Africans gave spirit to their fights by resuscitating Ogun, Chango, and Legba and by composing new divinities. The maroon's line of flight is conjugated with the line of the sorceror's "beyond": a space beyond the visible that is also beyond colonial reality, a projection of a world both past and to come.

What makes the Haitian Revolution radically different from the French and American Revolutions is the specific way in which it was deeply infused with an Afro-diasporic political spirituality. At the end of the eighteenth century, subversion was diffused, networks of dissidents were organized, and solidarities and secret commitments were forged during nocturnal Kalenda dances and Vaudou gatherings. Marronage is secret in the literal sense of "secreting" a form of life, a way of operating. It began under cover of night when, taking advantage of the darkness, slaves slipped away from their "dwellings" (plantations and shacks) in order to commune in dances, prayers, and secret oaths. The mystical families ("mystical" because initiates of religions of Afro descent are considered to be sons and daughters of the gods) that were born during such nocturnal meetings constituted so many clandestine microcosms: parallel societies that continually worked over, infiltrated, and subverted the enslaving order on the sly.

> Throughout the history of Haiti, secret societies constituted an expression of popular resistance in the face of the tyranny and disorder of the state. Appearing during the colonial period, resurging at the start of the nineteenth century... they perpetuated the spirit of marronage and were etched into the imaginary of Vodou.[23]

The secret always plays a creative and dynamic role in any form of dissidence we can imagine: there are practices of secrecy (passwords, encryption, sung itineraries, etc.), an experience of the secret (often an experience of the sacred, since the secret constitutes a kind of forbidden knowledge), and a community of the secret (between the conspirators whom it binds together). In the context of the slavery system, cults and secret societies constitute privileged forms of popular resistance; in fact they serve as the unifying fixative among the enslaved, freemen and freewomen, and maroons. In Haiti, the nocturnal alliance between marronage and Vodou is best observed in secret societies. From secret Vodou brotherhoods to stealthy maroon gangs, the same minor mode of existence, the same poetic stance, the same opaque power is deployed: at night one plots, dances, dreams, prays, writes, debates, and gives sacrifice. Much like those of African descent, the artisans and proletarians of Europe, too, had recourse to the night's opacity and to the encryption of whispers. Dissidence always proceeds from a rupture of the temporal continuum: rupture of the conqueror's story, but also rupture of the alienating cycle of work and rest.

> The Society of Iron-founders, formed in 1810, is supposed to have met "on dark nights on the peaks, moors, and wastes on the highlands of the Midland Counties ... Awe-inspiring oaths and initiation ceremonies were probably fairly widespread.[24]

The rupture of the temporal continuum induced by the breakbeat of Afro-diasporic rhythms corresponds to a diffraction of space and a multitude of surprising spatialities (space–time of the cult, the tale, the martial dance, etc.). But with the phenomenon of maroon secession the fight against the slavery system enters into a strategic phase, which displaces the theater of operations and makes it durable. As a collective form of the fugue, "secession" is territorial resistance: it forms a body with a labyrinthine territory whose meanderings and uneven terrain constitute so many natural allies for the rebels. The maroon does not flee, he dodges, evades, vanishes; and through this folding back he metamorphoses and makes an "outside" for himself: the quilombo, the palenquero, the mocambo, the *péyi an déyo* ...

Whether it follows the rectitude of a geometric line or the winding path of a river, whether fixed or moving, whether material like a wall or spiritual like a series of invisible forces (spirits and protective ancestors tarrying in the rocks, animals, rivers), a border enacts the spatial inscription of a human collective in a given territory. Because it establishes and delimits a territory, a heterotopia that short-circuits the order of the enslaving system, maroon secession necessarily produces borders. But borders are maintained only through their own effacement. In fact the maroon frontier must mark and code the community's territory without leaving "visible" traces, without giving the colonial apparatus of capture landmarks by which it could orient itself. And thus we see why the defensive system of maroon communities appears from the outset as a system of camouflage. Maroon secession is paradoxical because, far from announcing the official birth of a new state, it consecrates a society of rebels in their act of going underground. It is a matter not of combatting the enslaving state but of warding off its very principle. Let the master never return to the heart of maroon society. In Haiti, the official story of the revolution has always been centered on the figure of the founding father of the nation; since the nineteenth century, every Haitian autocrat inscribed his power in the glorious lineage of Toussaint Louverture, of Dessalines, of Christophe. This is one reason why we must call into question a certain masculinist and elitist conception of anticolonial struggles.

> This idealization of the rebellious, even revolutionary slave tended to favor the masculine struggle at the expense of the feminine one and underestimate less visible forms of struggle and resistance thanks to which the vast majority of slaves survived and a minority of whom, including many women, obtained their freedom ... other historians... preferred to highlight discreet or "subtle" resistance to show that it was more effective in the long term than violent revolt, which, barring a few exceptions, inevitably led to massive, harsh, and exemplary repression.[25]

To get past the Spartacus syndrome – this mania for seeing the rebel male slave as the ultimate model for the struggle against slavery – the resistance of Afro descendants must be conceived of as a continuum that ranges from the slowdown of work processes at one end to maroon secession at the other – and the latter includes both fistfights and suicides on the slave-trading ships. Thus we need not oppose the *nègres* who supposedly remained quietly on the plantations to those others, the *nègres marrons*, who would have been heroic. For one thing, this would exclude the subtle forms of resistance developed by black women: the wealth of ways in which their memory was transmitted, their pharmacological knowledge and its associated cosmologies,[26] their influence over masters in the role of *cocotte* or "favorite," infanticide as a gesture of paradoxical love (magnificently depicted in Toni Morrison's splendid *Beloved*), and so on. Apart from these forms of resistance in a minor mode, there were certainly many women who knew how to confront the colonial and enslaving system with armed resistance when necessary: Anacaona (a Taïno princess and the first woman maroon of the Americas), Nanny of Jamaica, Solitude "the Mulatto Woman" of Guadeloupe, and Harriet Tubman, the "Moses" of the Underground Railroad...

Ethics of subtraction

MEMENTO

To contemplate images of the Earth illuminated at night
To observe the phosphorescent synapses that sparkle across its
    surface
And envelop us without our knowing
To grasp that we live under an invisible dome
To mourn the demise of transgression as the last heroic gesture of
    resistance
To mourn the full virile light of confrontation
To cultivate the shadow of forests
To extend the fog of the marshlands
To drip along the fault lines of volcanic ridges and jagged mountains

There, you have the barbed wire fence, I cut, I'm cutting and going inside. The scanner is raised to check the truck. I look to see if there are police. I open the truck and climb inside. If no one sees me and there are no dogs, then it's good. The dog is the last monitor. If the dog doesn't catch my scent, I'm on my way to England.[27]

This is how a young Ethiopian refugee describes his attempts to climb on board a ferry leaving Calais. In the digital era, the primed nose and fangs of the enslaver's mastiff have taken on the features of a mobile and netlike border that can no longer be confused with the territorial limits of the nation-state. The borders have become "smart," veritable microprocessors in their own right, which continually overreach the edges of nations and proliferate even deep within domestic territory, until the least access point is transformed into a space that is either public or private and every human element of a flow becomes a suspect. To separate the grain from the chaff, we have finished by expanding to the whole of humanity procedures that hitherto were used only for "illegal" bipeds: the recording of fingerprints, biometric inquisition, the identification of "risky people."

The smart border has become a central element in the system of capitalist predation and in the new algorithmic governmentality. It plays an essential role in producing, through a whole series of structures (for example, a judicial apparatus, transnational institutions like Frontex, camps and internment centers), a kind of humanity easily pressed into labor and disposable at will. This is the figure of the "migrant," who becomes from now on the object of a perpetual manhunt designed to keep him outside the law, in a stateless and pariah condition close to that of the slave. Journalistic reporting on the slave markets in Libya pulls a sensationalistic veil over something that, far from being an exception, has become the norm: the dehumanization of "infiltrators" as a result of triage procedures. In December 2013, the disinfection of naked migrants via power hoses on the island of Lampedusa provoked indignant reactions throughout international media: no one could help being reminded of procedures used in Nazi concentration camps. That the world no longer sees anything sacred in the nudity of a human being (Hannah Arendt) is the great scandal that gives rise to all the others: the traffic in human organs, the imprisonment of children in detention centers (sometimes in separation from their parents), the expulsion of refugees to countries with autocratic regimes where they risk torture and execution, and so on.

With the ongoing abolition of the right to asylum at the international level and the acceleration of the sixth mass extinction of living beings, what is starting to slip away from our grasp is the very possibility of refuge. Marronage, the pursuit and production of an "outside" to a society of enslavement, needs only to be reinvented, because it mobilizes the active sense of utopia implicit in "refuge" in a world ruled by the manhunt and the pillage of the living, from which we have not yet escaped. Maroon secession refers to a "cosmo-poetics" (from the Greek *kosmos*, the "world" in the beauty of its order, and *poiēsis*, the process of "making," "production"): it is the production of a world, creation of an outside that will have worth as a refuge and a concrete utopia for all those who remain in captivity. The quilombos represent in fact "a constant appeal, an incitement, a flag for black slaves."[28]

This point cannot be overstressed: the refuge does not preexist the fugue that produces it, "secretes" it and "encrypts" it [*chiffre*] it.

The art of the fugue, only one of whose modalities is represented by the historical experience of marronage, is the "sub-version" of an inside (be it the colony or our control society), even if the latter may strike us as closed and hopeless. The fugue is not an illusory transgression into a transcendent outside, but the secretion of a subterranean version of reality, clandestine and heretic. We are rightly told that we must play the chameleon, scramble the procedures of identification and profiling, by a text from 2016 protesting plans to bury nuclear waste at the Centre Industriel de Stockage Géologique (Cigeo) in Bure, a commune in the Meuse department. Using subterfuges, the one who fugues or flees produces herself as a simulacrum, makes herself a "transfuge"…

> A strategy of general and collective resistance may consist in rendering oneself indiscernible. … We have to be willing to transform the tactics and the roles that we play … according to the circumstances, the relations of force … Rioter one day, legalistic citizen demanding accountability the next day, crazy dancer the day after that.[29]

In these dark times when control structures proliferate, forms of resistance benefit from being stealthy rather than head-on. To act out in the open is to offer a point of attack to multiple powers that subject us and to expose oneself to being captured, discredited, criminalized. Marronage is therefore less a matter of seizing power than one of subtracting from power. "Furtive" tactics are in fact tactics of un-seizing: they leave opponents grasping at nothing but a void. I have given the name "fugue" to this corrosive power with which marronage erodes apparatuses of capture and the simulacra that they produce. When I use this word, I mean a form of life and of resistance that, far from engaging in the shining face-to-face exposure of heroic revolt, effects a retreat in the darkness, a continual dissolution of the self. The fugue is an ascesis: the paradoxical art of defeat – an "un-doing" [*dé-faire*] that is applied as much to dominating authorities as to their reverberation in our deepest interiority.

What meaning would a maroon life have today? That, I believe, of a truant who never stops evading the love of power and the fascist becoming[30] that it implies.

To adopt death itself,[31] the powers of darkness and organic disintegration, in order to better be reborn in the wavering light of uncertain dawns…

7

Lianas Dreaming

Spectral prelude

What is the scale of breathing? You put your hand on your individual chest as it rises and falters all day. But is that the scale of breathing?... And if the scale of breathing is collective, beyond species and sentience, so is the impact of drowning. The massive drowning yet unfinished where the distance of the ocean meant that people could become property, that life could be for sale. I am talking about the middle passage and everyone who drowned and everyone who continued breathing. ... I am saying that those who survived in the underbellies of boats, under each other under unbreathable circumstances are the undrowned, and their breathing is not separate from the drowning of their kin and fellow captives, their breathing is not separate from the breathing of the ocean, their breathing is not separate from the sharp exhale of hunted whales, their kindred also. ... Breathing in unbreathable circumstances is what we do every day in the chokehold of racial gendered ableist capitalism.[1]

A specter haunts globalized humanity: the specter of collapse. At the end of summer 2018, the first high school climate strikes took place. Beyond any "for" or "against," an unsettling cry: "No one wants to study for a future that will not exist!" What good is going to school, if we are fated to have shortages of water, air, flora and fauna, and even the ancestral humus of humans? This cry of childhood and

youth is less a cry of despair than a demand for justice and for
action.

Conspiring

Most cosmogonies present us with floods, exoduses, exiles in quest
of a promised land. What would a world be like in which there were
no longer any refuge, either for humans constrained to flee their
countries or for the mass of living beings menaced by the ferocious
exploitation of their environments? Poetry is a celebration of the
earth, a celebration of the sky, a celebration of the cosmos. It is a
great "yes" to life, but it is precisely this "yes" that requires us to
say "no" – to testify to the world's intolerableness, squalor, and
devastation. The cosmo-poetics that I am sketching in this chapter
represents one way among others to both summon and ward off
the ongoing "cosmocide" (a neologism created by Sony Labou
Tansi).

Even before acting, we must find inspiration: catch our breath,
pay attention to this air that we breathe, that envelopes us, that
moves through us and escapes us. "What is the scale of breathing?"
In extending our kinship to marine mammals, Alexis Pauline
Gumbs begins by breaking the circle of human confinement, to
extend the breath of our existences to the planetary level.[2] In her
disorienting "guide to un-drowning," she celebrates the heritage
of "undrowned" lives: the black lives that survived the Middle
Passage, but also the black lives of marine mammals (dolphins,
whales of different types, etc.) that have survived generalized
predation. "Blackness is more expansive than the human"[3]... A. P.
Gumbs' text strikes me as a genuine manual for "conspiration":[4]
a call to share our breath and the cyclonic forces that frustrate all
confinement.

Above a gutter overflowing with detritus, two children: one
seated cross-legged, the other on his knees, in a posture of suppli-
cation (see Figure 3). While the girl, enveloped in a pagne, has
free hands and a partially uncovered face, the boy's hands and
forearms are completely swaddled in cloth. Only the top of his
head emerges from a madras scarf. At the level of his mouth, we
see a connecting tube hanging empty: a simulacrum of a breathing
aid to ward off suffocation. A little bottle of hand sanitizing gel sits
beside the girl's thigh and is covered with a white-lettered label: "I

Figure 3. *Breath*. Painting by Gaël Maski. © Gaël Maski, 2020.

can breathe." A distorted and provocative echo of George Floyd's last words… In Kinshasa, there are only black lives, but some of them are more important than others: they are on the other side of the street that partitions the canvas, in these new residences under construction where the success of an Afropolitan bourgeoisie is displayed.

In a series of five paintings entitled *Psycho corona*, Gaël Maski grapples head on with the event of COVID-19.[5] What psychology does the "corona" entity create? As the painting *Breath* illustrates, social distancing ("protective measures") already existed in Kinshasa in the form of an insidious apartheid: a proliferation of walls, barbed wire fences, and secure residences that kept undesirables at a distance. The reinforcement of the fragmentation of urban space is the first way in which COVID's temporality is expressed. If the pandemic provided an occasion for the affluent middle classes to reconsider their relationship with work, for the disinherited mass from the poorer neighborhoods it meant a deepening of precarity, as survival became even more haphazard. In fact the privileged neighborhoods of Kinshasa intensified their reliance on deliveries and online shopping, in an effort to limit contact with the zones of infection – the shantytowns. This process by which the wealthy parts of town were immunized required their inhabitants to be anaesthetized: a rising tide of insensibility toward the fate of their neighbors, to which the Congolese artist draws our attention. This anaesthesia – this work of death at the very heart of our lives – is a worldwide phenomenon, nourished by each of our renunciations. The fear of contamination reactivates the fear of uprisings by the damned...

"Humans are biological risks"

If you are, in a general sense, well equipped to confront a massive attack of zombies, you will be equally well prepared to deal with a cyclone, an epidemic, an earthquake or a terrorist attack.

Dr. Ali Khan, Centers for Disease Control[6]

Since its outward spread from Wuhan, China, where it first appeared in November 2019, COVID-19 has brought the pathogenic effects of the plantation into the full light of day. What I mean here by "plantation" is the combined systems biological risks of monoculture and industrial farming[7] that, because they weaken the living environment, are bound to bring about the proliferation of infectious agents and parasites – the ones that affect plants as much as the ones that affect animals and humans. The first reason why capitalist exploitation inevitably produces ecocides is that it forces a radical simplification on ecosystems – a process of biological purging. As Anna Lowenhaupt Tsing emphasizes in *The Mushroom at the End of the World*, the plantation was designed to facilitate the suppression of all beings that could not be identified as profitable.[8] The emergence of COVID-19 clearly demonstrates that the border between forests, plantations, and metropoles is in the process of vanishing, which can only encourage zoonotic illnesses and their accelerated spread at the global level, via increasingly rapid and interconnected transport networks. And the extinction of the border between "wild" environments (where autochthonous people continue to resist) and globalized societies signifies nothing but the extinction of this "outside."

Contemporary capitalism can be defined as integrated world capitalism, because it tries to assure that no human activity on the planet will escape its touch. Since one might think that it has already colonized every surface of the planet, the essential aspect of its expression today involves new activities, which it attempts to overcode and control.[9]

Faced with the COVID-19 syndemic[10] and the asphyxia it provokes, integrated world capitalism proposes to submerge us even further in its digital matrix: our health will consist in an immunized future, without contact, anaesthetized. "Humans are biohazards, machines are not," as Anuja Sonalker, the CEO of a US firm that specializes in contactless technology, announced triumphantly at the start of 2022. This future, Naomi Klein proposes, "claims to be run on 'artificial intelligence,' but is actually held together by tens of millions of anonymous workers tucked away in warehouses, data centres, content moderation mills, electronic sweatshops, lithium mines, industrial farms, meat-processing plants and prisons."[11] Behind the "smart" smokescreen, the e-future feeds the fires of e-slavery.

The collapse of the dream

Face down on the warped and cracked hull of an overturned canoe, a black man lies, petrified by sleep, in the posture of a swimmer (see Figure 4). The sleeper is dressed in nothing but a pair of bathing shorts and a life jacket. He is suspended between two shores: those he has left and those that he may never reach. To sleep means never being sure one will awaken: the canoe seems ready to disintegrate... The image obeys the logic of dream inversion. Not only has the ship overturned, but it is painted with the sign of the conquistadors: the same red cross, symbol of the military–religious Order of Christ, that adorned the huge sails of the caravels used by Christopher Columbus to reach the Caribbean in 1492. Jean-David Nkot has a taste for paradox; he continually juxtaposes heterogeneous space–times, as a way of restoring the opacity of lived time to the experience of a flat surface. Space is nothing but condensed time, sedimented memory, telluric geology covered in the froth of days. In *L'Effondrement du rêve* (*The Dream's Collapse*), it is to a shipwrecked sub-Saharan that the Cameroonian painter gives the task of reminding us that the "great replacement" – of which European intellectuals and identitarian movements are so frightened – has already taken place: the Europe that emptied itself unrestrainedly across the globe's entire surface for centuries,

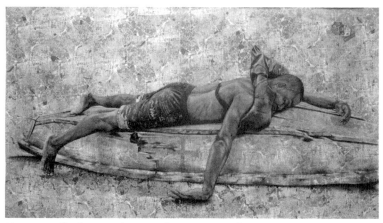

Figure 4. *Effondrement du rêve* (*The Dream's Collapse*). Painting by Jean-David Nkot. © Jean David Nkot, 2020. Courtesy the artist and Jack Bell Gallery, London. https://afikaris.com/products/bp-effondrement-du-reve-com?lang=fr

causing quite a few cosmocides, should not be surprised today that the world comes back to haunt it. But, unlike the conquistadors, contemporary "explorers" from southern countries do not leave these countries bearing arms, to impose their faith and carry out "civilizing" work; they set sail as survivors, with no equipment but the dream of a better life.

> In Gabon, as in the Congo ... the "night husbands" ... are figures in dreams who have sexual relations with men or women while they are sleeping. They provide those they visit with extraordinary jouissance and the experience is so physical and powerful that at the same time they transform them into "zombies" in real life. These people are no longer capable of working, or of maintaining stable relationships in their professional, family, or love lives... This "thing" that inhabits them renders their everyday existence very difficult to bear. A relationship of slavery is established. Their bodies no longer belong to them, but they are incapable of resisting its grasp and thereby liberating themselves... the "night husbands" are all these obstacles and frustrations that are transformed by the dream work into faceless entities, without name, without age, and even without gender... [This phenomenon] gets to the root of the African dystopia, wherein something that should render people happy is transformed during the night, in the darkness, into a factor of disintegration, of dehumanization and of death.[12]

"Afro-dystopia"[13] is the name of the dream which moves sub-Saharan migrants, the name of this "life in the dream of the Other" – that of commodities – which renders everyday life detestable and pushes one to leave at any price, to become a foreigner not only to one's own land but also to oneself, by letting oneself be governed by the dream of an Other. *The Dream's Collapse* – the dissipation of the mirage of Eldorado – can be an opportunity if it makes room for a creative detour, if it obliges us to learn how to "breathe differently," as A. P. Gumbs encourages us to do.[14]

"The medium is the message": the canvases of J.-D. Nkot are priority mail, according to their postage stamps. In this artist's universe, postage stamps [*affranchisements*] allow the process of liberation to be visualized in the form of a "correspondence," a capacity to respond to the questions raised by a situation. The painting *The Dream's Collapse* proposes to free us from the phantasmagoria of capital, to pull us out of the grasp of the "Babylon system," to make the shipwreck into an entrance ramp for "Dreaming": dreams as cosmo-poetic experience. The time of the dream is the space of an initiatory quest through an ocean of virtual existences where a multitude of temporal currents interpenetrate, while breaking with the homogeneity and the linearity of western temporality. Like the breathless deep dive of marine mammals, dreaming is an experience of immersion that presupposes a change of plan, the toppling of reality's surf into its unsuspected depths.

> The slogan that the *Big Brother* TV show uses – "You decide" – captures perfectly the mode of control by feedback that, according to Baudrillard, has replaced old centralized forms of power. We ourselves occupy the empty seat of power, phoning and clicking in our responses. TV's *Big Brother* had superseded Orwell's Big Brother. We the audience are not subjected to a power that comes from outside; rather, we are integrated into a control circuit that has our desires and preferences as its only mandate – but those desires and preferences are returned to us, no longer as ours, but as the desires of the big Other. Clearly, these circuits are not confined to television: cybernetic feedback systems (focus groups, demographic surveys) are now integral to the delivery of all "services," including education and government.[15]

This holds not only for the dream of Eldorado, but also for the simulacrum from which we must disconnect. By "simulacrum" I mean the continual generation of synthetic entities and environments that simultaneously dispense both pleasure and the feeling of security. Late capitalism is a womblike capitalism,[16] which exerts control through immediate jouissance (which it models and promotes), comfort, entertainment, "benevolence," but also through the fear and anguish that are linked to the perpetual possibility of ruptured connection (the loss of access imposed automatically as a punishment by rating systems). More and more often, control takes the form of an addiction to "artificial paradises" (synthetic environments).[17] Thus the dream is ambivalent: to put it schematically, the "Dreaming" is pitted against the "simulacrum"...

"The boat is sinking"

I like to read *The Dream's Collapse* as a premonition of the "fall of development" that Sony Labou Tansi yearns for. With formidable irony, the Congo poet's "Sealed Letter to the People of the North and Company" articulates one of the terrors that motivate contemporary ecological movements: the "survival of a drinkable future."[18] On the 500th anniversary of the "discovery of America," in 1992, Labou Tansi took up his pen to make things absolutely clear. If the poet insists that a "fall of development" is necessary, it is because, in a world with finite resources, the sacralization of the endless growth of infrastructures, commercial production, and associated styles of consumption can do nothing but push back the borders of disaster.

> Respected people of the North, your development is costing us too much. The time has come to change this development. You no longer have ears to hear. You no longer have eyes to see. No longer any dream to foresee. But our duty is to say with all the remaining force we can manage that after having been aggravated for five centuries, this is enough... Just as we waited for the fall of the Berlin Wall and the bureaucracies that fed into it, we are now waiting for the fall of development. Consumerism is not up to the task of being God. It is too stupid to last for two hundred years... The boat is sinking. You may yet turn a deaf ear to the ecological cataclysm, you may continue to hide the economic rot and dissimulate the extent of social disorder, but the death of thought is waiting for you, and the end of the dream is knocking on your door, because your development is morally unsustainable, and your wasteful economies are unjustifiable from the simple standpoint of reason. On all three planes: moral, ecological, and logical, the North has destined our planet to collective suicide. ...

We have come to the crucial moment when we must learn to reinvent everything: concepts, approaches, habits, methods, tools, nations, spaces... everything visible today must be reinvented. Because this is the only possible way we might still ward off the cosmocide of our planet... The quantification of everything has rendered you deaf and blind to life... You have forgotten that the only thing we have left to dream for is the survival of a drinkable future.[19]

If the notion of the Anthropocene is problematic, this is above all because it presupposes the existence of a unified and uniform humanity, collectively responsible for the unfolding dysfunction. Can one compare the carbon footprint of Papuan, Amerindian, or Touareg societies to that of our western societies (and of capitalist globalization), whose development has relied on the consumption of the world in the morbid form of commodities over the course of centuries? Let's get to the point: for many peoples of the South, the end of the world has already taken place. It was brought about with Christopher Columbus's initial landing in the Caribbean in 1492, and was then repeated many times, from Tasmania to Patagonia, by way of the Congo basin. What the conquistadors and their descendants present as "discovery" was lived by local peoples as the death of the gods or the falling sky: in the space of one century (from 1492 to 1600), massacres, slavery, devastating ecocides and epidemics caused the population of the American continent to drop from 60 million to 5 million inhabitants (and these estimates evolve with ongoing research).[20] Thanks to the massive regrowth of forests that this brought about – a regrowth linked to the size of the landmass left fallow by the disappearance of those who farmed it – this genocide impacted the climate: it was the principal factor in the Little Ice Age that extended across the northern hemisphere. Must we consider that "humanity" was always, then, a geo-climactic power? And if the answer is yes, which humanity are we talking about? The surviving humanity of the indigenous peoples or that of the colonists, who could affirm themselves only through the effective negation of those peoples?[21]

The experience of the cybernetic desert

Somewhere... a blank white space, shapeless, without thickness, shadows, or texture, transparency of a pure virtuality in which the

only reference points are two stately red armchairs, well uphol-
stered, positioned on one side and the other of an old television set.
After a program loads, Morpheus explains to Neo that the matrix
is a "neuro-active simulation" that generates "reality" and therefore
controls it. "Welcome to the desert of the real," he concludes.[22]
In the cybernetic regime, places, with their opacity, their force of
inertia, and their zones of friction vanish behind the anticipatory
envelopment that is offered: a "smart environment." Thanks to
the transfer of data from connected bodies in real time, there is no
longer any gap between the virtual world of algorithms and the
physical world of objects. Even before you formulate a wish, the
blinds are raised, the coffee is started, the vacuum cleaner runs. You
can't remember where you put your toothbrush? The smart toothbrush gives off a signal. If there is too much sugar, your smart cup
sends you an alert regarding your glycemic level, while a notification
from Doctolib offers you a time slot for a medical appointment. As
over the course of time the interconnection of objects, databases
and artificial intelligences accelerates, the desert grows: territories
and their inhabitants become superfluous. The experience of the
digital desert is the experience of the negation of place: the milieu in
which you evolve no longer offers any resistance to your action, but
rather pre-empts it in an entirely "benevolent" way. The very speed
of the responses that are brought to you on the basis of a predictive
analysis of your behavior annihilates the space and time it would
take you to act for yourself, to steer your own path: the magic of
cybernetics (in ancient Greek *kubernētikē* was "the art of steering,
governing").

> The society of transparency manifests itself first and foremost as a
> *society of positivity*. Matters prove transparent when they shed all
> negativity, when they are smoothed out and leveled, when they do
> not resist being integrated into smooth streams of capital, commu-
> nication, and information. Actions prove transparent when they
> are made operational – subordinate to a calculable, steerable, and
> controllable process.[23]

Beyond the spectral becoming of a humanity cultivated like a
plantation crop and plugged into a global cybernetic dream, the
Matrix provides us with a perfect allegorical image for the operative
mode constitutive of capitalist and colonial modernity: creation *ex
nihilo*. Creation from nothing: from the virgin surface, from the
empty white space that one has produced on one's own, because the

existence of the other – nature, women, indigenous people, *nègres*, proletarians – has been reduced to nothing, and as a consequence of this very reduction. From the negation of the alterity of the "Indian" to the negation of the alterity of reality itself, we recognize the same process of nihilation, repeated indefinitely. Whiteness is the color of nothingness: an annihilation brought to the point of incandescence by digital transparency.

Cybercapital, a mutant power

From here on, with the rise to power of an "algorithmic governmentality"[24] that rests on the massive exploitation of big data, power bears less on the actual body than on its potential trajectory, over which modeling techniques guarantee predictive control. Digital shadows double, pre-empt, recapitulate each of our steps and our clicks, each of the tiniest signals we give off; these are the million and one profiles that, starting from databases outside our control, surreptitiously infiltrate, haunt, and govern our lives through notifications and alerts, but also via barely perceptible infrared signals. In the *Matrix* trilogy, the disclosure of reality before Neo's eyes, in the form of an uninterrupted cavalcade of lines of code, conveys perfectly the totalitarian dimension of the world's digitization. The best way in which a power can assure its grasp of an "environment" is to generate it – to be its matrix or seedbed – so that it can then inscribe the procedures of government into its very texture: let subjects follow only circuits that have been preprinted, even if they maintain the illusion of free will. The "smart city" or the "safe city" is the dream of a nourishing and protective matrix, a space integrating a whole network of surveillance cameras, detectors, and biometric trackers into its very structure. The future Eve is a cyborg city animated by clouds of artificial intelligence and connected objects; synthetic archangels constantly watch over us, exhaust our still unformulated wishes, and warn against every possible and imaginable risk – including that of an "event."[25]

Capital always operates in a colonial way: being an infinite process of wealth accumulation, it can be perpetuated only through the continual conquest of new territories to exploit. But what happens when it has already colonized every surface of the planet? It recomposes by extending its empire to fields of activity and to dimensions of existence hitherto left to the side or unnoticed, and finishes by colonizing time itself (lived experience), particularly the future – which is a matter of transforming it into "prediction products," as Shoshana Zuboff analyzes in *The Age of Surveillance Capitalism*.[26] The digital revolution has compounded the integrative power of capitalism to the point of instituting it as a viral power. With the exponential digitalization of the world and of our lives, the capitalist order has become a cybernetic order. Cybercapital is that mutant power that integrates the totality of technological apparatuses into its self-sustaining loop by replicating them, and goes even so far as to contaminate and recombine our own subjectivity: our very life becomes "capital," a financial product whose price fluctuates in each of our interactions, thanks to continual evaluations. Without a doubt, the growing synergy of capital and control is best expressed by the generalization of digital rating systems, whose logic is simply exploited by Chinese "social credit," albeit accused of being totalitarian.

Control addict

> Imagine that a human being (you can imagine this to be yourself) has been subjected to an operation by an evil scientist. The person's brain (your brain) has been removed from the body and placed in a vat of nutrients which keeps the brain alive. The nerve endings have been connected to a super-scientific computer which causes the person whose brain it is to have the illusion that everything is perfectly normal. There seem to be people, objects, the sky, etc; but really all the person (you) is experiencing is the result of electronic impulses travelling from the computer to the nerve endings.[27]

Far more than Fukushima, COVID-19 makes clear what an important procedure "confinement" has become, not only for managing risks and government but also for the production of "reality" itself. The destruction of the sensible world is at the base of modern thought, as we learn from the speculative fiction of *annihilatio mundi* ("annihilation of the world") in Hobbes, of the "evil genius" in Descartes, and so on. This nihilism constitutive of modernity that Nietzsche diagnosed in detail increasingly takes the form of an effective negation of our conditions of existence. To a certain extent, the modern subject is nothing but the residue of the world's destruction. For Husserl, pure consciousness was best revealed through a thought experiment concerning the world's disintegration – a proliferation of discordances in the flux of perceptions:[28] the subject was envisaged as a simulator of worlds. The western subject is a trigger of atomic fissions…

The basic unit of capitalist rationality is the individual (in Latin, *individuus* means "indivisible"). This individual – a human atom – is produced only through an operation of confinement: a deliberate extraction from its surroundings and its memories, its common goods and communities, indeed its very body. In many ways, Descartes' *cogito* is the same as the egoistic individual of classical liberalism. The biopolitical paradigm of "contact-free" interaction[29] is therefore only the most advanced expression of capitalist confinement: the extraction of a brain ("you may suppose it is your own") from its flesh (the "contact" interface) and its surroundings, a brain that will be plunged into a vat, a brain destined to have relations with the world and with its own alter egos only through cybernetic plug-ins. "The bravest new world," of which the latest avatar is the smart city, is an expanding incubator driven by the "mad genius" of capital.

> To reclaim a real political agency means first of all accepting our insertion *at the level of desire* in the remorseless meat-grinder of Capital. What is being disavowed in the abjection of evil and ignorance onto fantasmatic Others is our own complicity in planetary networks of oppression. What needs to be kept in mind is *both* that capitalism is a hyper-abstract impersonal structure *and* that it would be nothing without our co-operation. The most Gothic description of Capital is also the most accurate. Capital is an abstract parasite, an insatiable vampire and zombie-maker; but the living flesh it converts into dead labor is ours, and the zombies it makes are us."[30]

Life delivered by intravenous drip and assisted breathing machines did not begin with COVID-19. The globalized state of medical emergency simply extended and amplified it. Through a thousand and one tubes, we consume a continual flow of emotions, moods, experiences, ideas, desires, and dream lives. Cybercontrol operates less through patriarchal discipline than through the mothering provided by benevolent environments: synthetic uteri soliciting a symbiotic dependency. This is why the drug addict has become the figure par excellence of contemporary subjection. In fact, control devices have given us access to a constant flow of sugary satisfaction on demand.[31] This is where the character of William Burroughs' "control junkie" comes from: the one who cannot give up control, but also the one from whom control has been taken away, who is possessed by the controls. The "night husbands" are perhaps not so exotic as one might imagine… Life in the era of cybercapital is a life in the cyberdream: the simulacrum.

> Junk is the ideal product… the ultimate merchandise. No sales talk necessary. The client will crawl through a sewer and beg to buy… The junk merchant does not sell his product to the consumer, he sells the consumer to his product. He does not improve and simplify his merchandise. He degrades and simplifies the client. He pays his staff in junk.[32]

The asphyxia that we feel today does not result simply from the aggravation of ecological crises; more profoundly still, it relates to the inscription of our existences in cybernetic feedback loops (of which the "health pass" is just one illustration among others) that aim at the elimination of all unpredictability. The continuous sterilization of the future that is now underway is also linked not so much to fatalism before the possibility of a collapse as to a paradoxical colonization of the future by cybercapital. If, in the rainbow-colored shadow of the past, the medium converses with the dead to clarify a trembling future, it is in the transparency of "real time" that cybernetic foresight scans the phantoms of the future so as to optimize the present. Cybercapital is a cyber-oracle (see P. K. Dick's novella *The Minority Report*): its expansion feeds on spectral futures, which it advances even as it forms predictive models of them. How can we project ourselves into the future, how can we imagine other worlds, when the future itself – our tendencies, our inclinations, the tiniest virtualities in our existences – have become the new Eldorado and are the target of an unprecedented data-mining operation, which generates profit for the occult powers of capital and creates a globalized state of emergency?

We are constantly occupied, always too occupied, never free from our thoughts, ceaselessly invaded by worries, tasks, notifications… the use of new technologies only reinforces our obsession with using time efficiently, with acting without a moment's waste, and this makes us less and less present to those we live with, so that we waste our time even as we think we are saving it. Now, if we do not live in the present, the present passes and we pass with it, up until the day when, on the threshold of departing, we understand that we have not lived. One can dwell in time only on condition of freeing it, freeing oneself from the industrial occupation and mining of one's attention; and this is something that takes place in acts of subtraction – in fugues, desertions, marronages.

Restoring the powers of the dream and poetry

Given the continual acceleration in which we are caught – this speed that abolishes distances as well as lived time in favor of a spectral "real time" – we are going to have to experiment with an "ecology of time"[33] that will restore its fertile opacity: the humus of plural memories. Going against the temporal grain might be one tactic in this ecology: it would make delay – deferral – into an art of creative differentiation.[34] An impromptu dance short-circuiting the programming of behavior! It is up to us to multiply the unaccented beats as if they were as many counterpoints and countershots to the algorithmic optimization of our existence. Going against the temporal grain also means retracing our past steps – beyond quantified time (time that is money) – until we are once again able to feel it in duration: the taste and the scent of a madeleine soaked in a cup of tea can thereby unfurl a life that one believed forever lost. At the crossroads of memory, imagination, and dream, we must cultivate these voyages in the invisible so that we may relearn how to dwell in time and open the possibility of alternative futures. Mental voyages, the first form of "virtual reality,"[35] are initially voyages in time: a dive into a sensorial maelstrom where that which is not yet, that which is no more, and that which might be overlap and mutually condition one another. Time is not possessed, it crosses through us and constitutes us; it is both birth and destruction, it is Shiva dancing! To accelerate is to age prematurely. It is in the time of the dream that the virtualities of an always present past are best realized. What is opposed to the cyberdream, the alienating fantasmagoria of capital, is the cosmo-poetic dimension of the dream, of which the Dreaming of the Australian Aborigines is one of the most remarkable expressions:

> For the Aborigines, the English term "Dreaming" refers at once to the eternal beings, to the mythic stories in which they are the actors, to their itineraries and geographical resting places, which have become sacred sites, and to the creative matrix that gives rise to them. "Dreaming" translates concepts coming from different

aboriginal languages ... which situate mythology and its narratives in a space–time linked to dreams. This dream matrix corresponds not to a golden age of the past but to a space–time that is eternal and becoming, to which one gains access through a kind of virtual portal, namely the sacred sites, the rituals, and above all oneiric practice. Many Aborigines say that the sites refer to images and sounds in a manner similar to that of radiation, vibrations, or waves... The mythic itineraries celebrated by rites in the form of chants, dances, and paintings on the body, on sacred objects or on the ground, are cognitive maps in the sense that these stories of performance encode information essential for the survival of society.[36]

Above and beyond its critical significance, the present chapter aims at nothing less than rehabilitating the powers of dream and poetry – 'rehabilitating' because the intelligence of the sensible bends the rainbow of possibilities. In Amerindian, Aboriginal, or Bantu cosmologies, the dream is not opposed to reality; on the contrary, it constitutes reality's most profound dimension. In the dream, contours and categories are blurred in order to make room for the flow of metamorphoses. "Indigenous" dream practices are not a picturesque daydream but a form of ethical and plastic imagination that, far from being opposed to memory, traces new lines of flight in it and thereby continuously reconfigures it in "image actions." Dreams, whether by day or by night, intimate hopes or collective mythologies, offer the possibility of experimenting with the living viewpoint [*point de vie*][37] of a bird, a tree, or a river, and provoke us thereby to care for what is both beyond and within ourselves. Initially it is through dreams that we "realize" that we can live only in relation to other terrestrial intelligences. "Cosmo-poetics" refers to this obscure dialogue, woven with metaphors and unexpected gestures, that we entertain in privileged moments with the totality of everything that vibrates. In order to explore the cosmo-poetic dimension of our existence, I propose the Dream of the liana. As ayahuasca testifies, the teaching of the liana is, first, an oneiric teaching (see Figure 5). We will therefore use the liana as a dream thrower...

Chimerical visions

I do not portray being: I portray passing... (Montaigne, *Essais*, 3.2, p. 611)

Tropical forests rarely offer clear vantage points – it is impossible for the gaze to dominate them! Once one penetrates such forests,

Figure 5. Preview footage from "Spectrographies: Contes de l'île étoilée" ("Spectographies: Tales of the starry isles"), danced by Les Écorcés – a collaborative and transdisciplinary work conceptualized by Dénètem Touam Bona and directed by Hugo Rousselin, 2022. Costumes of bark, lichens, mosses, and wisteria plants by the Carole Chausset Company. Production: Centre International d'art et du paysage de l'île de Vassivière. Performers involved in the project: Myriam Mihindou (Gabon-France), Daniely Francisque (Martinique), Florence Boyer (Réunion). © Dénètem Touam Bona.

moreover, space is so completely broken up by the profusion of vegetation and by indistinct forms that the field of vision is brutally reduced. The stealthy populations who live there rely more on hearing than on sight; they evolve in a world of correspondences where the cooing of an antshrike reveals the passage of a tapir, where the melody of a cocoa thrush signals the presence of jocote fruit. This text, which coils and detours like the liana, interweaving heterogenous elements, draws on this kind of musical logic. It is not a matter of writing on lianas but with them, of being traversed by them, powered by their unpredictable zigzags, pierced by their improbable twists, disoriented by their arabesques to the point of no longer knowing who is speaking in you or in what person to conjugate. You could run through these lines like a "jungle" and let yourself be caught up in a vegetal fugue, a profusion of tracks that constitute as many variations on an endlessly elusive motif. Some trails are hardly cleared and force us to retrace our steps, to go back through passages that we had already used but that have a totally different look when approached from another direction or at a different hour of the day. Tremblings rather than certitudes...

> From the midst of these stagnating and unwholesome waters, forests arise, that are as ancient as the world, and so choked up with *lianes*... that the strongest and most intrepid man cannot penetrate into them.[38]

No wisdom without measure, it is said. Now the liana belongs to a kind of excess: that of titans, primordial divinities of the original world, from a time of both innocence and chaos. How can a plant as disorderly as the liana be *wise*? Only if by wisdom one means the clandestine and wily knowledge that appears in tales and witticisms, the Chinese shadows and acrobatics of Jako,[39] the eel dances[40] and subway graffiti of hip-hop artists; all these sleights of hand that, starting from thin air, enchant the lives of those who watch carefully, lest they be dispossessed of everything.

From the Caribbean to Papua New Guinea, the inextricable meshwork of lianas resisted colonial penetration. First obstacle in the quest for Eldorado and in the establishment of the plantation regime, the liana is the serpent, the vegetative hydra that, in the colonist's eyes, turns the tempting virgin forest into a green hell. Twisting and contorting everywhere, the forked tongues of lianas can emit only the wisdom of a monkey: a gay science that, in the flash of a grimace, transforms the suffering of oppression into peals of laughter. Far from excluding madness, the wisdom of lianas integrates it as a motivating element of its teaching.

What is [in popular culture] called "wisdom" (*sabedoria*) may be defined as a stratagem ... and as trickery ... Innumerable ways of playing and foiling the other's game (*jouer/déjouer le jeu de l'autre*), that is, the space instituted by others, characterize the subtle, stubborn, resistant activity of groups which, since they lack their own space, have to get along in a network of already established forces and representations.[41]

Because they never go straight, lianas can only inspire a canny wisdom – steeped in stratagems and the play of masks – which mocks the code of honor of gallant warriors. Also, the wisdom of lianas points less to diplomacy than to an art of striking blows practiced by the most diverse kinds of creatures (octopus, spider, turtle, banyan, chameleon) and by the "humble peoples" of every age. By invoking the wisdom of lianas, I am therefore only returning to an immemorial gesture: that of drawing from teachings, in the form of tales, about the thousand and one malicious tactics of the living being.

If I have chosen the liana as the main motif and totemic plant in this chapter, this is not simply in order to play around with a certain colonial imaginary or to enthuse over the botanical properties of these delicate vegetative forms, but rather and most significantly to pay homage to the *lyannaj* of the archipelagos of Martinique and Guadeloupe. This term, derived from the Creole *lyann* (and related to the French *liane*), designates practices of solidarity and resistance inscribed in the historical experience of marronage – the arts of the fugue of enslaved peoples. In the Americas and the islands of the Indian Ocean, descendants of Africans draw an intimate connection between relationships of care for the land and the heritage of the *nègres marrons*, their liberatory use of the forest as a refuge, as a space of camouflage and self-reconstruction. It was at the dawn of the sixteenth century, on the island of Hispaniola (divided today into Haiti and the Dominican Republic) that the Spanish adjective *cimarrón*, "untamed" – the etymon of the French *marron* – was first used: at that time it designated a domesticated animal that had fled to return to life in the wild. By extension, the colonists qualified fugitive slaves as *négros cimarrónes*. Marronage is thus a process of de-domestication,[42] drawing its breath from the very subversiveness of the living. By "forest" I mean not so much an "environment" as the surge of that truant life in us that always opposes the curbing movement of humiliation and servitude, be it constrained or voluntary.

Among the traits of the liana, I want to foreground the way in which it allows us to imagine relations in terms of pulsation and living lines. But before we go any further in that direction, a qualification is in order: as a matter of botany, "liana" does not correspond to any rigorous taxonomic category. If we had to sketch a liana while taking into account the more than 130 botanical families that contain crawling and climbing species, the drawing would have to illustrate characteristics of palm trees as well as of roses, ferns, vines, conifers, and more. Therefore, in the proper sense, the liana does not exist: it only exists in a figurative sense. But what is in question here is precisely the liana as figure, as trope, as turn of speech and as adroitness, as gesture and as bodily movement (the ancient Greek *tropos* meant "turn," "direction," "course," "way"). Because figures are schematics assembled from the most recognizable features of a landscape, of an animal, of a political function (e.g. the scales of justice, the crescent of the moon), they do not refer to something given but constitute a call into existence.[43] Likewise, the kung fu master is not interested in the "objective reality" of the dragon; what matters to him is the way this chimerical figure appears in its movements, modifies its field of forces and perception, amplifies what a body can do. The dragon is neither symbol nor substance; it is a moving relation between a multitude of elements such as the fluid and rippling movement of the serpent (combined with the infinite spiral of its moults), the ferocity of the tiger, the alchemical power of fire, the devastating and fecundating power of the flood, and so on. I approach the liana in the same spirit, and the reality of the book that you have in your hands is, in a certain manner, only the effect of its figural existence.[44] This rebellious vegetal being immediately subverted the colonial mania for cataloguing living things into ethnicities with watertight borders. Thus the liana refers less to a being – an identity – than to a certain way in which vegetal pulsation explores and unfolds a territory as it advances, by tracing unexpected paths in it and securing the correspondence between a multitude of strata and forest dwellers.

Although it borrows its characteristics from a biological reality, the liana nevertheless remains a chimera in the sense that, like the

thunder serpent of the Hopi in Arizona, like the Greek Sphinx
with its woman's face, lion's body, and eagle's wings, or like Mami
Wata, the siren of the black Atlantic, it combines heteroclite, indeed
contradictory elements in one and the same figure. The advantage
of the notion of "figure" by comparison to that of "image" is that
it preserves a relationship with gesture: a calligrapher or a dancer
is said to execute figures, regardless of whether these figures leave
a lasting mark on a material support. I am not using the liana
as a representation or symbol, but rather as one of these African
masks that come to life only when they are deciphered and invest
us with their powers. The loops and knots created by lianas at the
heart of territories – loops and knots that they deploy by writing
themselves into the landscape, and as they do so – belong to the
genre of Möbius bands, where the right side and reverse side,
fiction and reality, cause and effect are interwoven and condition
each other, in a movement that expands space–time. Our understanding of the agency of an image[45] is still imprisoned within the
mechanical conception of causality that Nietzsche considered to be
a "grammatical illusion"[46] overshadowed by theology (God as first
cause, as first agent of a creation *ex nihilo*). Therefore through the
lianas' intertwining we are also trying to understand how forms of
agency can be interwoven: in other words, we are trying to understand the "intra-action"[47] of humans and other living beings, of
living milieus, of artifacts, images, and so on.

My use of the liana thus obeys a "chimera principle":[48] it
results from reflection on condensation in thinking (a procedure
shared by metaphor and the oneiric image) that is also linked to
a certain experience of visual ambiguity. "Tiger shark," "snake
liana" (*serpent-liane, Tinospora crispa*), "vine snake" (*liane-serpent,
Thelotornis*), "frog man," "buffalo toad," "spider monkey," "moon
fish" ... our language brims with chimerical expressions that testify
to the sensory excess of the living over our categories of thought.
Because it proceeds from an act of "seeing as," poetry is without
doubt the best way to express the chimerical dimension of our
worldly experience: I can see the liana as an anaconda, as a cosmic
umbilical cord, as the flow of a river, as the silk of a spider, as the
winding, cryptic language of a shaman, as the moving circle of the
community, as Ariadne's thread, or even as the bite of a whip. Here
it is not a question of distinguishing different visions but, much to
the contrary, of playing on the polyphony that is folded into the
heart of this figure. At every point of the zigzag path that I propose,

the liana unfurls like an *imago agens*,[49] a form of artificial intelligence that allows the figuration not merely of thought's content but also of thought's operations, memorization, or imagination.

The wisdom of lianas is simultaneously textile and choreographic. It is textile insofar as (in some way) the liana consists of nothing but a play of threads[50] that, in linking together multiple points of living [*points de vie*] – monkey, spider, Tarzan, hair, hydra, forest, resurgence, *nègre marron*, plantation – generate unprecedented constellations. And it is choreographic insofar as this wisdom is a matter of passing from one figure to the next, without a definitive resolution. Now this movement of permanent transfiguration – together with the configuration of the metamorphic body – is nothing but dance itself. It is precisely because the liana is a chimerical entity – a sketch, a movement in suspense – that it calls us to take up the thread once again, to pursue the dream, to reactivate its movements of subversion with our own fugues.

> How often, asleep at night, am I convinced of just such familiar events – that I am here in my dressing-gown, sitting by the fire – when in fact I am lying undressed in bed! Yet at the moment my eyes are certainly wide awake when I look at this piece of paper; I shake my head and it is not asleep; as I stretch out and feel my hand I do so deliberately, and I know what I am doing. All this would not happen with such distinctness to someone asleep. ... As if I did not remember other occasions when I have been tricked by exactly similar thoughts while asleep! As I think about this more carefully, I see plainly that there are never any sure signs by means of which being awake can be distinguished from being asleep. The result is that I begin to feel dazed, and this very feeling only reinforces the notion that I may be asleep.[51]

In his search for an Archimedean point, an absolute certitude, a first truth on whose foundations he could finally build a science worthy of the name, Descartes makes doubt into a war machine against sensible experience. But how can I deny that these hands and body are mine, unless I were to behave like certain kinds of madmen? To the objection that it would be madness to doubt everything, Descartes responds with the argument from dreams: "As if I were not a man who sleeps at night, and regularly has all the same experiences while asleep as madmen do when awake." This is how modernity disenchanted the dream, plucked away its powers (as a path of access to the radical alterity of animals, spirits, the dead, etc.) in order to reduce it to an "argument" – a bit of incriminating evidence – in the trial that results from the encounter with the world as it appears to us (only what is calculable is "objective" or "real") and the magic it contains. Dream and madness will constantly serve as models in western philosophy's effort to demonstrate the blindness of belief or "superstition," and thereby to discredit the ancient cosmologies that peopled the woods, the marshes, the mountains, and the rivers of Europe with dragons, mermaids, dwarves, leprechauns, trolls, and other fabulous entities.[52] The wisdom of lianas, on the other hand, takes the side of fabulation and is first manifest as an oneiric wisdom that, through the hesitancy that it imposes on "rational" evidence and certitude, introduces fissures into the sealed enclosure of "reality."[53]

> Once Zhuang Zhou dreamed he was a butterfly, a butterfly flitting and fluttering around, happy with himself and doing as he pleased. He didn't know he was Zhuang Zhou. Suddenly he woke up, and there he was, solid and unmistakable Zhuang Zhou. But he didn't know if he were Zhuang Zhou who had dreamed he was a butterfly or a butterfly dreaming he was Zhuang Zhou.[54]

To draw a blank

> Words can be like tiny doses of arsenic: one swallows them carelessly, they seem to have no effect, and then lo and behold their toxic effect eventually makes itself known.
> Victor Klemperer, *LTI*, pp. 15–16

Nothing is more familiar than drawing a blank: you reassure yourself by saying that you will remember, that it's the effect of emotion or fatigue. This name that you have forgotten and that was just on the tip of your tongue, as if all the better to mock you, will eventually emerge. But it is more problematic than you dare to admit: you have memory problems... This is not just absent-mindedness, as when you begin some action and realize suddenly that you no longer know why you are running upstairs, a book or a knife in your hand. This is something more troubling, the sentiment of being only a surface, without depth, without access to your own opacity, without being genuinely anchored in what came before, as if your memory were just a notebook with pages crossed out, slashed, unreadable. And this recurrent sentiment that you have just landed in this body, that you were thrown there by chance, that the wrong signal flashed, that the limbs that are moving under your impetus are only pretending to obey you, that they are not your own, that you are not in your place but just passing through, perhaps even already passed... After a whole slice of life whitened by the chalk of integration, after the permanent injunction to forget yourself, to efface yourself behind your own back, you are no longer anything but a zombie. So you sleep, you wander around, you let yourself go adrift in the secret hope of someday breaking these invisible threads that rule your body.

You no longer know when this started, this more or less conscious refusal to correspond to the role and place you were given. Your revolt was silent and immobile, and came less from confrontation than from evasiveness. "That child is a real little savage!" How many times did you hear these words from the lips of adults deliberating over your case? You didn't like talking, you didn't want to let yourself be caught in other people's terms, these invisible links that hobble us, encumber our movements and our thoughts, and thereby tend to determine who we are.

The first thing that you liked about Tarzan was his muteness.[55] You had the impression that both of you shared a similar defiance regarding language. One could therefore be an apeman and a hero! That was you, the lord of the jungle swinging from vine to vine, on the other side of the screen, living a life as wild as it was free: no pants, no shoes, no red lights or forbidden directions, none of these apartment buildings scraping the horizon of Paris – a life that could be fully expressed only beyond words, in the hurricane cry that you dreamed of letting loose yourself, in the middle of the street or in the tunnels of the metro.

Your father, as black as the men you were watching on the screen of your little television, must have been sitting right next to you, and yet you were never able to associate him with Tarzan's blacks. You cannot remember what kind of face he made at the sight of all these superstitious, stupid, and above all abysmally docile creatures. How could you have imagined that he might have felt humiliated by the fact that you yourself, like the young Caribbeans described by Fanon, identified completely with Tarzan? How could you have seen your father as a *nègre*, when he was all revolt, when he spent his evenings discussing revolution with his exiled comrades, when he terrorized you simply with his look and, in your eyes, was the strongest and most courageous man in the world, a hero – nothing more banal for a boy?

The day after *Tarzan the Ape Man* was on television, something strange happened in your little 15th arrondissement school. It was as if the film were following along, or rather as if it followed *you*: the monkey imitations, the cries of *umgawa*, *cheetah*, *bamboula*, or "go back to your jungle" were flying everywhere. That was the moment when you realized that you had not been included among the victors, in the triumphal procession of Columbus, Cook, or Livingston.

You wanted to disappear under the ground, scrub, scrub, and scrub once more, with soap, with detergent, with bleach, this skin that could not be yours; you wanted to sand it down until every bit of darkness was removed, until you became transparent. All in vain; this filthy color does not come off like that, it sticks to the skin like motor oil: you were nothing but a pathetic seagull stuck in a black spill. Sometimes just a little impact was all it took, a little shock wave, to break the mirror and crack your face to the point where you could no longer recognize yourself. How many shocks in a lifetime? ... But perhaps there is nothing more precious than this brittleness of being, because only at the moment when everything cracks does what is woven inside of us – all these shadows by which we are inhabited – bubble up to the surface, so that we are open to metamorphosis.

Sometimes it so happens that our life itself escapes us, that it becomes foreign to us, like a dog that one thought would always be loyal and that, taking advantage of a day that happened to be stormy and crackling, went off to meet with the wolves and then returned to that wild life that a millennium of training should have effaced from its lineage. But this void in life that breathes us in, we can convert it into subtraction: to every capture, oppose a withdrawal, the insubordination of a laughter that makes us fly into sharp pieces – unassimilable. That is the lesson you take from these *nègres marrons*, these men and women who, in their mad dash to escape from the attack dogs, tore off their servants' uniforms for the ribbed shadow of foliage.

You had to run, then, in order not to lose your balance on the hanging thread; run and, beneath the incandescent friction of the wind, shed your dead skins – your slave skin; run and rip the vine from Tarzan's hands, to make it into the most precious of allies.

Tearing the liana from Tarzan's hands

To draw a blank when one is black – and all the damned are black, in other words denigrated[56] – is to be infected by a necrosis that attacks the fibers of our memory; it is to be worked over by the bleaching of one's history to the point of denying oneself at times, appearing onstage in *peau noire, masques blancs* – "black skin, white masks." By *blanc* I mean neither a being nor a thing, and not even a privilege, but simply the operation of annihilation: the laundering of memories and of subaltern territories with an eye to occupying them. Every imperial occupation requires that the land in question should be a *terra nullius*, a "no one's land": a nullified land, a space emptied of the lines of life that once embroidered its geography. And Tarzan is nothing but the name of this old complicity that ties ecology to empire in the dimension of amnesia – a name for the production of blank pages on which, in good faith, the story of a salvific mission might be inscribed. In fact we must remember that it was in the name of white supremacy that colonial imperialisms reduced "indigenous" worlds, rich in histories that went back for millennia, to a virgin nature that must be protected and, above all, made fruitful. Natural reserves, those resuscitated Edens, are simply complements to mining or plantation agriculture. In both cases, "man's exteriority with respect to the environment permits either its sacralization or its exploitation."[57] But "God is dead!" in such a way that all sacralization can be converted by capital into surplus value, and this for the greater profit of globalized tourism. As the Amazonian leader and thinker Ailton Krenak observes with a raised eyebrow, "what starts as a park ends up as a parking lot."[58]

Tarzan was born in 1912, from the pen of the American writer Edgar Rice Burroughs, who had never seen anything of Africa but a reconstituted indigenous village – a human zoo – during the 1893 World's Columbian Exposition in Chicago. Like the "apeman," the first African nature park fulfilled the prophecy of an immaculate wilderness: the Albert Park[59] was created in 1925 in the Belgian Congo, at the instigation of trophy hunters, specimen collectors, and colonial administrators who wanted to reserve exclusively to themselves the big game that they claimed to be saving from autochthonous people – from their poaching, their destructive agrarian and pastoral practices, their "overpopulation." In the tropics and other "savage" regions, the other side of environmental protection – for which Tarzan stood as a heroic figure – was the dispossession and the dehumanization of entire communities, even though their lifestyles were essential to the viability of the so-called environments. Nostalgia for the Garden of Eden made customary lands into blank hells...

> These institutions [UNESCO, the World Wildlife Fund, and others] are organizing the naturalization of a whole part of the continent at gunpoint. By this I mean the dehumanization of Africa: turning territories into parks, forbidding agriculture there, excluding humans, making their fields and their pasturelands disappear in order to create a supposedly natural world in which humanity does not exist. And this combat for a phantom Africa changes absolutely nothing about the destruction of biodiversity.[60]

In our own day, it is in the reserves of bipeds nostalgic for the arboreal life of their ancestors that the memory of Tarzan is honored in the sharpest and most singular way. In fact there is not one treetop theme park in France that fails to include a "Tarzan's leap" or a "Tarzan's vine": in general that's the culmination of the course, the last drop into the void reserved for the most heroic of Sunday explorers. Take note: *one does not leap from liana to liana*! This is the most elementary principle in an equatorial forest. The lianas are not ropes hanging in the air, they are the roots by which these plants draw up the water and minerals without which they could not climb. And when they hang from a branch, we are dealing with fragile new growths diving toward the earth, to anchor and fortify themselves down there. Finally, more often than not lianas are interwoven, sometimes to the point of forming inseparable mats, like hair. Considering some of these basic points as one mentally revisits the Tarzan films might be a first step toward detoxification...

> First we must study how colonization works to *decivilize* the colonizer, to *brutalize* him in the true sense of the word, to degrade him, to awaken him to buried instincts, to covetousness, violence, race hatred, and moral relativism; and we must show that each time a head is cut off or an eye put out in Vietnam and in France they accept the fact, each time a little girl is raped and in France they accept the fact, each time a Madagascan is tortured and in France they accept the fact, civilization acquires another dead weight, a universal regression takes place, a gangrene sets in, a center of infection begins to spread; and that at the end of all these treaties

that have been violated, all these lies that have been propagated, all these punitive expeditions that have been tolerated, all these prisoners who have been tied up and "interrogated," all these patriots who have been tortured, at the end of all the racial pride that has been encouraged, all the boastfulness that has been displayed, a poison has been distilled into the veins of Europe and, slowly but surely, the continent proceeds toward *savagery*.[61]

Unlike the mushroom, the rhizome, or the lichen – figures of the living dimension often mobilized to think the world differently[62] – there is no innocent approach to the liana. Let us only pull a thread; a whole body of colonial imagery falls down on us. Thus ripping the liana from Tarzan's hands should not be understood as an act of revenge. It is not just a matter of rehabilitating a mode of vegetal existence far richer and more complex than the apeman's acrobatics might lead one to believe but also a matter of coming back to oneself, of extracting oneself from a bad dream: for example, from these irrepressible imagistic associations that lead me to let out an absurd yodel as soon as I weigh myself against the void with a rope in my hands. It would be very simple if this "white," this dominant male, were completely foreign to me, but it is always in those moments when I least expect it that it comes back to me in the form of the most innocuous acts, such as a Tyrolean pseudoshout.

Cutting the thread of a toxic imaginary without remaining faithful to the very principle of power that one claims to be contesting is not so easy; one does not decolonize oneself through decrees or dramatic stances. Believing that one can start over from square one, that it takes only a revolution (moral, artistic, political, technological) to turn the past into a *tabula rasa* and erase an era's worth of evils, is one of the greatest illusions of our modernity. Accepting the wisdom of lianas presupposes that we patiently untangle the threads and undo the knots of stupidity with which we, as well as they, have been associated. Although lianas are an important element of the colonial imaginary, in their very manner of existing they offer something that can help to short-circuit it: the movements of return and refolding, drifting, twisting, and distorting to which they invite us are nothing but movements of subversion. In the eely undulations by which they evade capture, I already glimpse the grimaces and the monkeying around of a carnivalesque life whose excess and unpredictability have always shaken the established order.

To be done with the Virgin

Amazonia, the Congo basin, the Melanesian archipelago, and so on: for the westerner, to trace the line of the equator with one's finger means activating a whole imaginary of the virgin forest, where the cannibal lives side by side with the South Seas maiden, *wahine*, the noble savage with the wild Amazon, Eldorado with the jungle's "green hell." Behind this figure of wild nature, which continues to haunt the scientific notion of the primary forest, there is a "denial of the humanity of autochthonous forest societies."[63] This denial cannot be separated from a denial of the historicity that is specific to the mechanism of colonialism: "the colonist makes history. His life is an epic, an odyssey. He is the absolute beginning," Frantz Fanon reminds us.[64] While the "barbarian" – who surged out of the steppes or the desert – is defined only in relation to a civilization that he tries to destroy or to appropriate, the "savage" – the inhabitant of the forest [*sylve* < Lat. *silva*] is perceived only against the backdrop of a mother nature from which, as an infant, he has difficulty detaching: he "has not sufficiently entered into history."[65]

If the tropical forests initially appear to us as virgin lands, this is because, in European eyes, they did not bear any inscription, any trace of history, monuments, roads, or cities worthy of the name. In the colonial tales, the nudity of woodland territories corresponded to the nudity of savage bodies. An immaculate landscape, Amazonia was treated by the conquerors as a blank page on which their mark could be made: every plantation wrested from the jungle, every outpost and city established, every road hacked through staged the great story of "civilization."

It is time for us to be done with this fable of the virgin forest, which rings out like a call to rape.[66] The expression "virgin forest," which appeared during the conquest of the Americas, brings to mind the biblical image of the Garden of Eden and the idea of a nature that is innocent, pure, and authentic because it has not yet been penetrated by humans: a nature constructed as passive and powerless, on the model of women in the ancient Roman world, who were subjected to the right of *pater familias*, the head of the family, over life and death. Virgin forest is not a harmless metaphor; in it we hear echoes of the Roman juridical principle of *terra nullius*, which, because it defined a piece of land as "masterless," legitimated its colonization in advance. The Christian doctrine of "discovery," formulated in the papal bull of 1455, stipulated that "any Christian king who discovers non-Christian lands has the right to proclaim them his own because they belong to no one."

Even before it functions as an ideological discourse, negationism is the very mechanism of colonization: it refuses to accept that the colonized can be inscribed on their own territory as anything but scenery, picturesque fauna, an ornamental and therefore superfluous element. We understand why, in *Tarzan*, the *nègres* function for the most part as backdrop and are almost out of the field of vision – creatures carved in the night of savagery, whose fall from a cliff or ingestion by a crocodile awakens no more compassion than the death of a pack animal. "Exterminate all the brutes!" concludes the white man's report on his civilizing mission at the end of *Heart of Darkness*.[67] It is not a long stretch from denial of humanity to genocide. In regions such as Indonesia or Amazonia, ecocide cannot be dissociated from the temptation of genocide: "It's a shame that the Brazilian cavalry hasn't been as efficient as the Americans, who exterminated the Indians."[68]

Colonization is geo-graphy – "earth drawing" – in the literal sense: the marking and shaping of a "pagan" land perceived as lacking sense, as a nothingness. "The map was a tool to 'domesticate' otherness using a set of soothing metaphors... Before the conquest, the environment of the First Peoples was still amorphous. It was up to the colonizer, an almost divine figure, to shape the space."[69] The colonial map ensures the legibility of wild lands and sketches out their destiny by assigning values to the elements (roads, ports, forts, navigable rivers, plantations) that will eventually permit them to be domesticated and given human form. But in the same movement it pushes the indigenous lines of life, which have long been written into that historical landscape, into a blind spot – into the nothingness of a blank space. For example, think of the ways in which, by their travels, their horticultural practices, their shamanic rituals, and the variety of their habitats, Amerindians turned the Amazon, over the course of millennia, not only into a vast garden but also into a cosmos: a world peopled with ancestors, animal spirits, dream beings, and elementary forces that continuously give meaning to the territories of life. Therefore the exponential multiplication of fires in the Amazon basin cannot be limited to the destruction of the "primary forest": it constitutes a true and proper cosmocide.

The September 2, 2018 conflagration in the National Museum of Brazil in Rio[70] is inscribed in the ongoing story of this endless cosmocide, which began with the arrival of the first conquistadors. There was nothing passive about the disrepair imposed on this edifice and its research center; this was not the result of negligence but of a deliberate policy (applied equally to everything in the public domain, in conformity with the mechanics of neoliberalism). Abandonment is one of the modes of sovereign power: a right to kill exercised through deferment or delay. To abandon means to banish from the commons: it exposes the one who is abandoned to the natural elements, to illnesses, to relocation, to deterioration, to death, whether we are talking about an individual, a historical building, documents and other memory storage devices, or populations. With this fire, material evidence for the territorial inscription of Amerindian communities and those descended from Africans also went up in smoke, rendering recognition of their civil, cultural, and territorial rights even more fragile.

Today Amazonia is being devastated by the same "civilizing mission" under the codename "development." In the purest colonial tradition, Jair Bolsonaro considers the Amerindians incapable of investing profitably in their own lands. So, by appropriating those lands for themselves, large landowners and multinational corporations would only open them up for the common good, while continually pushing back the edges of "savagery." This scorched earth policy corresponds to a politics of burned memory that aims at the accelerated production of a virgin and homogeneous surface ready to be disemboweled, scarred, squeezed to the last drop by the faceless conquistadors of globalized capitalism. We must therefore question the *blanc* in its relation to forgetfulness and to the extraction of memories, a process that also requires the extraction of natural resources and human resources; question it as a modality of the inscription of colonial power. The *blanc* is an operation that annihilates other worlds, an act zombifying bodies and other territories.

> I attest to this: the world is not white; it was never white, cannot be white. White is a metaphor for power, and that is simply a way of describing Chase Manhattan Bank.[71]

Whiteness is not just a metaphor for power, but also for a geography of nothingness. The colonist's gesture of inscription simultaneously scrubs away indigenous memories and whitens history in a such a way as to expunge its crimes, while consecrating the civilizing hero. The virgin surface, the *terra nullius*, the white space on the map, is the myth of colonial or "modern" power par excellence,[72] which can operate only by making the active forces of the past into a blank slate the better to be able to shape, subject, and exploit indigenous bodies and territories. Michel de Certeau reads *Robinson Crusoe* as a novel about writing, about the specifically capitalist power to make inscriptions by which the West is defined. This modern form of power operates from the start by giving writing a grip over indigenous lands and over the commons in general.[73] First and foremost, it is on a white page that the modern subject, the conquering ego, imposes its will, thereby disqualifying indigenous voices as well as the minor knowledges of the peasant, the artisan, the wise woman (criminalized as a "witch"), all relegated to the suspect shadows of orality.

> The awakening of Robinson to the capitalist and conquering task of writing his island is inaugurated by the decision to write his diary, to give himself in that way a space in which he can master time and things, and thus to constitute for himself, along with the blank page, an initial island in which he can produce what he wants.[74]

If the blank as a form of forgetfulness constitutes an essential step in the mapmaking process, this is because it participates in a mechanism of desire, an erotics of predation: one re-drapes an indigenous land in a veil of virginity – the innocence of something without history – in order to rape it all the better. As Matthieu Noucher stresses, "the agents of colonization participated in a whitening of the maps when they effaced certain landmarks in order to build an empty space from scratch, a space they could conquer."[75] The whiteness of maps is the product of a strategic operation laundering history, bleaching away the memory of old territories.

The right to opacity

> We despair of the chaos-world. But this is because we are still trying to discern in it a sovereign order that would once again bring the world-totality back to a reductive unity. ... This is why I call for the right to opacity for everyone. I no longer have to "understand" the other, that is, to reduce him to the model of my own transparency, in order to live with this other or to build something with him. Today, the right to opacity is the most obvious sign of non-barbarity.[76]

Édouard Glissant did not invent a "poetics of relation"; he exhumed it directly from the opacity of the living world. Hence his passion for the primordial bubbling of the mangrove, where our distinctions, our categories, our labels are perpetually being blurred. The opacity of the living, our own opacity, is nothing but the infinite intertwining of lines of life and their sedimentation. The poetic work consists precisely in deploying this opacity by allowing it to be traversed by the chthonian powers it contains, powers that reveal the irrepressible growth of trees, lianas, and other plants as much as the growth of communities and peoples that rise up in the forest's retreats.

Every time when my own mother wanted to talk to me, she first had my wife or my sister come and said to them, "I have a desire to talk to my son Amadou, but first I would like to know which of the Amadous that lives in him is currently there.[77]

According to a Bambara proverb, "the persons of the person are multiple within the person." In sub-Saharan cosmologies, the multiverse is located in the heart of each human, who understands vegetal, animal, climactic, and mineral elements within him or herself, entering into combinations in perpetual movement, while each one produces singularities: "persons." Hence the legitimate question of Hampâté Bâ's mother concerning "which of the Amadous" she should get ready to meet. The lianas allow this proliferation of constituents in a person to be conceived using the figure of entangled lines of life. This is doubtless one meaning of ancestrality: being anchored in lineages that extend, through resonance, beyond the human lives that precede us, to the totality of the living and to elementary forces.

Listen to Things
More often than Beings,
Hear the voice of fire,
Hear the voice of water.
Listen in the wind,
To the sighs of the bush;
This is the ancestors breathing.

Those who are not dead are not ever gone;
They are in the darkness that grows lighter
And in the darkness that grows darker.

> The dead are not down in the earth;
> They are in the trembling of the trees
> In the groaning of the woods,
> In the water that runs,
> In the water that sleeps,
> They are in the hut, they are in the crowd;
> The dead are not dead.[78]

The ancestor is the shadow, which duplicates each of our steps and reminds us that one never starts from nothing, that we are not individuals as much as knots of relations.[79] To make a path in the world is always to pick up on stories and circumstances that we have not chosen, but that offer us a unique working material while giving our lives a weight that is both ambivalent and necessary – a heaviness that at once burdens us and carries us. It is by cultivating this mangrove that dwells in us and goes beyond us – a jumble of lines of growth and decomposition – that we bring about the unforeseeable: unsuspected versions of one's "person."[80] It is not a matter of becoming oneself – as if this "self" were already there,[81] as if existence had only one dimension – but rather one of taking the risk of diffracting oneself by exposing oneself to uncertainties and to the multiplicity of this world's functions and possible stories: as Fernando Pessoa enjoins, "be plural like the universe!" It is legitimate to want to affirm oneself; it is even an ethical and political exigence in contexts of systemic violence toward minoritized groups and communities. But how, then, can one avoid falling into ossifying logics of identification (such as the logic of the closed identities of colonial ethnicity or, better still, the logic of the segmentation of markets and of the "personalization" of marketing) that tend to obstruct the sealing of alliances between subaltern movements? Beginning from the "black question," Léonora Miano points – quite rightly, and with some irony, too – to the illusion of authenticity characteristic of all forms of essentialism:

> Among sub-Saharans and people of African descent, the higher ranks of essentialism have come to be occupied by convinced racialists, who forget too quickly that these conceptions were not part of the vision of the world held by their sub-Saharan ancestors, to whom they have dedicated a cult... Their logic is to sub-Saharan thought what wax cloth is to the continent's homegrown textiles: a European fabrication, so well assimilated that it is confused with the ancestral patrimony, which it has finished by replacing.[82]

If *who* I am can surprise the most loving mother (as we see in the extract from Hampâté Bâ), this is because the "who" is more like a musical motif – always contextualized by the circumstances under which it is executed – than like the permanence of an essentialized identity. This does not mean, however, that one can become everything and anything, because every material, including that of existence, presents lines of force and systemic constraints. A "matter of existence" that would put up no resistance to our arbitrariness – to the free will of the postmodern consumer of identities – would be as inconsistent as the avatars of social networks. My opacity – all these lines that traverse me and make me escape my own surface – is precious because it preserves the possibility of withdrawing from all programming, including my own.

The right to opacity proclaimed by Édouard Glissant is also inscribed in the art of camouflage and of disappearance practiced by the *nègres marrons*. If the modern map is the instrument by which territory is domesticated, then to live in the shadow – in the blank space of maps – is, under certain circumstances, to bury oneself in the humus of an unconquerable earth: to interact with it so intimately that one almost melts away. Although they are the great forgotten people of cartographic projects in Guiana, the Businenge (the maroons of the Guianas) do not present themselves as victims of an "invisibilization." In fact they manifest a centuries-old defiance toward institutionalized categories of knowledge and recognition. In their case, living in the white parts of the map means extirpating oneself deliberately from the map of the whites. It means remaining faithful to the stealthy mode of life and of resistance which allowed their ancestors to survive and hatch an ombrophilous culture. Indeed the borders of maroon territories could be maintained only through their own effacement, the continual scrambling of the masters' radar.

Art of the arabesque and camouflage

> The steamer toiled along slowly on the edge of a black and incomprehensible frenzy. … The earth seemed unearthly. We are accustomed to look upon the shackled form of a conquered monster, but there – there you could look at a thing monstrous and free.[83]

Before they ever raised an obstacle to the colonist's march, lianas – and the trees they weave together – obstructed his sight, his plans. During Marlow's return up the Congo River, the anxiety that eats away at him is initially as indecipherable as the shores he passes: he perceives nothing but vegetal "frenzy." The captain is not confronted with a "primary forest" but with a primal fear. This fear is not new; it has always gripped "civilized" people in the face of undomesticated territories. In *Heart of Darkness*, Conrad sets the mouth of the Thames from Roman times into resonance with that of the Congo in Belgian times. "Natural walls": this is the expression that Julius Caesar used in the *Gallic Wars* to evoke the shadow of forested cliffs – the first impediment to the penetration of "civilization." In fact Celtic peoples cultivated the art of melting into these "tenebrous" forests in order to trace lines of defense there and weave them into refuges.

> At the very moment when the demon alights on the surface, it ceases to be a surface at all, and the lines apparently drawn on it become threads that trap the demon as if in a spider's web."[84]

Far from being nice innocent plants, during the course of their evolution lianas have developed a thoroughly mystifying strategy of transforming their own bodies and the spaces they traverse into indecipherable geographies: the dreadlocks of future Zions... One of the first things the lianas teach is how to turn one's territory into an encrypted space. And when I say "lianas," I am not thinking only of crawling and climbing plants, but more generally of the plant world's power of alliance and art of the arabesque. Etymologically, "liana" evokes *lien* ("bond"); or, more precisely, the plant designated by the term "liana" presents the same ambivalence as the notion of the bond. Bonds connect us to one another, but they can also close up around us like nets. Because they weave the trees together and hang in canopies, lianas – like the mycelium in another plane – work to produce the tropical forest as a polyphonic body, but they can also become "threads that trap the demon as if in a spider's web":

> Nature protects the *sertanejo*, renders him an indomitable Antaeus... the *caatingas*[85] are an incorruptible ally of the *sertanejo* in revolt... They arm themselves for the combat, take the offensive. For the invader they are an impenetrable wilderness; but they have numerous paths by which they are accessible to the backwoodsman, who was born and grew up there. ... Spreading out, on the run, [the soldiers] plunge headlong into the labyrinth of boughs and branches.

Tripped by the slipknot lassos of the creeping *quipá* vines, they fall, or else are brought to a standstill, their legs held motionless by the powerful tentacles. They struggle desperately, until their uniforms are in tatters, in the feline claws of the macambiras with their crooked thorns.[86]

Camouflage – blending, to the point of vanishing, into the living environment in which we evolve – presupposes an ecology of feelings: feeling the wind, the sun, the rain, the elements penetrate us through every pore and embracing the cycle of their mutations; perceiving until one becomes imperceptible. The *nègre marron* is the fugitive par excellence, the one who traces without leaving any trace. The *nègres marrons* are the ninja *nègres* who perfectly master this art of metamorphosis and self-dissolution. By their virtuoso gestures and movements, by their rhythmic dislocation, maroon bodies purify themselves, efface themselves, and make themselves virtual in the suspense of an ungraspable blue note:

> No note is attacked straight; the voice or instrument always approaches it from above or below, plays around the implied pitch without ever remaining any length of time, and departs from it without ever having committed itself to a single meaning. ... The denying or withholding of all signposts.[87]

The "blue note"[88] is the musical expression par excellence of the subterfuges by which black peoples twist time and transmute this rhythmic pulsation, which pushes them to hammer the ground and split the air. All the musical forms of the African diaspora bear the maroon imprint of an art of the swerve, a practice involving the scrambling of references and traceable steps. During the period of slavery, the fugitives of "Negro spirituals" undertook quite concrete escapes: those of the Underground Railroad, the largest network of escaping slaves in the Americas. What made this clandestine organization, which involved black and white abolitionists as well as "refugees," so distinctive was that it bent the technological model of the railroad to establish an encoded cartography of flight routes (including "emergency exit paths" in case of discovery by the slave hunters) and of hiding places.[89] All this was in the encrypted language of the railway (refuges baptized as "stations," fugitives as "goods," guides as "conductors," etc.) and of the Bible. Spirituals like "Follow the Drinking Gourd" constituted manifest songlines, that is, sung itineraries (musical maps) with precise notations such as "Where the great big river meets the little river/Follow the drinkin' gourd" (i.e. "where the Ohio crosses a small river, follow the Big Dipper.") Likewise, the song "Wade in the Water," which appears to be a biblical parable – "wade in the water, God is gonna trouble these waters" – instructs the fugitives to do everything possible to conceal their footsteps.

> In a sense, it can be said that travel themes in the blues rearticulated the collective desire to escape bondage that pervaded the musical culture of slavery. Travel was one of the central organizing themes of the spirituals. Traveling liberators (as in "Go down, Moses/Way down in Egypt land/Tell old Pharaoh/To let my people go") and signposts for travel (as in "Follow the drinking gourd/And the old man is a-waiting/For to carry you to freedom/Follow the drinking gourd") are common subjects of the spirituals. Images of trains (as in "The gospel train is coming/Get on board, little children, get on board") and other traveling vehicles (as in "Swing low, sweet chariot/Coming for to carry me home") are also abundant in the spirituals.[90]

The Underground Railroad is a "ghost train" (thus a "chimera"): a sublime subterfuge, a simulacrum that operates by poetic encryption, the twisting of language, the distortion of the dominant system (like the one Jimi Hendrix imposed on the national anthem of the United States). It was by repurposing the postal system, by getting himself *affranchi* ("franked" and "liberated") in the form of living cargo – a container he designed and where he hid during a 26-hour journey on 23 March 1849 – that the fugitive slave Henry Box Brown won his freedom. This was a true sleight of hand (worthy of the ruses found in folk tales), which earned him the surname "Box." Fuguing is not fleeing before oppression but producing one's own disappearance in a haze of tricks and fabulations. To escape the grasp of the forces of order or to slip away through the smallest interstices requires a rigorous practice of twisting, distorting, and contorting languages and bodies. The motif of the "underground" is indissociable from contemporary subcultures. They feed on the idea of the subterranean, of the tunnel as a liberatory space and path – a motif running through all African–American literature of the United States, in novels such as Ralph Ellison's *Invisible Man*, in *Rite of Passage* and *The Man Who Lived Underground* by Richard Wright, or, more recently, in Colson Whitehead's *Underground Railroad*. The carnivalesque dimension of these works – which make us see the world from the vantage point of the basement, in a sort of reversal of the white's high-altitude point of view – is mirrored in the upside-down world of hip-hop dancers who spin on their head. From Josephine Baker to KRUMP, the grimace[91] evokes the same twisting and distortion, applied this time to the face and to the roles that the *nègre* is supposed to play on the social scene: it expresses the impact of oppression (a grimace of pain) as much as the menacing irony of the black person wearing "blackface" (which began as a way to frustrate racist stereotypes and the codes of good society by exaggerating them).

> Live with your head in the lion's mouth. I want you to overcome 'em with yeses, undermine 'em with grins, agree 'em to death and destruction, let 'em swoller you till they vomit or bust wide open.[92]

Indissociable from marronage, the techniques of camouflage thus extend even to the way in which slaves twisted the master's language. Because it pushes the French language into polyphonic and polyrhythmic variations,[93] Creole can encrypt and render the most seditious speech "chimeric." *Tembe*, the sculpture of the Businenge (the maroon peoples of Guiana and Surinam), is doubtless one of the most beautiful plastic expressions of the creative dimension of subterfuge (this word derives from the Latin *subterfugere*, "to flee from under/secretly"): even today, marronage is pursued in the intertwining of sculpted wood. Here the fugue, inasmuch as it is a rhythmic principle of encryption and variation, is directly inscribed in the furrows of a threshing basin, on the head of an oar or the seat of a bench. Like so many paths or vines, the wood ribbons turn, dive, resurface above and below one another, thereby offering a vertiginous experience to the gaze. The artist's virtuosity is measured by her capacity to confuse the marks she leaves behind. Beyond the meaning that certain motifs may carry in the eyes of the community or the artist who created them, the composition formed by the entangled bands of the *tembe* certainly carries a talismanic dimension, like all labyrinthine figures.[94] By disturbing the viewer, the intertwining protects whatever might otherwise be exposed…

From time immemorial, clandestine communities have learned to forge alliances with vegetal powers that, in dissolving the "surface" – the overarching view of those who are dominant – into inextricable threads (see the earlier extract from Ingold, p. 142), deploy a protective maze: a zone of offensive uncertainty. Lianas provide a figure for the composition of a vegetal mesh that offers cover and refuge to witches and heretics, to *nègres marrons* and *cangaceiros*, to Zapatistas and Zadists, to all the dissident communities that defy the grasp of state and capital.[95] Thus the wisdom of lianas leads us toward a practice of alliance between "minor" forms of life. These modes of existence are minor not just because they are minoritized, disqualified, criminalized by dominant norms and powers, but also because they evoke an art of the fugue: games of legerdemain, with multiple variables and levels (secretive habitats, encoded languages, masked identities) that elude any classification. Because of its musical meanings (in polyphony, as a baroque form), the notion of fugue manifests the creative dimension of flight and of different forms of "fugitiveness" in general (avoidance, camouflage, clandestinity, etc.). My goal is to think of the fugue on the basis of the experience of a maroon body, a fugitive body, and to develop a musical and choreographic conception of resistances.[96]

> A minor key is always interlaced with major keys – the minor works the major from within. … neither the minor nor the major is fixed in advance. The major is a structural tendency that organizes itself according to predetermined definitions of value. The minor is a force that courses through it, unmooring its structural integrity, problema-tizing its normative standards.[97]

To live in the minor mode, to live in "fugue," is to join with forms of life and resistance that subvert the dominant order by imposing creative variations on it. This is how the minuet, the quadrille, the contra dance, the mazurka, and many other dances of the European colonizers were transfigured by the creative reworking that the lives of the wretched imposed on them: the *nègres* played them on the basis of other worlds and in light of other ends. In that way they effected a subversion – a subterranean version – of the master's divide, to the point of giving birth to unexpected songs and fields of force such as the *gwoka* of Guadeloupe, the *bèlè* of Martinique, the *kaseko* of Guiana, the *maloya* of Réunion, or New Orleans jazz: soul music to awaken the dead and to unleash lives!

In the seventeenth century, the memoirs of a former governor of Surinam recounted his defeat by the Saramaka, a community of *noirs marrons* whom he compared to the Lernaean Hydra, which grew two new heads for every head that was severed.[98] While the western sovereigns identified with Hercules (who, through his twelve labors, incarnated the civilizing hero), these "same rulers found in the many-headed hydra an antithetical symbol of disorder and resistance, a powerful threat to the building of state, empire, and capitalism."[99] The proliferation of lianas is the vegetal equivalent of the proliferation of the Hydra's heads: a concrete illustration of the inexhaustible character of resistances in a minor mode. Like the image of the chimeric monster's serpentine body, lianas continually renew their assault on the paths and lands cleared by the conquistador, the missionary, the planter. If the Hydra arouses fear in kings, this is not just because it symbolizes a resistance that grows in number each time it returns from the ashes. The Hydra's multiplying tentacles also represent the specter of an alliance between heterogeneous subaltern groups: the colorful and rebel multitudes formed by pirates and *noirs marrons*, dispossessed peasants and itinerant laborers, house servants and prostitutes, religious dissidents and trappers.

Power(s) of the vine

The dynamics of the *lyannaj* are a matter of combining and gathering together, of binding, connecting, and relaying everything that found itself broken apart [*désolidarisé*] ... Beyond demands related to purchasing power and profiteering, remarkably large masses of people of all ages, all social backgrounds, and all sectors of activity found themselves side by side in impressive parades, nighttime assemblies, and enthusiastic vigils where songs, dance, music, open speech, and forgotten forms of cameraderie were liberated.[100]

In the Creole languages of Martinique and Guadeloupe, *lyann* ("liana") is a living line that binds a circle together and makes it into a collective body – *fo nou lyanné, nou an lyannaj*. But it also traps those who are dominant, encircling them in a fine web of continuous conjurations that range from escapes and acts of sabotage all the way to general insurrection, not to mention mystical ceremonies and the selection of plants to be found in "the blacks' garden" [*le jardin nègre*].[101] In Guadeloupe and Martinique, ever since the times of slavery and resistance against it, the word *lyannaj* recalls the powers of the forest, with which an alliance is forged in every movement of renewed existence. Most of the time the leaders of seditious movements were priestesses and *quimboiseurs* ("witch

healers"), masters of the knowledge and use of plants. Thus we
should not be surprised that, in 2009, a large social and political
movement against the cost of living on those islands (prefiguring
in certain respects the Yellow Vests movement in France) took
the form of a Lyannaj Kont Pwofitasyon ("Solidaristic Movement
against the Profiteering System").[102]

The *lyannaj* evoked by Breleur and the other writers of *Manifesto
for Essential "Products" [Manifeste pour les "produits" de haute
nécessité]* in 2009 was born in the fields, where it originally referred
to a kind of skill or dexterity, namely the weaving motion by which
enslaved people sewed together the sweet reeds of Babylon – the
sugar canes. Through a strange reversal, *lyannaj*, the technical
gesture essential to exploitation, dispossession, and the vampiri-
zation of enslaved bodies, became the most remarkable expression
of solidarity, creativity, and of liberating bonds: those of poetry,
song, work, and mutual aid societies, Afro-diasporic cults and
rhythms. As target and primary material for an apparatus of capture
and exploitation, the *nègre*'s body serves as the primary theater of
operation. In its beginnings, the subversion of *lyannaj* starts with an
internal variation of a movement that has been imposed on bodies:
let this movement, which ties together the cane bundles, also be able
to bind the wretched to one another! Thus *lyannaj* refers to the very
first counter-plantation practices.

It is in fact on the basis of the plantation itself, through a
redirection of its bloody discipline – whose principal slogan was
the snap of the whip and the spit word *nègre* – that the first retali-
atory acts were deployed: unexpected desertions, feigned idiocies,
damaging instances of negligence, thefts of provisions or coin,
slowdown of the work rhythms, the sabotage of machines, whispers
that decoded the master's language and predicted his imminent
demise, and so on – all the way to the fire of revolt. *Lyannaj* makes
use of a whole corpus of internalized know-how, a stealthy assembly
of allied bodies. It is not a matter of brandishing an identity as
Mandingo, Kongo, Yoruba, Ashanti, or Sakhalave in the master's
face, but of taking place and of making a space, of giving birth
to new versions of the world, to an opaque and unpredictable
pluriverse, on the basis of the chaos of intertwined memories and
powers.

But then why use the vegetal figure of the liana as an aid in
thinking about the emergence of a "we"– a decompartmentalized
community – that embraces the greatest variety of individuals

and groups? Doubtless because the liana has a formidable gift for intertwining; it is the loquacious plant par excellence. As it has no trunk (no self-supporting structure), its escape toward the heavens is possible only because it leans on others, because it mixes itself with others, while simultaneously mixing them with one another, as "a matter of combining and gathering together, of binding, connecting and relaying everything that found itself broken apart." The *lyannaj* is a way of composing forces and forms, a composition in the minor mode, a vegetal fugue. By its vertiginous trajectory, the liana incarnates the power to "traverse" and be nourished by whatever it crosses through (and vice versa): the strata of the subsoils, the teeming of (de)composed lands, the inverted collapse of ferns and tropical trees.

In the end, the liana is no thing but this race to the light, a race launched from the humid and opaque flesh of the undergrowth, to meet up with the emerald drapery of the canopy. The liana's movement is at once philosophical and poetic; it obeys the principle of detour and correspondence: in all manner of creative variations, by zig-zagging here and there, above and below, through the interstices of boulders or the springboard of stumps, the *lyannaj*'s line of flight runs through all the forest's layers with neither priority nor hierarchy, giving a supportive setting to forms of life with no connection a priori. Processional ants, praying mantises, howler monkeys, epiphytes tumbling toward the earth, expansive mosses, a multitude of living beings borrow and re-create the fractal routes of the *lyannaj* at every moment.

Mistresses of the crossroads, certain lianas are the privileged allies of the shaman, who "dreams" while secreting the confused words of whatever lies beyond the visible realm. This is how ayahuasca works. As the paradigmatic expression of the spirit of the forest, it reveals secret correspondences between the multiple dimensions of reality – a "string theory." The aerial tangle of lianas, like the subterranean lattice of roots and mycelium, makes the forest into a shifting and metamorphic canvas; by comparison, our cybernetic networks and forms of artificial intelligence are only pale approximations. The textile workshop of lianas introduces us to a cosmos in constant reinvention, to a cosmo-poetics of the fugue.

Lianas teach us not how to "land," as certain masters of terrestrial life urge us to do,[103] but rather how to draw back a bowstring: how to cultivate the tension between earth and sky. Making the sky bend to the earth and vice versa does not happen without friction, however, since lianas, like ropes,[104] stick together only as a result of the friction between their fibers. Moreover, one cannot reduce the characteristic activity of lianas to the establishment of relations. In fact there are also toxic bonds, because the ability to develop attachments gives rise to freedom only if one is also capable of breaking them, or even of striking them forcefully – with the bite of a vine whip (as in the expression *fouté lyann*; "to put the screws on someone") – when their grasp tightens up once again. There is no *lyannaj* without secession from those who obstruct us, gag us, choke us, coopt us, swallow us up. The liana weaves together beings and elements only when its movement ruptures terrestrial gravity: its swing toward the sky is the leap of the monkey who transmutes weight into buoyancy.

> "But," remarked the towering Hanuman, looking around him, "who will be able to withstand the formidable pressure that I will exert on the earth at the moment of my leap"?[105]

To leap is not to deny the weight of constraints and evils but, on the contrary, to make them into a force of weightlessness: the more intense the pressure, the higher the leap will reach. In the Hindu pantheon,[106] Hanuman is defined by his mental agility as much as by his bodily dexterity. Son of the wind – Vayu, the vital breath that animates all things – the monkey god puts his power of uprooting in the service of life: nothing, no bondage, can resist his breath. This same power to tear things from the ground conditions the liana's "poetics of relation."[107] Of the entire botanical kingdom, lianas are the plants whose will to ascend is the strongest, which is why they are the first to begin exploring after a tornado, a fire, the fall of trees, or the abandonment of a plantation create openings in the forest cover. The prodigious growth of lianas is possible because of large vascular channels, often visible to the naked eye, which give rise to an incomparable hydraulic thrust. In lianas more than in any other vegetal being, growth and flux, the driving force of a plant and the momentum of a river work together (when cut, a section of "water liana" that is shorter than one meter gushes at least a liter of water). I am trying to think through the irrepressible push of life within and outside us beginning from this torrential sap, which makes lianas lifelines in the proper sense; trying to think through this preexisting and perpetual insistence on returning, even after rape, pillage, enslavement, destruction and fire – the insistence on sprouting and resprouting that Anna Lowenhaupt Tsing calls "resurgence." Resurgence, not *resilience*,[108] because this is not a question of adapting oneself or of returning to an initial state: every crossing is a transformation (including a transformation of the environment being crossed), every fugue unfurls a cycle of metamorphoses, and both the liana and the fugitive hope to rebound to a place where, in their upwelling toward the surface of the canopy, they can no longer be cut off.

In her introduction to *The Feral Atlas*, Anna Lowenhaupt Tsing defines "feral" ecologies as ones "that have been encouraged by human-built infrastructures, but ... have developed and spread beyond human control."[109] For her, this is always a matter of questioning the possibility of life among the ruins of capitalism: what happens to a plantation of oil palm trees, an industrial lot, a hydroelectric dam, or an entire city when they are deserted by humans and left to their own devices? What transformations happen to the creatures that were cultivated or raised there, what new ecologies appear in those locations? "Feral" refers to the living world's becoming maroon, its concretely unpredictable character. The movement by which the living thing "feralizes" can give birth to new worlds – like these abandoned offshore platforms in the Gulf of Mexico that have become coral reefs – but also to fierce ecologies. Just as the *nègres marrons* who returned to wreak havoc on colonial society after they had escaped from the plantations ("a human infrastructure project"), living beings who escape our infrastructures can also be devastating to our globalized societies (COVID-19 being the latest example).

Stretching the string of a battle bow

Asclepius, the god of healing, has a snake twined round his staff as a symbol... It is significant, however, that even this most exalted and detached god has his roots in the nether world of the departed souls, where the living snake has an abode. The earliest tribute of worship is paid to him as a serpent. The snake twined round his staff and he himself are one and the same – a departed soul that goes on living and reappears in the form of a serpent.[110]

Most of the time, plants are referred to only within the context of "benevolence" and "care." To a certain extent, this angelic vision of our relationship with the vegetal world (and with the living world in general) perpetuates the colonial and capitalist construction of the living environment as powerless (nature as innocence, as inoffensive virginity). Meanwhile, even today, many autochthonous people in struggle and many dissident communities cultivate an aggressive way of using the plants found in their surrounding territories. When they declare, "we are not defending Nature, we ARE the nature which is defending itself!" the Zadists of Notre Dame des Landes call for an exit from the position of exteriority and distance that characterizes mainstream ecology, always haunted as it is by the shadow of Tarzan: a patriarchal vision of how nature is to be protected.

"One of the great successes of European states was not to forbid the use of hallucinogens and poisons, but to make them disappear even from memory," the historian and epistemologist Samir Boumediene points out.[111] Toxicity is not a negative aspect of plants that must be eliminated; rather it is in keeping with the very principle of their therapeutic virtues and their capacity to amplify our experience of the world. Thus one can understand the psychedelic (i.e. "mind-revealing," from the Greek *psuchēn dēloun*, "to make the spirit visible/clear") power of ayahuasca, also called "the purge,"[112] only on the basis of its toxicity: the "vision vine" (also called "death vine") teaches only through the ordeal of death, because the truths it delivers (in a ritual framework) demand a metamorphosis, a new birth. This is what we learn from Davi Kopenawa's story about one of the steps of his initiation as a shaman, in which his experience of *yakoana*, a psychotropic powder extracted from the leaves of the *Virola elongata* bush, is described. We must understand that there are many uses for these sacred plants, just as for the rituals and cosmologies that frame them, but all of them presuppose some form of death and (re)birth.[113] Moreover, the teaching of "wisdom plants" consists in the experience they produce in the initiate.

> It is true that sometimes the *xapiri* [forest spirits] terrify us. They can leave us for dead, collapsed on the ground and reduced to a ghost state. ... They simply seek to weaken our awareness, for if we were merely alive like ordinary people, they could not make us think right. If we did not become other ... it would be impossible for us to see things the way the spirits do! ... The spirits of the leaves, lianas, and trees are the first to come clean us. ... We return to being newborns, still red with the blood of our birth! ... Then the spirits lose our thought and language in order to teach us theirs. Next they make us

learn the pattern of the forest so that we can see it like they do and protect it.[114]

The word "toxic," which comes to us from the Greek *toxon* ("bow"), speaks of a bow and arrows steeped in poison. Nothing could be more accurate. The toxicity of plants is anything but accidental; it is the product of a self-defense strategy, a complex chemical technology that human groups have always known how to turn to their advantage. Lianas are rightly counted among the most powerful plants in terms of alchemical knowhow: in the Amazon, the Amerindians use them to prepare curare (for hunting with blowguns) as much as to make wade fishing possible (sprinkled in water, the hali hali liana of the Wayanas of Guiana provokes a deadly narcosis in fish, which allows them to be gathered from the surface).

Nature is such a potent symbol of innocence partly because "she" is imagined to be without technology.[115]

The Greeks had only one word to refer to something that behaved both as a remedy and as a poison: *pharmakon*. This ambivalent power was symbolized by the serpent (a kind of animal liana) coiled around the staff of Asclepius. That which cures may also kill, in such a way that care may itself prove to be offensive or take the form of counteraction, of something "returned to sender."[116] In central Africa, the *nganga* – the seer–healer of the Bantu-speaking world – is the very person who may become a *ndoki* – a witch who secretly causes harm – once night has fallen.

In the healing rituals of the Piro, as among neighbouring Amazonian peoples, the shaman – having taken an infusion of the hallucinogenic vine known as *ayahuasca* – becomes conscious of brilliant snakelike designs that appear to cover his entire field of vision.[117]

Whether we are considering the shamans of the Mexican deserts, the *Mãe-de-santo*[118] of northwest Brazil, or the *ngangas* of the Congo basin, to enter in relation with wisdom plants such as peyote or "devil's weed"[119] can indeed be dangerous: it is not a matter of using their therapeutic properties, but of negotiating with the powers that teach and care, *potencias*[120] of life and death over those who invoke them. Neither ayahuasca nor iboga (a bush from Gabon, *Tabernanthe iboga*) are perceived as hallucinogenic plants, but as the very spirit of the forest, by those whom they enable to see the "invisible" (which has nothing to do with the "supernatural") – the close net of relations and memories in which every life is registered. "We do not come into the world alone," writes Paul Claudel. "To be born [*naître*], for everything, means to be born in affinity with everything [*con-naître*], co-born. All birth is knowledge [*con-naissance*]."[121] The "wisdom" of lianas consists precisely in this inscription of knowledge in the living world. The poetic co-birth is a joint birth, an intuition of our relatedness to other living beings. To be co-born (*con-naître*) into the world is to join its perpetual birth. And what the West calls "ecology" is nothing but this feel for correspondences: the sensible apprehension of relationships embedded in a single biome (mangrove forest, tundra, savannah, steppes) of heterogenous elements and entities.

> Long before these words [of ecology] existed among [white people] and they started to speak about them so much, they were already in us, though we did not name them in the same way. For the shamans, these have always been words that came from the spirits to defend the forest.... In the forest, we human beings are the "ecology." But it is equally the *xapiri*, the game, the trees, the rivers, the fish, the sky, the rain, the wind, and the sun! It is everything that came into existence in the forest, far from the white people: everything that isn't surrounded by fences yet.[122]

The shaman and Amazonian leader Davi Kopenawa explains clearly that, for peoples like his own, the Yanomami, ecology does not constitute a separate dimension of existence; it is indistinguishable from its very texture: "the words of ecology... were already in us." Kopenawa defines this "us" as a knot of correspondences between humans and "everything that came into existence with the forest": "the *xapiri*, the game, the trees, the rivers, the fish, the sky, the rain, the wind, and the sun." To exist is to be inscribed from the very start in the meshes of the living and of elementary forces. This inscription is manifest in the most banal gestures, those of gardening, fishing, basketwork; in a way of moving through the forest while being attentive to the signs of an approaching storm (such as a cloud of flying ants), or in unthinkingly tossing away the kernel of the mango one has just eaten in a small clearing where a new tree might spring up. But one must not mistake this ecology, integrated as it is into a way of being, for a pure form of immanence: the "words of ecology" are in fact more than human, they were,

for the shamans, "words that came from the spirits to defend the
forest." Far from being reduced to beings of pure light, the spirits
with which the shamans communicate also represent the sensory
form of a fear that no effective ecology can do without: in truth,
these entities embody the forest's own capacities for self-defense, as
well as the terrible powers of the cosmos in comparison to which
every human order appears laughable. In the black communities of
the Pacific coast of Colombia, mangroves and forests are inhabited
by *visiones* such as the Madre de Agua, a siren who leads her prey
beneath the waves, or La Tunda, a sort of woman vampire who
traps young men in wooden mazes and madness. These spirits are
also called *espantos* in Spanish – "horrors." As with the *xapiri* of
the Yanomami, the fear and laughter that the *visiones* inspire[123]
give consistency to a complete ethic of relationships with the living
world – a wisdom of lianas – which is once again threatened by the
constant advance of urbanization and agroindustrial plantations.

> The *visiones* do not protect just the forest's visitors but the forest
> itself, by means of the menace they cause to weigh on those who
> traverse it, and above all on those who destroy it... the *visiones*
> tend to disappear over time, with the approach of huge palm oil
> plantations, the cutting of trees, the bulldozing of paths and of
> urbanization, which reduces the spirits along with the space of the
> forest.[124]

A living milieu is not limited to poetic correspondences; it also
constitutes a field of forces, with its disymmetries, frictions, and
fault lines, and with the subterranean impact of polar vortices,
warm currents, seismic waves, sunstorms, and other planetary
and interplanetary phenomena. These phenomena reveal that all
apparent harmony is shot through with chaos (the second principle
of entropy in thermodynamics). The Yanomamis have always lived
in fear of a new "falling sky" (their foundational myth), and they
never stop laughing about it, because laughter and fear come from
the same tremor. Under cover of the tree canopy, behind the apparent
fixity of things and beings, there rumbles a flow of metamorphoses
at once comical and menacing, echo of the early times when humans
were still indistinct from animals or continually transformed into
one another: from anteater to crocodile, from crocodile to human,
from human to toucan, from toucan to agouti, in a series of carnivalesque transfigurations. It was only after this series of fantastic
turnarounds, transgressions, and tribulations – which still arouse

hearty laughter in the Yanomami – that the ancestors lost their status as "humanimals." This definitive "fall" into human skin was experienced as the founding misfortune. The initiation of young shamans consists entirely in reactivating, through techniques of trance and dance, the simultaneously animal and human condition of the earliest ancestors. This is why shamans (like other masters of the invisible) are, initially, those who pass between worlds (human–non-human, living–dead, etc.); and they cross such borders only by transgressing them,[125] reintroducing indistinction and chaos into a cosmos that would otherwise be threatened by sclerosis and asphyxiation. In the West there is a tendency to present shamans as great sages, "guardians of nature"; but this is to forget that in the first place they are masters of disorder: pre-eminent fighters in the battle of the imaginary, cosmopolitical figures who inspire revolts and indigenous movements even today.

> In the war between invisible forces that is unfolding in the Americas, psychotropic substances render the greatest outrages possible: seeing things that must not be seen, imagining that other worlds can yet be made... Disorder is dreamed before it surges up, and when it is dreamed it is already disorder. From the neighborhood poisoner to the mystic leading a revolt, it is often by calling on voices and dreams that the decision is made to introduce dissonance into the colonial world's operations. And this considerable power can be obtained with just a few plants.[126]

Autochthonous peoples and communities of the African diaspora have expanded this "science of relations" that the West calls "ecology"[127] and put it to work using certain imaginative traditions (complex oneiric practices, various forms of trance and hypnosis) intensified with the help of psychotropic plants, corporeal techniques such as dance, intricate forms of enunciation[128] such as spellcasting songs, and all of these in combination with artifacts (masks, drums) and ritual structures (tent, circle, marked space) that lead to a perception of the world that is synesthetic (affecting the senses as a whole) and pluriversal (diffracting the universe into a multiplicity of versions and temporalities). It is because these customs have ethical implications from the start (integrating perspectives other than those of the subject and his or her limited community) that they can nourish political spiritualities. In fact the only reason why "indigenous" cosmologies constitute cosmopolitics is that, when they elaborate their mode of existence (their habitats, hunting and fishing techniques, ritual practices, etc.), they take extra-human lives into account – recognizing them as part of an extended kinship group. If our relation to Earth is so destructive, according to Kopenawa, this is because we no longer know how to dream, in other words to project ourselves into other forms of life in order to correspond with them and thereby to understand our position in the fabric of the cosmos. Thus there is an intimate relation between how a society treats its living environment and how it deals with its dreams. But how can we short-circuit the alienating parameters of our dreams and fears?

Mikhail Bakhtin explains that in medieval and Renaissance Europe, carnivals and popular festivals had the function of warding off not just cosmic fear but also its instrumentalization by worldly powers. European popular cultures found the resources both to confront world-shaking dread (epidemics, climactic changes, earthquakes) and to subvert the established order in a certain relationship with the cosmos – namely a relationship of symmetry and correspondence (the Renaissance doctrine of signatures) between the body's microcosm and the macrocosm of the earth (and celestial spheres). How many uprisings, how many popular rebellions by peasants, small tradespeople, forest wardens, and artisans against taxation, conscription, the church's monopoly on truth, or the nobility's control over the land were born from the very dynamic of inversion and parody with which the carnival confronted every dominant society – that is, when the carnival did not turn into a historical curiosity but still kept its utopian dimension of a reversal of the world from below, by the body and the "humble folk"?

> We must take into consideration the importance of cosmic terror, the fear of the immeasurable, the infinitely powerful. The starry sky, the gigantic material masses of the mountains, the sea, the cosmic upheavals, elemental catastrophes – these constitute the terror that pervades ancient mythologies, philosophies, the system of images... It is used by all religious systems to oppress man and his consciousness. ...The struggle against cosmic terror in all its forms and manifestations did not rely on abstract hope or on the eternal spirit, but on the material principle in man himself. Man assimilated the cosmic elements: earth, water, air, and fire; he discovered them and became vividly conscious of them in his own body. He became aware of the cosmos within himself.[129]

At the start of every initiatory quest – and life counts as one! – there is a poetic experience: the grasp of the world as living totality, the intuition that all the elements surrounding us, working through us and making us up – vegetal, mineral, water, air, magnetic waves – respond to one another, intertwine, and form a same and single "cosmos." The wisdom of lianas consists not just in the experience of these cosmo-poetic bonds, but also in the capacity to pull them taut as a battle bow. This is why, inasmuch as lianas stand in for all plants and allied biomes, I see them as expressions of the auxiliary spirits that assist "natives" in their pioneering struggles against the complete commodification of the living world and homogenization of its modes of existence. The martial art of lianas can take all forms, ranging from cluster bombs made of amaranth[130] to the subversion of western law by autochthonous cosmovisions,[131] all by way of maroon secession. Neither priority nor hierarchy: everything can be added to the fire, with the grace and agility of a monkey!

In March 2017, after more than 150 years of struggle, the Maori were victorious in their fight to obtain recognition of the Whanganui River as a living entity.[132] This victory shows that the cosmologies of autochthonous peoples constitute genuine cosmo-politics and not picturesque archaisms, destined to disappear either through the definitive triumph of the universal rationality of techno-scientific knowledge or by being absorbed into the market of à la carte spiritualities and technologies of personal development. The parliament of New Zealand did not recognize the rights of nature as an abstraction (a western fetish) but of the "complex person" Te Awa Tupua taken as an "indivisible and living whole … incorporating all [the river's] physical and metaphysical elements."[133] In the Te Awa Tupua law and the concrete arrangements it implies, the Maori did not just obtain rights according to preestablished norms, they put in question the very frame of juridical and political recognition, as well as fundamental notions such as "person," "territory," or "property." What this law protects, then, is not "the environment" as much as a Maori cosmovision that, through the modes of existence to which it leads (habitat, horticultural practices, rituals), contributed to forming a cosmo-poetic territory where the totality of lives is perceived as being in resonance: "I am the river, and the river is me" is the Maori formula. From this point on, every wrong inflicted on Whanganui River will be considered a wrong inflicted on the Maori communities that live near it only because the river lives in them. The living world, rather than being protected, thus becomes a political subject: it is fortified once again by the "enchantment" of a juridical fiction. In Te Awa Tupua we must see the visage of an existential territory, an effective chimera: a figure that contains within itself a whole pluriverse – a plurality of elements and dimensions articulated on one another – and combines, in its possible formulations, the conjugated powers of juridical enunciation and the dances, songs, and ritual practices of the Maori.

The fabrication of defenseless lands

> Within each of these two approaches [exploitation of the environment and protection of the environment], what prevails is always a logic of extraction: in the first case, the concrete and material resources producing pure energy, perhaps later to be transformed into money and to permit the expansion of the West's modern way of life; in the second case, immaterial resources also created from energy – this time subjective and spiritual – impregnating the entire collective with its stubborn and wild scent.[134]

If the dominant form of ecology is often complicit with the interests that destroy living environments,[135] this is because it continues to defend the rights of nature "in general," forgetting that an abstract nature is "still life" [*nature morte*]. The abstraction of the western notion of nature is just the refraction, on the theoretical plane, of the extraction processes that define capitalism. Conceived of in opposition to culture, nature appears "authentic" in the West only in the form of the nature reserve – a typically western artifact. And when "autochthonous peoples," those we used to call "savages" or "natives," sometimes meet the same end as nature parks and the animals cooped up in them – namely a life under glass, as in certain reservations for "natives" of North America and Australia – this is because they are thought to share in the same naturalness that for a long time banished them from humanity. The same idea of an intact nature – purged of its connections to lives, practices, and human memories – leads certain NGOs, with the complicity of local governments, to chase entire communities out of "nature zones" that have become sanctuaries.[136] In the dualism of nature and culture that structures the western imaginary and its mode of thought, no symmetry exists between the two terms. As Frédéric Neyrat tells us, this dualism has always been used to negate nature's alterity for the benefit of technology.[137] The evolution of the very notion of environment symptomizes the destruction–recreation of nature: "working environment," "smart environment," "virtual environment," and the like. Western cosmology is a necrology: death dwells in our gaze on the living world...

> [The white people] think that the forest is dead and empty, that "nature" is there for no reason and that it is mute. So they think that they can take it over to destroy the houses, paths, and food of the *xapiri* as they wish.[138]

Who could believe that nature has no voice and that it has nothing to say, when the first music is that of the Earth? The whispers, the clangs, the cries, the cawing of the "great animal orchestra"[139] are modulated in relation to the rhapsody of the winds and waters, changes in terrain, details of the landscape, factors like humidity or aridity. And the whole of this "biophony" forms a sonorous landscape, a landscape in flight, a jazz landscape. Here no partition is defined in advance; rather we find an improvisation, a continuous variation, which is that of the living itself. "'Whites' think that the forest is dead and empty": how to explain such a fatal vision of nature?[140] In her film *Tu crois que la terre est chose morte* [*You Think the Earth Is a Dead Thing*], Florence Lazar outlines several elements of a response to this question by using the testimony of those who live in the territory of Martinique, its small farmers, ecological and cultural militants, researchers and practitioners of traditional medicine (particularly experts in the pharmacopeia of "maroon plants").[141] Here we can see that the plantation is indissociable from a necropolitics, from the production of soil as something dead, a result obtained through the intensive deployment of chemical death – in this case, the pesticide chlordecone. But the work of death was already registered in the very mechanics of the plantation.

> In their sixteenth- and seventeenth-century sugarcane plantations in Brazil, for example, Portuguese planters stumbled on a formula for smooth expansion. They crafted self-contained, interchangeable project elements, as follows: exterminate local people and plants; prepare now empty, unclaimed land; and bring in exotic and isolated labor and crops for production.[142]

As a system of monoculture, the plantation – the structuring birthplace of modern agriculture – demands the extermination of everything that is not sugarcane, bananas, cotton, or tomatoes, everything that cannot be converted into commodities and capital. We are dealing here with a radical purge, in which living environments are reduced to replicated lines of vegetal clones.[143] The slave labor plantation consisted of "fields emptied of all life." But, for a complete picture of the system, we must also keep in mind the masters' phantasm or their ideal of a completely flexible workforce: this ideal consists of humans emptied of all unruly life, so that all that remains is a force to be used by others. From the point of view of Haitian Vodou, the real witchcraft was not carried out by *nègres* but by the white sorcerer who, by annihilating their consciousness and memory (an act of colonial alienation in Fanon's sense), transformed humans into livestock. The figure of the zombie[144] provides one of the best tools not only for thinking of the condition of enslaved peoples but also for reflecting on the necropolitics proper to capitalist exploitation, of which Fritz Lang's 1927 masterpiece *Metropolis* remains one of the most striking expressions. The zombie, in fact, offers a gripping vision of the work of death within the living being itself: a work of unbinding, of disentanglement, of "decomposition" whose single goal was the extraction of maximal profit from the earth and from exploited organisms (including human beings). See Figure 6a and 6b.

In the wake of Marx, Anna Lowenhaupt Tsing defines "alienation" as a form of disentanglement that facilitates asset production:[145] the living being – plant, animal, or human – is separated from its life process, from the environment in which it lives, entangled in a multiplicity of other lives. This is the disconnection that makes the exiled African into a "mobile asset" – a *bien meuble* – according to the Code noir (Black Code), the decree instituted by Colbert in 1685 to regulate slavery. What the *lyannaj* of the Antilles[146] works against is this work of death as a decomposition of the living world, this zombification. A wisdom of lianas may mean recomposing a vegetal community in the *jardin nègre* but also reinventing a "land of the ancestors"[147] (a maroon community) in the interstices (i.e. the marshes, mountains, or forests) of colonies. The wisdom of lianas is knowledge about the bonds that unbind. For those colonized, ecology has no meaning apart from the ecology of liberation, and is indistinguishable from the very movement of re-creating existence. An enslaved person is no one: the slave trader scratched out his line of life; he no longer has any lineage, either ancestors or descendants, and this makes him into someone unborn and a member of the walking dead. The shipping company and various masters have

Figure 6a and 6b. *The Tears of Bananaman*. Installation by Jean-François Boclé, 2009–2012. Galeria Passage Crista, Puerto Limon, Costa Rica, 2021. © Jean-François Boclé.

burned their initials onto his skin. His life hangs only by a thread, and the master is the one who controls this thread, always ready to sever it, to exercise his right of life and death, which makes the enslaved into a dead man with a suspended sentence. This is the unanchored, roughly textured body, the archive of physical cruelty that the dances, songs, arts, and rituals from the African diaspora are going to try to piece back together. As a process,[148] marronage is already waiting to explode within the mine, the plantation, or the master's mansion, in a wrenching movement that will permit the enslaved to deploy new dimensions of existence and thereby escape his or her tomblike body. Play the slave, but cultivate the maroon – the feral life – in order to rearm the body.

> Throughout the period of slavery, the disarmament of slaves was doubled by a veritable discipline of bodies to keep them in a defenseless state, which involved the imposition of punishment for the slightest militant gesture. This process finds its philosophical principle in that which constitutes the essence of servile condition: a slave is anyone who does not properly have the right and duty to preserve himself.[149]

Just as there is a procedure for the "fabrication of unarmed bodies" that is linked to the establishment of the modern state and colonial systems, there is likewise a fabrication of *defenseless lands*. The disarmament of nature is the historical and political construction of its powerlessness. "Dead, empty, without reason, mute"; in just a few words, Kopenawa presents the principle of the disarmament carried out by western modernity. Let us recapitulate:

- "disenchantment":[150] nature is mute;
- analytical "decomposition" of the world: nature is dead and empty.

The disenchantment of nature is indissociable from the techno-scientific rationalization that silences its polyphony so as to reduce it more easily to geometrical extension, to a mechanism of calculable forces, to exploitable resources, to ecosystemic services that must be managed. Beyond its theoretical and ontological aspects (mechanist conception of reality, mathematization of the world, reinforcement of metaphysical dualisms, etc.), this disenchantment also represented a massive exorcism of nature, orchestrated by religious and political powers that took the form of the greatest "witch hunt" of all time.[151] From the end of the Middle Ages to the eve of the American Revolution, tens of thousands of women were persecuted, tortured, and delivered to the bonfires.[152]

The cursed share of plants

By disqualifying the botanical and therapeutic knowledge of the common people (a field in which women were the primary experts), the Inquisition's war machine allowed a corporation of men – the medical corps – to establish a monopoly over truth about the human body for the benefit of the state and capital, in order to construct and regenerate the sacred body of the future nation. This dispossession of women – and particularly of their "bellies" – corresponded to the dispossession of peasant communities through the enclosure movement,[153] the dispossession of indigenous communities as colonization advanced, and, to be sure, the dispossession of black bodies when deported Africans were reduced to slavery. Each time, reference to the devil played a key role in the mechanics of these acts of dispossession. Infamous beings must always bear the weight of their own infamy, their own fall outside humanity – the blessed circle of those whose lives count and have significance. Although produced by the dominant order, damnation is presented as the necessary consequence of the very life of the damned. "I can condemn you to slavery because you are already damned, and the evidence is this skin, which is as dark as your soul," explains the master to the *nègre*. But before it was applied to the *nègre*'s shadowy skin (in the racializing process of slavery),[154] damnation belonged to the obscure world of forests. The forest's damnation is where the damnation of the "savage" was born – and this word, "savage," comes from the Latin *silva*, "forest."

> Bestiality, fallenness, errancy, perdition – these are the associations that accrued around forests in the Christian mythology. ... In the tenebrous Celtic forests reigned the Druid priests; in the forests of Germany stood those sacred groves where unconverted barbarians engaged in heathen rituals; in the nocturnal forests at the edge of town sorcerers, alchemists, and all the tenacious survivors of paganism concocted their mischief. ... Age-old demons, fairies, and nature spirits continued to haunt the conservative woodlands, whose protective shadows allowed popular memory to preserve and perpetuate cultural continuities with the pagan past.[155]

The Christian church and the Roman Empire (from which, to a certain extent, it took the reins) share a defiant attitude to the forest [*sylve*]. The forest is a disturbing place – disturbing for the capacity for sight and identity, disturbing for the perception of space and time. Landmarks and distinctions are scrambled there; and metamorphoses are suggested, burgeoning with illusions that are as frightening as they are tempting. This is a place for the hermit's ordeal by dreaming! In medieval England with its ballads and popular legends about outlaws, the forest acquired a carnivalesque dimension: it is nothing but an inverted, travestied, and deceptive world. In the eyes of those in power, the forest is marked with the seal of rebellion: it is always virtually beyond the law, inasmuch as it designates the "outside" of the law – and the word itself comes indirectly from the Latin adverb *foris* (< *foris*, "door"), which means "outside," that is, "out of doors." But this "outside" cannot be dissociated from the order it contests any more than the shadow can be dissociated from the light – which means, correlatively, that the shadow of forests can grow in cities (even in "smart" ones)...

In the unending branchwork of trees, the men of God read the mark of the devil – his fork – and saw his divisive, slanderous activity. What is diabolical is the vertiginous overgrowth of the forest: an anarchy of matter that breaks down the unity of truth, the hierarchy of beings, the sovereignty of light. To unify Europe under the sign of the cross, the church made satanic figures out of Pan, the half-human, half-goat divinity of nature, and out of elves, fairies, leprechauns, and all the other spirits of the woodlands. But by the same act, the church attested to this chthonic presence that dwells in the earth and renders it capable of sowing panic[156] among the most powerful armies. It is this very fear that the Indians, the blacks, and the mixed-race populations of the Americas exploited when, in turn, they saw their spirits, their gods, their sacred plants being diabolized by the colonial and ecclesiastical powers: "*Coca mia*, with Barrabas, with Satan, with the limping devil, with the devil of the fishermen, that of the merchants, that of the scholars, and many others still."[157] The archives of the Spanish Inquisition testify to the fact that the indigenous peoples converted diabolization into a seditious force, damnation into election. In trials for sorcery or poisoning where the accused was said to have "consorted with the devil," healers and indigenous or black wise women proclaimed their alliance with "the Enemy" as a challenge thrown at the figure of the masters; and such alliance ran from summoning the Devil to fornicating with him. For the colonized, attaining the power to create fear meant being able to exorcise the fear of the master, indeed to liberate oneself from it: no longer to lower one's eyes, no longer to tremble, no longer to kneel, no longer to shut up, no longer to obey, and, when the occasion arises, to strike back.

> To his surprise [Macandal] discovered the secret life of strange species given to disguise, confusion, and camouflage, protectors of the little armored beings that avoid the pathways of the ants. His hand gathered anonymous seeds, sulphury capers, diminutive hot peppers; vines that wove nets among the stones; solitary bushes with furry leaves that sweated at night; sensitive plants that closed at the mere sound of the human voice; pods that burst at midday with the pop of a flea cracked under the nail; creepers that plaited themselves in slimy tangles far from the sun. ... Macandal, the one-armed, now a *houngan* of the Rada rite, invested with superhuman powers as the result of his possession by the major gods on several occasions, was the Lord of Poison...chosen as he was to wipe out the whites and create a great empire of free Negroes in Santo Domingo.[158]

The epic of Macandal is the best symbol for the offensive dimension that the use of plants acquired in the context of marronage. Around 1750, for about twenty years, this fugitive African sowed terror among the colonists of Saint-Domingue by organizing a systematic campaign of poisonings and rebellions. The terror inspired by poison is directly linked to the secret character of its mode of action. Invisible, it can take any form: its "secretions" can be instilled equally well into food, into drinks or spices that are ingested, or into rivers where people cool off. Because it propagates through a vast network of complicities (field hands, overseers, domestics, freed blacks, maroons, etc.), poison strikes like the plague: it contaminates, corrupts, gnaws at colonial society down to its foundations. Macandal's poisoning campaign brought the tensions between masters and enslaved people to their climax, thereby preparing the way for the general insurrection of Saint-Domingue.

Prophetic visions and liberation movements

> *Exus* are slaves who do not accept their destiny, who rebel against their masters and kill them with poison or witchcraft.[159]

If by "devil" one means the spirit of rebellion – this force that pushes us to contest the father's order, God's order, the master's order – it could well be that the colonists were right to see the work of Satan in the secret religions of the *nègres*. Even today, the male and female devils whose costumes we don or whose images are brandished during the popular festivals and carnivals of Mexico, the Caribbean, or Colombia bear traces of a challenge hurled at authorities and oligarchies. In Afro-Brazilian religions such as Candomblé and Umbanda, Exu is the master of crossroads, the divinity who opens and closes roads, including the ones that lead from slavery to freedom; and this is because he guarantees relationships with the other gods. As Stefania Capone points out, Exu is the *agent provocateur* par excellence, the trickster[160] who introduces disorder through his transgressions, and therefore the possibility of change, indeed of revolution. In the Mississippi delta, impregnated as it is with "hoodoo" traditions, the local equivalent of Vodou, it is said that the apprentice bluesman[161] who wants to become renowned must sign a contract with Papa Legba (the Devil) at a crossing of roads (a precise place) and times (a precise hour). Rituals, but also insurrections, begin by invoking Exu or Legba. The unfolding of rebellion always proceeds from the rhythmic unleashing of bodies: no movement of liberation without the liberation of movement! Thus it happened that, one stormy night in August, in the French colony of Saint-Domingue, the maroon Boukman celebrated the ceremony at Bois Caïman assisted by Cécile Fatiman, a mambo or Vodou priestess. The terrible uprising of 1791, the founding event of the Haitian Revolution, broke out under the auspices of the Lwas (Vodou divinities).[162]

If the abolition of slavery is not reduced to the signing of a decree, if abolition is understood as an ongoing process of liberation, then it must be recognized that the first abolitionists were the enslaved themselves. But how are we going to understand their version of history, when most of the archives that have come down to us are those of the masters?

For the Africans who lived through the experience of deportation to the Americas, confronting the unknown with neither preparation nor challenge was no doubt petrifying.

The first dark shadow was cast when they were wrenched from their everyday, familiar land, away from protecting gods and a tutelary community. But that is nothing yet. Exile can be borne, even when it comes as a bolt from the blue. The second dark of night fell as tortures and the deterioration of the person, the result of so many incredible Gehennas. Imagine two hundred human beings crammed into a space barely capable of containing a third of them. Imagine vomit, naked flesh, swarming lice, the dead slumped, the dying crouched. ... But that is nothing yet.

What is terrifying partakes of the abyss, three times linked to the unknown. First, the time you fell into the belly of the boat. For, in your poetic vision, a boat has no belly; a boat does not swallow up, does not devour; a boat is steered by open skies. Yet, the belly of this boat dissolves you, precipitates you into a nonworld from which you cry out. ... This boat is a matrix, an abyssal womb. The mother of your tumult.[163]

It is precisely in order to overcome this abyss – the erasure of memory and of personal being – that Édouard Glissant calls on a "prophetic vision of the past," a vision committed to restoring the action and the humanity of "bare migrants" (the deported Africans) and their descendants by recomposing them on the basis of the least trace, the tiniest residue, the slightest vibration. The reason why historians could never have a monopoly on the exploration of the past is that the "lives without traces" of the enslaved demand a work of resurrection and re-creation that is in fact proper to the poet, the storyteller, and the witch artist. Every piece of blues, every samba, every Santeria ceremony constitutes in itself a creative commemoration of the time of the slave trade, of slavery and of struggles. The sufferings, battles, dreams, and voices of enslaved people literally resonate in the musical, choreographic, and ritual archives of the black and Creole Americas. On the island of Cuba, *nègres* lashed back against the damnation of enslavement (Ham's curse)[164] through the poetic counter-magic of the mambos (Bantu ritual songs). Dancing to certain salsa standards such as *las siete potentias* ("the seven powers") means dancing with the Orishas, Afro-Cuban divinities – Chango, Elegua, Obatala, Ochun, Ogun, Orula, Yemaya – whom the initiates summoned through mambos and congas in order to ward off [*conjurer*] the damnation of the *nègre* and to unbind their conjugated powers.[165]

> So it is better to speak
> remembering
> we were never meant to survive.[166]

Even though they knew know to appropriate the ideas of the Enlightenment and turn them against their own authors, ideas alone were not what enabled blacks to leave the shadows of slavery.

Despite the fact that they were not meant to survive, they were first guided and supported by the glimmers of incorporated cosmologies, that is, by the "powers" – *potencias* – contained in the movements of the enslaved bodies themselves: glints of the ancestors, the Orishas, the cosmic forces that illuminated the suspended lives of the enslaved with the help of the activating rhythms of memories. These were "glimmers" because their liberatory light could not be allowed to attract a master's attention: limited to a candle, the light of the moon, at most a dying fire – the minor light of the powers of survival that whisper under the cover of the forest or in the clandestine night.

Beyond their spiritual and therapeutic goals, the Afro-American religions (Vodou, Santeria, Candomblé, Palo Monte, Xango, etc.) constituted genuine arts of memory – iconographies in movement – mobilized repeatedly, with an eye to struggles and strategic situations. Each Orisha has its own rhythm, its own graphic and choreographic signature.[167] Thus Oxala, the god of creation and of death, because he is the oldest, has *igbin* as his rhythm: the very slow rhythm of a snail. Omolu, the divinity of the earth, of bruises, illnesses, and cures, has a very heavy step, because she bears the weight of evils. Oya, the goddess of wind, storm, and thunder, manifests herself only in an extremely rapid and turbulent dance. To each Orisha there correspond scents, colors, plants, foods – an entire microcosm. And each of them is diffracted into a multitude of variants, depending on the entities with which they enter into relation and the situations to which they are summoned. Afro-American religions are accompanied by an entire botanical and therapeutic savoir faire, a complete cosmo-poetics of the living world:[168] ecology here is not reduced to a discourse but truly put into practice for the sake of a different relationship to the world.

The question is not one of belief – to know whether these Orishas exist or not – but rather of experimenting with the fashion in which these figures function. The same holds for the kung fu master mentioned in the introduction to this chapter: the dragon exists through the movements it induces in me, through the way in which it amplifies certain aspects of my existence, but also through the fact that (whether I know it or not), it inscribes me, to various degrees, in the centuries-old memories of a singular practice and vision of the world. Resuscitated by the rhythms and memories of resistance, each Orisha illustrates a way of "enlianning" oneself with the living world, with dimensions of existence, with elements of the cosmos.

For example, one can understand the renewal and increasing power of the black movement in Brazil from the start of the 1980s – with the revalorization of maroon communities such as the quilombos or of movements such as capoeira, *batucada*, and so on – only if one considers the movement of critical renewal the cosmo-poetics of Candomblé, Macumba, Xango, and Ubanda ultimately aimed at.

If the subversion figured by the liana's movement is both textile and choreographic, this is because it is not produced *ex nihilo* but originates in a creative return to gestures like that of Spartacus,[169] whose implications overflow their original contexts. Take the case of the "epic" of Njinga, the Angolan queen who, in the sixteenth century, confronted the Portuguese as much on the plane of the discursive arts as on that of the art of war. When she entered into battle against the colonial power, her kingdom took the form of a quilombo: retrenchment into the forest coupled with guerilla tactics. It is this gesture of bending a rebellious territory back onto itself, in a movement of retreat – a woodland secession – that the Quilombolas, themselves *nègres marrons*, continually renewed and reinvented in the context of the Brazilian slave system. Thus we must stop separating memory from imagination in our thought. We can only imagine, project ourselves into anticipated scenes and alternative futures (such as the quilombo in relation to the plantation) on the basis of lived and transmitted experiences: this is a memory that will be reconfigured by the very action that sets it in motion.

The spider's dance

Nothing illustrates the veiled cultural resistance of subordinate groups better than what have been termed trickster tales. It would be difficult, I think, to find a peasant, slave, or serf society without a legendary trickster figure, whether in animal or human form. ... Only by knowing the habits of his enemies, by deceiving them, by taking advantage of their greed, size, gullibility, or haste does he manage to escape their clutches and win victories.[170]

Although they belong to different domains (vegetal and animal), both the liana and the spider's silk thread allow us to conceive of life as a textile process. As the Greek myth of Arachne testifies,[171] the spider is the paradigm of the weaving animal. In many sub-saharan cosmologies, it plays the role of a trickster (Ananzé, Téré, Wanto, Didobé, etc.): constructing its web at the intersection of angles or in the dark folds of dwellings, it belongs to the liminal powers whose ambivalence and versatility it shares. Like Legba or Exu, the spider is a master of transitions: malicious and hard to catch, it is always situated in the interstice between the worlds it puts in relation. In many parts of the Caribbean and the Guianas, it appears under the name of Anansi.[172] The spider's net and the *lyannaj* of the liana share the same dynamic of "unifying and assembling, of binding, connecting, and relaying everything that found itself broken apart":[173] the shores of the Americas and those of Africa, the past and the future, the living and the dead, and so on. The powers of imagination and of memory are closely combined through the figure of the spider; it holds in its web the totality of what has been, but it also unfurls the infinite tangle of possible versions of a history, thereby reminding us that every situation is rich in unfulfilled virtualities. By their knowledge of the "strong," by their ruses, their simulacra, and so on, the "weak" can always turn relations of force in their favor; such is the wisdom sprinkled through tales about Anansi that are recounted on the banks of the Maroni River by the Businenge of Guiana, or on the slopes of the Blue Mountains by the Maroons of Jamaica.

The storyteller is a weaver, the one who has always known that history gains value only by being retold, through its variations, through this to-and-fro movement, which makes sure that it has a weave, a texture, and a life. A history is always made up of intrigues, knots, and balls of string whose circumvolutions are inextricable, so that we are forever condemned to lose our thread. Moreover, history can only be baroque or jazz, can only be composed in a minor key, written on the sly, played, sung, and fine-tuned during endless jam sessions. "Our" history is the mobile constellation of our wanderings, as well as all the strata that, in their very intertwining, compose the ground on which our soles of wind unfurl. The art of Anansi does not consist in playing the game of the dominant order, but rather in showing that the latter hangs by a thread and that our sole task is to rework once again the motifs prefigured in the folds of monumental history, the one in which the descendants of the conquistadors drape themselves. The ultimate goal of that history, after all, is to ward off the polyphony of events, to put out their embers under the tombstone of a linear and "objective" narrative such as the inexorable march of civilization's progress, the retreat of savagery's borders, the development and improvement of territory, the modernization of infrastructures, and so on. In any country, official historiography (national novels rather than critical historical knowledge) continues to be inscribed in the lineage of chronicles of kingdoms and empire. This is a history dedicated to the glory of the state and to the oligarchical interests it serves – the state, which destines to infamy and silence those who dare to resist it by living outside its grasp.

> Where we perceive a chain of events, he sees one single catastrophe which keeps piling wreckage upon wreckage and hurls it in front of his feet.[174]

If Walter Benjamin sees progress itself as a "catastrophe," this is because it is the simulation software run by the dominant order. Progress is the triumphant march of the victors, whose stories and majestic choirs – with a contempt proportional to their consciousness of the duty being fulfilled – destroy the voices and actions of the conquered by turning them into so many survivals, archaisms, superstitions, zones of "non-law," or "communalisms" for which there is no longer any place. Triumphal arches are always built on the bones of the oppressed. Thus it was that the Third Republic did everything to close the cursed chapter of the Paris Commune once and for all, beneath the massive foundations of Sacré-Coeur, the same place where the massacres were carried out that ended the libertarian secession of Parisian commoners during the bloody week of May 21–28, 1871.

> To the respected philosophers we would like to say that civilization taught us nothing if not that ruin spreads just like fire: indefinitely, on the beaches and toward the interior, toward the heights and in the hollows. The history of colonialism as a central chapter of modernization is the history of the exposure and constant reiteration of ruin as the landscape of progress and of progress as a promise of approaching ruins. In our twisted language, modernization is linked to ruin, along with burial, imposed silence, subordination, genocide, forced labor, theft and effacement.[175]

In a messianic and revolutionary conception of history, "the rigid divisions between future and past thus themselves collapse, unbecome future becomes visible in the past, avenged and inherited, mediated and fulfilled past in the future."[176] Every event contains a dimension of the "not yet": unfinished dreams, lost possibilities, aborted hopes. This is why the "uni-verse" does not exist: the world is pregnant with that which has not yet been accomplished, it can only be a "pluri-verse." All the unruly people relegated to the solitary cells of history will live again in us each time we call on them – one chooses one's ancestors – or each time we break the temporal continuum, in order to rediscover traces of their practices, their conceptions, their experiences. It is not a question of imitating them, but of drinking from their insurgent ardor. "Nothing that has ever happened should be regarded as lost for history," Walter Benjamin reminds us: there is no gesture, action, life – as miserable as its author might be – which cannot be saved by a story, a dance, a song, a barricade.[177] It is through creative mythologization that any community whatsoever recovers the power to act. The vocation of our concrete utopias and our active chimeras is not to validate states of affairs ("objective truths") – which means a present that is often intolerable – but to outline unsuspected futures.

> I had the distinct impression that I was watching the universe being born, galaxy upon galaxy... [The spiders] were *my* introduction to the spirits, to the magic afoot in the land. It was from them that I first learned of the intelligence that lurks in nonhuman nature, the ability that an alien form of sentience has to echo one's own, to instill a reverberation in oneself that temporarily shatters habitual ways of seeing and feeling, leaving one open to a world all alive, awake, aware. It was from such small beings that my senses first learned of the countless worlds within worlds that spin in the depths of this world that we commonly inhabit, and from them that I learned that my body could, with practice, enter sensorially into these dimensions.[178]

According to the latest advances of astrophysics,[179] galaxies are interconnected through filaments of hydrogen and black matter, thereby composing an infinite cosmic fabric, in constant expansion. What we call the universe is thus made from constellations of fabrics that resonate with one another. The Milky Way, our galaxy, does not wander randomly through space; it is embedded precisely in a cosmic netting whose filaments, whose secretions of hydrogen and black matter it borrows, a little like a spider in its web.

> Every subject spins out, like the spider's threads, its relations to certain qualities of things and weaves them into a solid web, which carries its existence.[180]

Figure 7. Dance scene from the choreographic creation *Démayé*, 2021. Choreography: Florence Boyer, Compagnie Artmayage/Florence Boyer. Conceptualization: Dénètem Touam Bona. Dancers: Florence Boyer (Réunion), Bérangère Roussel (Martinique). Photo: Ronan Lietar.

The dance of the spider (see Figure 7), which, with its steps and movements, knits a territory into which it is then inscribed, this dance on the wire is a figure for the living being as a *mayaz* operation (*mayaz* evokes "netting" in the Creole language of Réunion).[181] The animal is not a machine obeying a stimulus but a "machine operator,"[182] who responds to signals with operations (perceptions and actions): far from being content to endure its environment (as in theories of adaptation), it agrees with it, co-produces it. The living creature is composed of a milieu the way one composes a painting or a melody, beginning with the selection and arrangement of elements that make sense for the species in question. According to their organic and sensory dispositions, a liana, a wasp, a bat, and a human "design" a world of their own, on the basis of certain registers of color and of sound, certain wavelengths, certain vibrations, certain odors, certain chemical compositions. This is what the great German biologist Jakob von Uexküll means by *Umwelt*, a "milieu" or "lived world."[183] Thus, on the analogy of the spider's weaving, von Uexküll conceives of the living being as a radiation, a deployment of perceptual rays, in such a way that even the reality of a wildflower sprig fluctuates according to the surroundings (sensory emissions) to which it is *exposed*: by turns, it will be a bouquet in the environment of a young girl, food around a cow, a path in the world of an ant. Hence the existence of a living being unfolds simultaneously on multiple planes, in the context of a multiplicity of sensible cartographies. The universe is necessarily "conjugated" in the plural: it is a pluriverse.

> The environments, which are as diverse as the animals themselves, offer every nature lover new lands of such richness and beauty that a stroll through them will surely be rewarding, even though they are revealed only to our mind's eye and not to our body's.
> We begin such a stroll on a sunny day before a flowering meadow... and we make a bubble around each of the animals living in the meadow. The bubble represents each animal's environment and contains all the features accessible to the subject [the creature]... A new world arises in each bubble.[184]

Thus the spider – and all living beings in general – secrete a web of sense along their entire trajectory: the "soap bubble" of a microcosm. For the single world of classical science, von Uexküll's ethology[185] substitutes a multiverse: the infinite variety of perceptual worlds, linked to one another in a vast musical score. In his eyes, the spider's web does not refer simply to the weaving of heterogenous elements (colors, odors, perception of movements); it also covers the field of forces within which each body is moved. In fact the spider is essentially oriented to the vibrations of its web and acts in relation to them. To locate its prey exactly, particularly when the latter adopts the defensive tactic of playing dead, the weaver turns musician: it plucks and strikes the strings of its silken nebula.[186] As a space of vibrations and as a sensory extension of the spider's own body, the web makes manifest the fact that an existential territory, an *Umwelt*, cannot be separated from the body that traverses it while simultaneously deploying it. Among Aboriginal peoples, the Dreaming brings about an arachnoid – in other words, a reticular or rhizomatic – relation to territory: a way of projecting knowledges and practices onto a geographic network.[187]

Regardless of their "civilizing" pretentions, architecture, urbanism, monuments, majestic buildings, and infrastructures do not make a living territory; they only make possible its economic and political management while exhibiting the sovereignty of dominant powers, in the viaducts, dams, tunnels, and acts of deforestation that they inscribe upon it. As the collective experiences of confinement have shown during the state of emergency linked to COVID-19, a city without the movement of retraced steps, mad dashes, murmurs, voices, and graffiti, without habits embedded in a world and without dreams that animate it, is nothing but a necropolis.

Like song or music, dance reveals space while leaving it to its own devices: it whispers space, hums it, subverts it while deploying a version of it that is subtle and heretical. If dance produces worlds to inhabit and not surfaces to occupy (infrastructures, monuments, equipment), this is precisely because it is the art of movement par excellence and of *survival*, that by which we acquire a surplus of life even in the least hospitable environments, by drawing on the gestures that precede us and on the resonances that work through us. Paul Valéry saw in dance "a general poetry of the action of living beings."[188] All creation, be it the generous gesture of sowing seed, the potter's sensual dexterity, or the acrobatic spinning of the spider, starts out as the meaningful action of dance. On the plane of elementary forces, choreography participates in the inscription of the land, its transmutation into existential territory. To approach landscape beginning from the perspective of a body in movement is to see it not as an environment but as an animated territory, a living milieu in which we are truly immersed. Life is registered in a landscape only by the *tracing* of living beings and of elements, "this tracing in advance of the letter," which Fernand Deligny mentions and which shapes landscapes as much as the bodies it embeds there, in successive layers.[189] Life has always been *geography* in some literal sense, a writing on the earth by means of the swarming, braiding, enshrining, stacking, and sedimenting of lines of life. Tim Ingold's argument that the earth does not preexist the living being begins with analyses of how burial mounds are formed: the earth is not a receptacle, a cooking pot into which the primordial soup of life is poured, as if by a miracle. The very ground on which we travel and build is itself a product of living:

> The very ground underfoot, in short, is a tissue of lines of growth, erosion, and decomposition. Far from separating the earth below from the sky above, the ground is a zone in which earth and sky intermingle in the perpetual generation of life.[190]

Very often, when we pronounce the word "earth," the first thing that comes to mind is a satellite photo: the image of a blue planet against an infinite black background. If, subsequently, we represent the world to ourselves from an extra-terrestrial standpoint, this is because we no longer truly dwell in it but have in fact become its spectators. As Frédéric Neyrat has shown in *The Unconstructable Earth*, geo-engineering and transhumanism – these forms of techno-prophecy that describe humans as temporary passengers on a spaceship – only push further a process of deracination from the lived world that began several centuries ago, with capitalism, colonization, and a mono-dimensional techno-scientific rationalization. The birth of the western notion of landscape attests to the logical conclusion of this process.

It was at the end of the fifteenth century that the term "landscape" appeared in France to designate a painting that represented an expanse of countryside. Since then, landscape has been persistently associated with a panoramic view, taken from a "universal" observation point (the modern western subject), dislocated from any given body and any given territory. Of course, landscape painting in the Renaissance must not be regarded as the origin of all our ills; it was just one element among others that, in the West, expressed the demise of the countryside as a "fellow traveler" and its transformation into a stage setting, a backdrop, a piece of scenery (as demonstrated in the compulsive practice of taking selfies in front of "nature scenes.")

To dwell in the world, which means in the interval between earth and heavens, presupposes dwelling in one's body. In my work on marronage, the radical privation of worldhood and of embodiment that characterizes slavery and is figuratively represented in the zombie has been my starting point for thinking about the body in movement and for meditating on its utopian powers. These powers include its capacity to produce an "outside" on the basis of the escape enacted through song or dance, even from within an asphyxiating "interior" such as the slave labor plantation or the urban ghetto. Oppression is first felt in the difficulty, or even impossibility, of breathing: "I can't breathe…" Krumping or the KRUMP – an acronym that stands for Kingdom Radically Uplifted Mighty Praise – was quite rightly born from a respiratory emergency: managing, through twists and unpredictable circumvolutions, to draw a breath against the military and policing straitjacket imposed on the young blacks and Latinx of Watts in LA in the first years of this century.[191]

> Krumping is a profound movement, not yet a commodity. It would seem that the world caused the birth of a dance from within,

authentically spiritual, a dance made to flush out the monsters and to voice the inarticulate dimension of words stuck in the throats of those who could no longer even scream. The only dancing worth doing. Before being a style, it was an invented ritual, a sort of extreme praise, the brutal contorsion of someone who refuses the contemporary straitjacket.[192]

Like the work songs of black people condemned to forced labor[193] – songs punctuated by the phrasing of breaths and the hammering of pickaxes – the KRUMP is inscribed among these forms of spirituality that emerge from the experience of dispossession and humiliation, from the test of suffering, exhaustion, the absurd. They are political spiritualities through their stubborn affirmation of soul power:[194] singing, dancing, shaking with rage and joy, even when one's body might be shackled! "For women ... poetry is not a luxury. It is a vital necessity of our existence," wrote the African–American poet Audre Lorde.[195] "Uplifted"... the raising up evoked in the acronym KRUMP reminds us of the same poetic necessity: not ethereal detachment but the power of uprooting from the cellar, from Gehenna, from the "zone of non-being." In homage to the liana's characteristics, it is this trajectory toward the light – as a "'yes' resonating from cosmic harmonies"[196] that I have tried to transcribe in the present chapter. The important thing is not so much to reach the surface of the forest canopy – which contains traps[197] – as to savor the thousand and one detours and the chiaroscuro required by the *lyannaj*'s powerful ascent.

> There is a zone of nonbeing, an extraordinary sterile and arid region, an incline stripped bare of every essential from which a genuine new departure can emerge.[198]

Finally, what is this liana, whose wisdom maddens more than it soothes? Doubtless a chimera... the liana is a Dream to be followed: a body that dances, a furtive body, a body of mist that condenses in the blooming of a gesture. Utopian body, archipelagic body, diasporic body inhabited by memories and plural lines of life.

The "liberation movement" brought about by marronage (including its manifestation as the *lyannaj*) must be taken in a literal sense: this is, first and foremost, a liberation of movement that sets afoot a dancing body – because every dance step may be the precursor to a blow, as Elsa Dorlin has proposed regarding martial dances such as the *ladjat* and the *damnyé* in the French Carribean, the *moringue* in Réunion, or capoeira in Brazil. Beyond and through the liana's twisting and subversive moments, there is at the same time the matter of celebrating the creative power of Afro-diasporic worlds born from "Creolizations," "swahilizations," chimerical processes: the wealth of Creole languages and gastronomies, jam sessions of jazz, seismic beating of *batucadas*, the syncopated sweat of funk, verbal battles of rap, mystical explosions of Rastafarianism. The exiled Africans and their descendants have brought off a moving victory over the societies from which they were excluded by imposing on them, little by little, the imprint of their creative flights.

Notes

Notes to Chapter 1

1 V. S. Naipaul, *The Middle Passage*, p. 183.
2 This was the political and military title of the governor in the Republic of the United Provinces, inherited within the House of Orange-Nassau.
3 Frédéric Bouyer, *La Guyane française*, pp. 297–298, 300.
4 Expression used by those who hunted them down: see John Gabriel Stedman, *Narrative of a Five Years' Expedition*.
5 Arts center dedicated to the work of Armand Gatti. I take the opportunity to thank Joachim Gatti and Pierre-Vincent Cresceri.
6 I'm thinking here of Creole languages and cuisines, martial arts such as capoeira or *damnyé*, work songs (which gave birth to the blues), Afro-Christian religions (Santeria, Vodou, Candomblé, etc.), and the creative forms of resistance that shaped in large part the cultures of the Americas, including that of their former masters.
7 Louis Sala-Molins, *Le Code Noir*, p. 169.
8 Frantz Fanon, *Wretched of the Earth*, p. 2.
9 [TN: The French *nègre* does not have an exact English correlate. Often translated simply as "black," the term is, however, less neutral than "noir," having insulting connotations that can be turned back defiantly on the European and former slaveholding cultures, in which it meant "slave" and served as a term of racial abuse. Its meaning, like that of similar terms in English, may shift

depending on evolving political tensions in the Francophone world where it is used and on the speaker's social position or attitude toward racism. I have left it in French in order to indicate that the author is using it polemically, in a historical context that is in many respects analogous (but not identical) to that of the former English-speaking colonies of North America and the Caribbean.]

10 [TN: The French adjective *marron* means "brown."]

11 I can already hear scandalized reactions such as: "but this was not genocide, since there was no intention to exterminate them! They did not do it on purpose..." Let us pray that no extraterrestrial nation has the idea of "discovering" us...

12 Édouard Glissant, *Le discours antillais*, pp. 180–181.

13 Elias Canetti, *Crowds and Power*, p. 384.

14 Malcolm X, "Message to the Grass Roots," pp. 10–11.

15 See Elsa Dorlin's pathbreaking book *La Matrice de la race*.

16 The anthropologist Mary Douglas shows that phobias related to dirt, impurity, and mixture play the role of a system that symbolically protects social order. See her *Purity and Danger*.

17 Moreau de Saint-Méry, *Description topographique...*, pp. 71–88.

18 Article 44 of the Code Noir promulgated in March 1685 by Louis XIV; see *Le Code Noir ou Edit du roy*. A properly colonial codification of social relations, racism is the nauseating fruit of the "black codes" of the slavery system; "juridical" codes which rationalized the unjustifiable.

19 Michel Foucault, *Discipline and Punish*, p. 218.

20 Excerpt from "Run, nigger, run," an African–American folk song of the 1850s (Louisiana version). For documentation, see https://en.wikipedia.org/wiki/Run,_Nigger,_Run.

21 A wild figure in the medieval West that symbolizes the return of fecundating forces in springtime.

22 Involuntary settlement of "native" populations on a given territory in order to impose forced labor upon them.

23 Jacques Stéphen Alexis, *Romancero aux étoiles*, pp. 156, 170, 177.

24 Père Charlevoix, as cited in Jean Fouchard, *The Haitian Maroons*, p. 300.

25 Girod-Chantrans (1786), quoted by Gérard Barthélémy, "Le Rôle des Bossales dans l'émergence d'une culture de marronage en Haïti," p. 841.

26 The figures of the Creole *nègre* and bossal *nègre* were initially colonial representations. Let us not forget that what often kept the Creole slave from definitively escaping was the more or less consistent kinship network that he or she was trying to preserve. To run away might mean abandoning very young children or parents who needed assistance and leaving them to the mercy of the master.

27 La Boétie, *Anti-Dictator*, p. 26.
28 Michel Foucault, "The subject and power," p. 342, translation modified.
29 Èvelyne Trouillot, *The Infamous Rosalie*, pp. 26–27.
30 Eric Hobsbawm, *Bandits*, p. 33.
31 Agamben, *Homo Sacer*, p. 105.
32 Stedman, *Narrative of a Five Years' Expedition*, pp. 282–283.
33 Michel Foucault, "What is critique?" p. 32.
34 The "press-gang" system: from the seventeenth century to the start of the nineteenth, the British Royal Navy and other European navies forcibly recruited any unemployed individuals in the ports. In general the recruiters resorted to trickery: they got their prey drunk and then kidnapped them.
35 Stedman, *Narrative of a Five Years' Expedition*, p. 66.
36 Gilles Deleuze and Claire Parnet, *Dialogues*, p. 136.
37 Fanon, *Wretched of the Earth*, pp. 10 and 51.
38 See Walter Benjamin, "Critique of violence."
39 It was on São Tomé, an island off equatorial Africa, that the Portuguese experimented for the first time with the slave labor plantation, toward the end of the fifteenth century. But in 1595 the fugitive slave Amador unleashed a general insurrection that resulted in the permanent destruction of the enslaving system on that island, although Amador himself died in action.
40 Jean Hurault, "Histoire des noirs réfugiés Boni de la Guyane française," pp. 77–78.
41 Lännec Hurbon, *L'Insurrection des esclaves de Saint-Domingue*, p. 31.
42 Stedman, *Narrative of a Five Years' Expedition*, p. 48.
43 "Many Politics," in Deleuze and Parnet, *Dialogues*, p. 135.
44 Fouchard, *The Haitian Maroons*, p. 272.
45 Jean Hurault, *Africains de Guyane*, pp. 20 and 22. See also pp. 92–93 in this volume.
46 Pierre Clastres, *Society against the State*.
47 "The Africans arrive stripped of everything, of every possibility, and even of their language. For the hold of the slave ship is the place and the time where the African languages disappear" (Édouard Glissant, *Introduction to a Poetics of Diversity*, p. 6).
48 "Creolization is the putting into contact of several cultures or at least several elements of distinct cultures, in a particular place in the world, resulting in something new, completely unpredictable in relation to the sum or the simple synthesis of these elements" (Édouard Glissant, *Treatise on the Whole-World*, p. 22).
49 Maryse Condé, *I, Tituba, Black Witch of Salem*, p. 3.
50 The treaties signed with the Dutch stipulated that the Maroons

would cease their attacks against the plantations in exchange for an annual tribute (of weapons, tools, and various goods), but also that they would return any newly arrived fugitive slaves to their masters. The N'djuka, allies of the Dutch, killed the military leader Boni and kept his community under their supervision for many years.

51 Richard Price, "Preface to the 1996 edition," in his *Maroon Societies*, p. xiv.
52 Victor Schoelcher was the principal architect of the decree that abolished slavery in 1848.
53 I.e. the army created by Toussaint Louverture to counter the military task force Napoleon sent in 1802 to re-establish slavery.
54 Dénètem Touam Bona, "'Écrire' Haïti...," n.p.
55 The case of French school textbooks is exemplary. Thus the history supplement on "Antilles – Guyane" for the use of more advanced high school [*collège*] students (a supplement edited by Hatier in 2001) devotes a long unit to abolition movements, but makes only a brief allusion to the phenomenon of marronage, via a citation of Voltaire's *Candide*. Likewise, one learns that the victory of black revolutionaries over the Napoleonic armies in Saint Domingue was connected above all with yellow fever...
56 Michelle Perrot, "Faire exister les acteurs de l'ombre," n.p.
57 I wrote this text in 2003, at a time when I was still learning about the history of slavery and knew nothing about the remarkable works by black feminist authors; these were not published in France until 2008, when Elsa Dorlin compiled and edited a groundbreaking anthology on this theme; see Dorlin, *Black Feminism*.
58 For the heterogeneous set of proverbs and maxims, songs, proclamations, prayers, and tales connected to the time of the "founding ancestors," see Richard Price, *First-Time*.
59 Nathan Wachtel, *The Vision of the Vanquished*, p. 213.
60 Frantz Fanon, *Black Skin, White Masks*, p. 206; translation modified. See p. 37 and n. 68 further down.
61 This was before the imposition, in 1969, of the communal system with the policies of development and "integration" that it presupposes: social assistance, medicalization, administrative control, compulsory schooling...
62 Naipaul, *The Middle Passage*, pp. 182–183 (the chapter title is "Surinam").
63 Alexis de Tocqueville, *Democracy in America*, p. 327.
64 Maurile de St.-Michel, *Voyages des îles Camercanes*, 1652, as quoted in Sala-Molins, *Le Code Noir*, p. 22; see also pp. 199 and 200 in this volume.
65 *Télérama* interview with the Martinican writer Raphaël Confiant, August 4, 1993, p. 7.

66 Fanon, *Black Skin, White Masks*, pp. 29–30.
67 Biringanine Ndagano, *Nègre tricolore*, pp. 136–137.
68 Fanon, *Black Skin, White Masks*, p. 206. See p. 31 and n. 60 in this chapter.
69 "'The one-drop rule,' which defines as black a person with as little as a single drop of 'black blood.'… It still is, according to a United States Supreme Court decision as late as 1986, which refused to review a lower court's ruling that a Louisiana woman whose great-great-great-great-grandmother had been the mistress of a French planter was black" (Lawrence Wright, "One drop of blood," p. 48).
70 "It is therefore demonstrated that the color of all rays when reunited is white. Black, consequently, will be the body which does not reflect any rays" (Isaac Newton, as quoted by Maurice Déribéré, *La Couleur*, p. 24; re-translated here back into English).
71 Richard Wright, *Black Boy*, pp. 48–49.

Notes to Chapter 2

1 "Go down, Moses" is a Negro spiritual inspired by the book of Exodus in the Old Testament. It was sung in the slave labor fields of the southern United States to announce the coming of a guide charged with leading fugitive slaves toward the "free" states of the North or toward Canada.
2 Marcel Dupré, quoted in Pierre-Petit, "Fugue."
3 A *fougue* is not a "flight" (*fuite*) but a "fire" (*feu*) in *Le nouveau Petit Robert*; see s.v. The word derives from the Latin noun *fuga*, which had a much richer sense than the French *fuite* ("flight").
4 Richard H. Hoppin, *Medieval Music*, pp. 370–374.
5 The black Caribs were a maroon people born from the encounter of Carib Indians (Kalina) with slaves who had escaped from shipwrecks off the coast of the Île St. Vincent. After two wars against the British, they were deported to Honduras, whence they dispersed over a large expanse of central America.
6 Gilles Deleuze and Félix Guattari, *A Thousand Plateaus*, pp. 277–278.
7 Stedman, *Narrative of a Five Years' Expedition*, pp. 279, 283, 284.
8 Ibid., p. 276.
9 Ray Bradbury, *Fahrenheit 451*, pp. 126–127.
10 Guillermo Cabrera Infante, *View of Dawn in the Tropics*, p. 8.
11 Thoreau, *Walden*, pp. 90–91.
12 Bradbury, *Fahrenheit 451*, p. 138.
13 Ibid., p .145.
14 Ibid., p. 146.

15 Here we are speaking exclusively about the marronage of "secession" practiced by *nègres bossales*. Newly arrived from Africa, these slaves – the ones who were least deculturated – were in the best position to reinvent a society in the seclusion of the forests. The Creole *nègres* (those born in the islands), for their part, tried rather to melt into the anonymity of towns and to pass for "freedmen."

16 Namely a singular conception of the world, to which Afro-American religions such as Candomblé, Santeria, or Vodou testify: in these religions African and Amerindian divinities, tutelary ancestors, animal and plant spirits, female forces of the rivers (e.g. *mamans d'lo* or *wata mama*), and Catholic saints were intermingled in complex cosmologies. [TN: See "Chimerical visions" in Ch. 7 for a discussion of river sirens such as Mami Wata.]

17 Benjamin Péret, *La Commune des Palmares*, p. 73. Throughout the seventeenth century, this quilombo held Dutch and Portuguese military expeditions at bay.

18 Candidates for emigration to America who could not pay for their crossing signed a contract of "indenture" that bound them to a future master for a period between three and seven years. In the British colonies, this system lasted until the middle of the eighteenth century and went hand in hand with a political strategy of ensuring the deportation of vagabonds, chicken thieves, street children, sex workers, and expropriated Irish peasants; in the case of these convict servants, the term was fourteen years of servitude.

19 Michel le Bris, *Le Grand Dehors*, pp. 309, 310.

20 Édison Carneiro, as quoted in Péret, *La Commune des Palmares*, p. 75. Also quoted in Ch. 6, p. 105 (with n. 28).

21 Le Bris, *Le Grand Dehors*, p. 310.

22 Alain Fleischer, *La Traversée de l'Europe par les forêts*, p. 25.

23 Almost 100,000 persons were deported. The Irish represented a significant proportion of the indentured servants in the English colonies of the Americas.

24 Michel Foucault, "Different spaces," pp. 178, 184–185.

25 "Relação das guerras feitas aos Palmares de Pernambuco no tempo do governador D. Pedro de Almeida, de 1675 a 1678," from Leonardo Dantas Silva, *Alguns documentos para a história da escravidão*, quoted in French by Gérard Police, *Quilombos dos Palmares*, p. 129.

26 Canetti, *Crowds and Power*, p. 342.

27 See Sally Price and Richard Price, *Maroon Arts*.

28 In the black English dialect of the American inner city, "funk" originally meant "stink"; it evoked the odor, the sweat of the *nègre* – a stigma turned into a positive value. Radically opposed to the fastidious, "proper" camp of the whites' cool jazz, "funk" music (e.g. free jazz) is characterized by "dirty" and primitive sonorities

in which interferences, shouts, and improvisations, sometimes
pushed to the point of collective trance, are important.

29 In order to prevent the police and the Hollywood unions from
   interfering, Van Peebles claimed to be making a porn film.
30 Angela Davis, *Blues Legacies and Black Feminism*, p. 70.
31 Reverend Calvin Fairbank, *During Slavery Times*, pp. 10–11.
32 Banks, *Cloudsplitter*, p. 408.

Notes to Chapter 3

1 Canetti, *Crowds and Power*, p. 210.
2 In this they are in contrast with films from the first half of the
  twentieth century such as *White Zombie* (1933) or *I Walked with
  a Zombie* (1943).
3 Frankétienne, *Les Affres d'un défi*, p. 9.
4 Daniel Maximin, *Lone Sun*, p. 60.
5 Friedrich Nietzsche, *On the Genealogy of Morals*, p. 61.
6 Radio Frequency Identification (RFID) is a technology that allows
  small electronic chips implanted into objects to transmit information to distant receivers through radio waves.
7 See Andrew Niccol, *Gattaca*. The general theme is the reduction of
  personal identities to biometric data, biometrics being a technique
  for the identification and authentification of persons on the basis
  of their bio-aspects – that is, bodily aspects considered to be
  unique and inexchangeable such as the iris, the retina, the voice,
  the fingerprints, the DNA. The cutting edge of this evolving
  technology is represented by the growing intrusion of businesses
  into the private lives of their employees and customers.
8 Laënnec Hurbon, *Le Barbare imaginaire*, pp. 292–293.
9 Report of a Polish officer during the rebellion of Saint-Domingue
  (1802–1804), in Fouchard, *The Haitian Maroons*, p. 176.
10 Patrick Chamoiseau, *Slave Old Man*, p. 74.
11 Victor Schoelcher, *Des Colonies françaises,* p. 102.
12 [TN: In French, *conjuration* has multiple meanings that seem in
   tension with one another from the English point of view; it has
   connotations of "casting a spell," of "urging" someone to do
   something, but also of "warding off" and, in some contexts, of
   "conspiring" or "plotting."]
13 From the vessel *Jeune Auguste*, reported in the *Gazette de Saint-
   Domingue*, February 9, 1791: quoted in Fouchard, *The Haitian
   Maroons*, p. 152; see also pp. 97–98 in this volume.
14 See Clastres, *Society against the State*.
15 [TN: The French verb *fuir* means "to flee" as well as "to leak."]

Notes to Chapter 4

1 Jean Comaroff and John Comaroff, "Naturing the Nation," pp. 645–646.
2 It's not a matter of saying that the situation of foreigners referred to as "illegal" or "clandestine" is the same as that of enslaved black people, but of understanding that they share a ghostly condition: they are perceived as shadows, as living in that shadow of the law (and therefore of humanity) that is always the shadow of crime. This happens in such a way that their very existence is necessarily culpable, which explains the massive efforts, in most countries, to incarcerate or confine them.
3 Barnabé Binctin, "A deux pas de 'la Jungle' des migrants."
4 We don't know whether these shadow warriors emerging from the dunes are men or women, and their camouflage gives them an animal or vegetable look, like that of crocodile men or leopard men in ancient African secret societies. A fish-woman – a mermaid – is a chimera; for further discussion around chimeras, see Ch. 7, pp. 126–128.
5 [TN: "Nyabinghi" designates the practices, rituals, and songs of some Rastafarian communities.]

Notes to Chapter 5

1 "Mayotte: Mort de 7 migrants dans un naufrage."
2 Since the establishment of the Balladur Visa between Mayotte and the Union of the Comoros in 1995, there have been more than 15,000 deaths of immigrants, according to estimates from the NGO Migreurop.
3 Françoise Vergès, *The Wombs of Women*, p. 7.
4 See Laurent Lagnau, "Pouquoi il faut s'intéresser aux îles Eparses."
5 [TN: The word *karibu* means "welcome" in the languages of the Swahili zone.]
6 According to the 2008 Petit Futé tourist guide to Mayotte.
7 [TN: Metropolitan France and its overseas territories are divided into *départements* (counties or regions) for electoral and administrative purposes. These units have equal constitutional status and representation in the National Assembly and may participate in EU elections, but the ability of *départements d'outre-mer* (DOMs, i.e. overseas regions) to make laws for their unique circumstances is limited.]

8 "Nature" and "nation" come both from the same Latin root, which is present in the verb *nascor, nasci* "be born."

9 In France's distant overseas territories (Tahiti, Guiana, Martinique, Réunion, New Caledonia, etc.), the continued use of the expression *métropole* is rather revealing: the Greek *mētropolis* was the "mother-city" that dispensed light and civilization to its "daughters," the colonies.

10 Although there are variations from one island to the next, indeed from one village to the next, one finds in this archipelago a common language (where the criterion for a language is mutual comprehension despite regional variations), common religious practices and familial lineages, and shared therapeutic and agricultural practices.

11 This is a fragment from a text produced during a writing workshop that formed part of my philosophy course in 2013 at the Lycée du Nord. There, on clear days, one can see the silhouette of the island of Anjouan.

12 Glissant, *Le Discours antillais*, p. 287.

13 Vergès, *The Wombs of Women*, pp. 5 and 25.

14 Cf. the title of Brian K. Vaughn's CBS series *Under the Dome* (2013–2015), inspired by an eponymous novel of Stephen King (2009). In that novel an entire city wakes up one day beneath a transparent dome, which divides the world into two. This has been the tacit effect of Mayotte's "departmentalization."

15 See also d'Estaing's 1974 declaration in "D'Estaing sur Mayotte."

16 The establishment of the Balladur Visa in 1995, the departmentalization of the island in 2011, and its "rupeization" (i.e. relegation to ultra-peripheral status) in 2014 were steps in this progressive entrenchment of the distinction.

17 From an opinion column by the author: see Dénètem Touam Bona, "Mayotte: Peau comorienne, masques français."

18 Isabelle Mohamed, "Les Comores existent-elles?" n.p.

19 Rémi Carayol, "Chasse à l'homme à Mayotte," 19.

20 The pamphlet can be found at http://www.linfokwezi.fr/mayotte-asphyxie.

21 Flash Info, January 19, 2016.

22 Anne Perzo, "'Décasages,' ces chasses aux clandestins condamnées par le tribunal administratif." Quoted from the June 4, 2016 edition of the newspaper *Le Journal de Mayotte*.

23 "Mayotte: La Chasse aux étrangers par la population est ouverte... et couverte."

24 See Glissant, *Le Discours antillais*, passim.

25 Philippe Triay, "Mahmoud Azihary," n.p. (Azihary, interviewed here, is the author of *Mayotte en sous-France*.)

26 Soeuf Elbadawi, *Un dhikri pour nos morts*, pp. 7–8 and 10–11.

27 The cycle of winds is what made the seas navigable.

Notes to Chapter 6

1 Mahmoudan Hawad, excerpts from "Détournement d'horizon" ("Horizontal Diversion") and "Buveurs de braises" ("Cinder Drinkers"), poems from his volume *Furigraphie*, pp. 134 and 67.
2 Yann Moulier Boutang, *De l'esclavage au salariat*, pp. 133–134.
3 Gazing at the crosscut trunk of a sequoia, Kim Novak points her finger at one of the tree's rings, which corresponds to one of her previous lives.
4 Martin Lienhard, *Le Discours des esclaves*, p. 24.
5 This quotation can be found online on Wikimedia at https://commons.wikimedia.org/wiki/File:Burnum_burnum_declaration.jpg.
6 Gary Victor, interviwed by Touam Bona, "'Écrire' Haïti..."
7 By "anarchism" I do not mean the western tradition (largely individualist and atheist), but the logic of the term, which presupposes the absence of a principle that would command a given reality on the basis of something exterior to it. Here it is important to understand anarchism as the refusal and the warding off of a power that would detach itself from society and would take the form of a separate authority (the master, the sovereign, the government, etc.) in order to direct and dominate social activities. See Pierre Clastres' analyses in *Society against the State*.
8 Hurault, *Africains de Guyane*, pp. 20 and 22. See also p. 22 (with n. 45) in Ch. 1 here.
9 Karl Marx, *Capital*, p. 342.
10 Jacques Roumain, *Masters of the Dew*, pp. 26–28.
11 Gérard Barthélémy, *Créoles–Bossales*, p. 172.
12 Alfred Métraux, *Voodoo in Haiti*, pp. 153–154; translation modified.
13 [TN: For further discussion, see Metraux, *Voodoo in Haiti*, p. 257. *Lakou* is a Creole transformation of the French *la cour*, "the courtyard," in Haitian. As for the meaning of *demanbré*, see Margaret Mitchell Armand, *Healing in the Homeland: Haitian Vodou Tradition*, p. 131, n. 9.]
14 Roumain, *Masters of the Dew*, p. 75.
15 [TN: Haitian Creole meaning "back country" or "backwoods," but here also "the other country."]
16 Fouchard, *The Haitian Maroons*, p. 152, quoting from in the *Gazette de Saint-Domingue*, February 9, 1791: also quoted Ch. 3 (see p. 61, with n. 13).
17 Roger Bastide, *Images du Nordeste mystique*, p. 47.
18 João Ubaldo Ribeiro, *An Invincible Memory*, p. 332.
19 Extract from the 1797 *Bulletin officiel de Saint-Domingue*, quoted in Fouchard, *The Haitian Maroons*, p. 225.

20 [TN: In Haitian Creole and Vodou, *konesans* means "intuitive knowledge" or "second sight." See e.g. Metraux, *Voodoo in Haiti*, pp. 63–64.]

21 [TN: The French verb *conjurer* means both "to conspire, plot" and "to ward off, avert." See Ch. 3, n. 12 on the polysemy of the French term *conjuration*.]

22 Wachtel, *La Vision des vaincus*, pp. 184–185.

23 André Corten, *Misère, religion et politique en Haïti*, p. 62.

24 E. P. Thompson, *The Making of the English Working Class*, pp. 509–510.

25 Aline Helg, *Slave No More*, p. 11.

26 Condé, *I Tituba, Black Witch of Salem*.

27 Translated and quoted from Nicolas Klotz and Elisabeth Perceval's 2018 documentary *L'héroïque lande, la frontière brûle*, which offers a poetic and political portrait of the Jungle in Calais.

28 Édison Carniero, quoted in Péret, *La Commune des Palmares*, p. 75; also quoted in Ch. 2, p. 46 (with n. 20). In this work, the surrealist poet compares the quilombo of the zone of Palmares in the Brazilian northeast to libertarian experiments such as the Paris Commune. In the seventeenth century, Palmares held off Dutch and Portugese military incursions for almost seventy years.

29 Anonymous, "La Meuse."

30 See Michel Foucault, "Preface to *Anti-Oedipus*."

31 To make peace with death, not to deny it – rather to suspend the negation of alterity.

Notes to Chapter 7

1 A. P. Gumbs, *Undrowned*, pp. 1–2. This book is a guide in which, with affection and humor, Gumbs parodies the popular US reference texts *Guide to Marine Mammals of the World*, published in 2002 by the National Audubon Society, and *Whales, Dolphins, and Porpoises*, a Smithsonian Institute handbook of the same year. She encourages us to take our marine mammal relatives as guides in "the art of not drowning."

2 "And by we, I don't only mean people like myself whose ancestors specifically survived the middle passage, because the scope of our breathing is planetary, at the very least." Gumbs, *Undrowned*, p. 2.

3 Ibid., p. 14.

4 From the Latin *conspirare* (< *cum* + *spiro*) "blow/breathe with."

5 For each canvas, he uses between 80 and 100 snapshots taken at different hours of the day. Thus he can play with different tones and variations of color and light. The very texture of his compositions is temporal: it spatializes a plurality of temporalities.

6 From Good, "Why did the CDC develop a plan for a zombie apocalypse?" [TN: The public education blog in question was later removed from the CDC's website.]
7 The plantation system created by the Portuguese in the African archipelagos of the Atlantic (Cabo Verde, São Tomé, etc.) in the context of colonial slavery.
8 Anna Lowenhaupt Tsing, *The Mushroom at the End of the World*.
9 Félix Guattari, "Le Capitalisme Mondial Intégré et la révolution moléculaire."
10 See in general Richard Horton, *The COVID-19 Catastrophe*.
11 Naomi Klein, "How big tech plans to profit from the pandemic."
12 Joseph Tonda, "En Afrique, l'argent se mange." See also Joseph Tonda, *Afrodystopie*.
13 A fantasm that has structured capitalist accumulation from the very start.
14 Gumbs, *Undrowned*, p. 106.
15 Mark Fisher, *Capitalist Realism*, pp. 48–49. [TN: "Dream(ing)" and "Dreamtime" (capitalized) are a rendition, in English, of the timeless state or virtual geography in which mythical events take place and that has been entered by successive generations of Australian Aboriginal artists and practitioners of traditional religion.]
16 It cannot be reduced to a form of patriarchy, but this does not mean that we are done with male domination and state violence.
17 The synthetic environments of leisure-related and work-related platforms (the difference between the two types is becoming less and less meaningful) are increasingly more important than legal or illegal drugs.
18 Sony Labou Tansi, "Lettre fermée," p. 166.
19 Ibid., pp. 164–166.
20 Jonathan Amos. "America colonization 'cooled Earth's climate.'"
21 See Las Casas, *An Account, Much Abbreviated, of the Destruction of the Indies*.
22 See Lily and Lana Wachowski, *The Matrix*.
23 Byun-Chul Han, *Transparency Society*, p. 1.
24 See the work of Annette de Rouvroy.
25 *L'Eve future* is a pathbreaking science fiction novel by Villiers de L'Isle-Adam, and it is well known as the inspiration for the film *Metropolis*.
26 Shoshana Zuboff, *The Age of Surveillance Capitalism*.
27 Hilary Putnam, *Reason, Truth, and History*, pp. 5–6.
28 A film such as Christopher Nolan's *Inception* conveys the idea.
29 This is the techno-immunizing version of Descartes' metaphysical solipsism.
30 Fisher, *Capitalist Realism*, p. 15.
31 The touch of a keyboard, of a touch screen, or of any other virtual

interface is always a controlling touch, which gives us the illusion of command.

32 William Burroughs, *Naked Lunch*, p. 201.

33 See "Citoyens de la ville-monde" and "Je ne suis pas un révolutionnaire," where Paul Virilio spoke about this claim of "grey ecology": "we have entered 'chronopolitics': henceforth, real time will win out over real space."

34 The creativity of the living being proceeds from a process of differentiation, of continual variation. The real time of cybernetics is dead time inasmuch as it tends to abolish the very possibility of the unforeseen, the accidental.

35 According to neuroscience, they represent 50% of our psychic activity. On this topic one can consult in particular the work of Alain Berthoz.

36 Barbara Glowczewski, *Rêves en colère*, pp. 43–44.

37 Expression used by the philosopher Emanuele Coccia in his *The Life of Plants*, p. 20. [Untranslatable play on the phonetic closeness between *vue* "view, sight" and *vie* "life": *point de vue* = point of view / *point de vie* = "point of life," "living point" – and, by implication, "living point of view."]

38 Abbé Raynal, "Present state of Peru," pp. 132–133 (Book VII, ch. 28); translation modified.

39 Jako is a figure in the Malbar (Hindu) community of Réunion who performs acrobatics during certain ritual celebrations in honor of Hanuman, the monkey-god.

40 These were dances performed by slaves and freedmen during the nineteenth century in New York, at St. Catherine's Market, in exchange for eels or money. These performances, which had a dimension of parody of the dominant order, constituted one of the principal sources for American popular spectacles. See W. T. Lhamon, *Raising Cain*.

41 Michel de Certeau, *The Practice of Everyday Life*, p. 18.

42 The first form of decolonization, since the body marks the first position to be freed.

43 For example, let us take the figure of the cross: it can be inscribed on the sail of a caravel just as easily as embodied in the organization of a colonial city (such as the towns in Spanish America called "Santa Fe"), or even in the ritual gesture of a faithful Christian. A figure is not so much a representation as an operation or performance.

44 On the implications and uses to which the notion of "figure" can be put, particularly in dance, visit the excellent site Pour un Atlas des figures, http://www.pourunatlasdesfigures.net/atlas.

45 See Alfred Gell's title *Art and Agency*.

46 "Formerly, one believed in 'the soul' as one believed in grammar

and the grammatical subject" (Friedrich Nietzsche, *Beyond Good and Evil*, paragraph 54, p. 257).

47 As Karen Barad explains, "the neologism 'intra-action' *signifies the mutual constitution of entangled agencies*"; "distinct agencies do not precede, but rather emerge through, their intra-action" (*Meeting the Universe Halfway*, p. 33). All this is referred to by Yves Citton in "Cartographies lyannajistes et politiques monadistes," p. 156.
48 See Carlo Severi's title *The Chimera Principle*.
49 *Imago agens* is an "image that acts" thanks to its striking, paradoxical character. This description applies to the construction of operative images, maps, and mental artifacts in the ancient Greco-Roman "arts of memory."
50 See Donna J. Haraway, *Staying with the Trouble*.
51 René Descartes, "Meditations on first philosophy," p. 13.
52 To be sure, there are exceptions such as Nietzsche, Montaigne, William James, Bergson, and many others.
53 Understood as the dominant order's claim that "there is no alternative".
54 Zhuangzi, *Complete Works*, p. 18.
55 I am referring here to *Tarzan the Ape Man*, the 1932 film made by W. S. Van Dycke in which Johnny Weissmüller played the lead role – a film inspired by Edgar Rice Burroughs's 1912 novel *Tarzan, Lord of the Jungle*.
56 From the Latin *denigrare* "blacken." [TN: In French *blanc* means "white."]
57 Nastassja Martin, *Les Âmes sauvages*, 2016, p. 56.
58 Ailton Krenak, *Ideas to Postpone the End of the World*, p. 25.
59 "Nature, including 'primitive' people as fauna in the timeless scene, was to be preserved for science, adventure, uplift, and moral restoration as proof against civilization's decadence" (Donna J. Haraway, "Race," pp. 255–256. "Nature" here refers to the Albert Park).
60 Guillaume Blanc, *L'Invention du colonialisme vert*, p. 16; see also Xavier Amelot, "La Forêt primaire."
61 Aimé Césaire, *Discourse on Colonialism*, pp. 35–36.
62 See particularly Deleuze and Guattari, *A Thousand Plateaus*; Lowenhaupt Tsing, *The Mushroom at the End of the World*; and more recently Vincent Zonca, *Lichens*.
63 Amelot, "La Forêt primaire," p. 109.
64 Fanon, *Wretched of the Earth*, p. 14, translation modified.
65 The original sentence reads: "The African [*l'homme africain*] has not sufficiently entered into history" (Sarkozy, "Le Discours de Dakar").
66 "The taboo is there in order to be violated," Bataille affirms in his *Erotism*, p. 64. The sacralization of "Nature" is therefore not really in contradiction with its exploitation.
67 Visionary novel by Joseph Conrad written in 1899, several years

before the twentieth century's first genocide – a policy of extermination perpetrated by the Second Reich between 1904 and 1908 against the Hereros and the Namas in the German colony of Southwest Africa (Namibia).

68 Extract from a 1998 interview with Jair Bolsonaro, in the newspaper *Correio braziliense* (see Bolsonaro, "What Brazil's president...").

69 B. Westphal, *The Plausible World*, pp. 130 and 145, translation modified.

70 This is, from an anthropological standpoint, the most important research center in Brazil (Eduardo Vivieros de Castro taught there); it contains the richest repository of artifacts and of ethnographic and linguistic documents concerning the Amerindians and Afrobrazilians: see Autres Brésils, "À propos de l'incendie au Musé National."

71 Excerpt from Raoul Peck's film *I Am Not Your Negro*.

72 The indissociable character of the "modern" and of the "colonial" is what authors of South American decolonial studies such as Enrique Dussel, Anibal Quijano, Walter Mignolo, and Arturo Escobar mean by "the coloniality of power."

73 Starting at the end of the Middle Ages, the process of enclosure in Europe expropriated small peasant communities by subjecting common lands to the law of private property (and its exclusions) – to the overwhelming benefit of the dominant classes.

74 De Certeau, *The Practice of Everyday Life*, 136.

75 Matthieu Noucher, "Le Blanc des cartes," p. 293.

76 Glissant, *Introduction to a Poetics of Diversity*, p. 45.

77 Bâ, "La Notion de personne," p. 182.

78 Excerpt from Birago Diop's 1947 poem "Spirits" ("Le Souffle des ancêtres"), pp. 152–153.

79 See Tim Ingold's brilliant analyses of the figure of the knot in *Lines*.

80 [TN: In French, *personne* also means "no one."]

81 In the form of a unique and unchangeable (authentic) essence, which must be rediscovered and protected with coaching mantras and manuals of personal development.

82 Léonora Miano, *Afropéa: Utopie post-occidentale et post-raciste*, pp. 69–70, 70–71 .

83 Joseph Conrad, *Heart of Darkness*, p. 38.

84 Ingold, *Lines*, p. 57.

85 A kind of cactus endemic to the region of the sertão in the northeast of Brazil. From the Portuguese "back-country" or "last land," the sertão is characterized by long dry spells, an arid climate, and a vegetation composed of cacti and spiny bushes. The *sertanejo* is a rural agricultural worker similar to an American cowboy.

86 Euclides da Cunha, *Rebellion in the Backlands*, pp. 191–195 (text rearranged for my purposes). At the end of the nineteenth century

a millenarian insurrection led to the creation of the community of Canudos in the Brazilian sertão. Da Cunha covered the epic of this "mud-and-wattle Troy" as a war correspondent, from November 1896 until the revolt's suppression in October 1897. Under the direction of the messianic leader Antonio Conselheiro (Antonio the Advisor), the Sertanejos – landless peasants, *cangaceiros* (social outlaws), freed blacks, Amerindians, deserters, and their families – defied the "order and progress" of the young Brazilian Republic and imposed heavy losses on its armed forces.

87 Quotation from Ernest Borneman, in LeRoi Jones (Amiri Baraka), *Blues People*, p. 31.

88 The "blue note" indicates the incompleteness of the last seventh (a semitone), which echoes only other sevenths. Through this lack of resolution [*suspens*], blues and jazz impart the feeling that there is no end, nothing definitive or completed.

89 In fact former fugitive slaves constituted a "community of refugees of the underground railroad."

90 Davis, *Blues Legacies and Black Feminism*, p. 70.

91 On the practice of grimacing, see in particular the work of the choreographer Latifa Laâbissi and the analyses of Isabelle Launay in Alexandra Baudelot, *Latifa Laâbissi: Grimaces du réel*. On the KRUMP, see pp. 177–178 in this chapter.

92 Ralph Ellison, *Invisible Man*, p. 16.

93 And in turn the practice of *bouladjèl* in Guadeloupe pushes these variations to culmination, by totally emancipating itself from "articulated" language. This art of percussive vocalization has developed in part as a response to the prohibition imposed on drumming during the period of slavery.

94 It is always a matter of throwing a predatory demon off the scent: the experience of marronage cannot be separated from that of the manhunt...

95 [TN: *Zadistes* are activists often associated with French ecological movements who occupy land targeted for various forms of development, usually in the countryside, and claim it as a "zone to defend" (ZAD, *zone à défendre*).]

96 See Chapter 2 in this volume and its first iteration as a magazine article in 2005: Dénètem Touam-Bona, "L'Espace d'une fugue."

97 Erin Manning, *The Minor Gesture*, p. 1. With respect to the concept of the minor and the infinitesimal, see also Deleuze and Guattari, *A Thousand Plateaus*; Étienne Souriau, *The Different Modes of Existence*; and Zonca, *Lichens*.

98 Just as every cut liana gives rise to two new ones, the top of the liana develops new roots wherever it falls over, and therefore produces a new stem...

99 Peter Linebaugh and Marcus Rediker, *The Many-Headed Hydra*, p. 2.
100 Ernest Breleur et al., *Manifeste pour les "produits" de haute nécessité*, p. 2 (back cover, by Patrick Chamoiseau).
101 Small plots of land allotted by the master to enslaved people for their subsistence. The overlapping growth of root vegetables, therapeutic plants, fruit trees, and so on on these plots already prefigured another world, which actively opposed the plantation model.
102 Bringing thousands of people into the streets for more than forty-five days in the spring of 2009, the Antillians organized themselves into picket lines, blocking roads and businesses and occupying traffic circles, public spaces, and work sites. See Pierre Odin, *Pwofitasyon*.
103 Bruno Latour, *Down to Earth*.
104 See Ingold, *Lines*.
105 Christine Devin, *Hanuman or the Way of the Wind*, p. 29.
106 Hanuman appears in cultures where the relationship with the monkey does not "denigrate" or "blacken" the human. See also the figure of Sun Wukong (the monkey king) in the literature and imaginary of China, the ancestral figure of "Zako" in Madagascar, etc.
107 This is the title of one of Édouard Glissant's books.
108 "After a forest fire, seedlings sprout in the ashes and, with time, another forest may grow up in the burn. The regrowing forest is an example of what I call *resurgence*" (Tsing, "A Threat to Holocene Resurgence Is a Threat to Livability," p. 52).
109 Anna Lowenhaupt Tsing et al., eds., *Feral Atlas*, n.p. For the French translation of the whole Introduction, see Anna Lowenhaupt Tsing, "La Vie plus qu'humaine."
110 Aby Warburg, "A Lecture on Serpent Ritual," pp. 288–289.
111 Samir Boumediene, *La Colonisation du savoir*, p. 431.
112 An ascetic dimension of the ritual experience of ayahuasca, which notably includes a long fast. One is very far from the image of a "flying trip."
113 Philosophy itself, in its dimension of spiritual exercise, consists of an apprenticeship in death. See in particular Plato's *Phaedo*.
114 Davi Kopenawa and Bruce Albert, *The Falling Sky*, pp. 83–84.
115 Donna J. Haraway, "Teddy bear patriarchy," p. 186.
116 *Ngangas* use mirrors in order to take advantage of such reversible powers.
117 Ingold, *Lines*, p. 35.
118 "Mother of the saints," priestess in the Afro-Brazilian religion named Candomblé.

119 Peyote (*Lophophora williamsii*) is a cactus with psychotropic powers found in Central America. Like "devil's weed" (genus *Datura*), it was diabolized by the Spanish Inquisition during the colonial period.

120 "Forces," a description applied to the Orisas – divinities in the Afro-Cuban religion known as Santeria.

121 Paul Claudel, *Poetic Art*, p. 40, translation modified.

122 Kopenawa and Albert, *The Falling Sky*, p. 393.

123 They are omnipresent in the tales, festivals, carnivals, and imaginary of these Afro-Colombian communities.

124 Michel Agier, *Vivre avec les épouvantails*, p. 73.

125 This is not the role of a diplomat whose special privileges allow him or her to benefit from the immunity of the diplomatic corps. Some authors make diplomacy into an ideal model of the human relationship with the living world. The pierced and porous body of the shaman really has nothing to do with the immunized body [*corps*] of the diplomat; nor does the shaman's cryptic language, which bears no relation to the ambassador's highly policed idiom and to the social pretenses it safeguards.

126 Boumediene, *La Colonisation du savoir*, p. 431.

127 Ernst Haeckel, the founder of this discipline, defined it in his 1866 *Generellle Morphologie der Organismen*, p. 286, as "the science of relations between organisms and the surrounding world, in other words, in a broad sense, the science of the conditions of existence."

128 Multiplication of persons and temporalities of enunciation, poetic turns of phrase (a "cryptic tongue"), the use of sensory deprivation and rhythms, etc.

129 Bakhtin, *Rabelais and His World*, 335–336.

130 Peasant communities in Argentina fabricated botanical bombs that could be used against soybean plantations; and they made them with grains of amaranth, a plant resistant to Roundup. By proliferating, this highly nourishing "bad plant" suffocated the soy plants and thereby allowed the local communities to reappropriate some land.

131 When I say "autochthonous" I do not have in mind the supposed authentic purity of a territory's first inhabitants, but the intimate relationship that may be established anywhere between a human community and "chthonic" forces, the elementary forces of the living world.

132 Estelle Pattée, "Nouvelle-Zélande."

133 "Te Awa Tupua (Whanganui River Claims Settlement Act) 2017, Part 2, Subpart 2. This part of the document can be found in English at https://www.legislation.govt.nz/act/public/2017/0007/latest/whole.html#DLM6831452.

134 Martin, *Les Âmes sauvages*, p. 62.
135 For example, consider the financing of nature reserves by oil or agribusiness multinationals – one among many forms of greenwashing...
136 See Blanc, *L'Invention du colonialisme vert*.
137 Neyrat finds the most extreme form of this negation in contemporary geo-constructivism, which claims "that the Earth, and everything contained on it – ecosystems and organisms – humans and nonhumans, *can* and *must* be reconstructed and entirely remade," thanks to the geo-constructivists' belief that "nature – as an independent entity and force – has been overtaken by the techno-industrial power of humanity" (Frédéric Neyrat, *The Unconstructible Earth*, p. 2).
138 Kopenawa and Albert, *The Falling Sky*, p. 390.
139 See Krause, *The Great Animal Orchestra*.
140 The "white" is also the *garimpeiros*, the independent Brazilian gold prospector (mixed, black, or indigenous), who devastates the forest and its waterways for the chance to become a full-fledged member of the "people of commodities."
141 Florence Lazar, *Tu crois que la terre est chose morte*. See also Malcom Ferdinand, *Decolonial Ecology*; Véronique Kanor's short documentary *Broyage de cannes* (https://www.dailymotion.com/video/xu0dux); and Jean-François Boclé's installation *The Tears of Bananaman* (here in Figures 6a and 6b).
142 Tsing, *The Mushroom at the End of the World*, pp. 38–39.
143 The "farming" of sugar cane is possible thanks to the cloning of a first individual.
144 In this context "zombie" is understood as the human being whose memories and lineages have been extirpated by the enslaver.
145 See Tsing, *The Mushroom at the End of the World*, p. 5.
146 And also the *maïouri* of Guiana, the *coumbite* ("combite") of Haïti, the *mayaz* of Réunion, etc.
147 "Little Guinea" in Haiti, 'Little Angola" in Brazil, "Little Congo" in Panama, etc.; in all the slaveholding colonies, the communities of *nègres rebelles* are presented as the reconstruction of a lost Africa, as a reinscription within the lineages of ancestors, and therefore as a reconstruction of a humanity negated by the refusal of kinship that slavery presupposes.
148 If we are to avoid giving in to a heroic and virilist vision, we have to distinguish the process of marronage (a process of continual subversion) from the condition of the "fugitive slave" or *nègre rebelle* who belonged to a maroon community.
149 Elsa Dorlin, *Se défendre*, p. 26.
150 Max Weber, "Science as a vocation," p. 13 defined modernity as

a process of rationalization: "the knowledge or the conviction…
that we are not ruled by mysterious, unpredictable forces, but
that, on the contrary, we can in principle *control everything by
means of calculation*. That in turn means the disenchantment of
the world."

151 The hunt was conducted mostly against midwives, healers, experts
in therapeutic knowledge who perpetuated "pagan" traditions of
a dialogue with spirits and plants, etc.

152 See the masterly essays in Silvia Federici, *Caliban and the Witch*,
and Elsa Dorlin, *La Matrice de la race*. See also Maryse Condé's
retelling of the Salem witch trials from the point of view of a
runaway slave in *I, Tituba, Black Witch of Salem*.

153 This was a process whereby the bourgeoisie, in formalizing the
laws of private property, appropriated common lands (fields,
woods, etc.). The enclosure movement started at the end of the
Middle Ages.

154 "This nation bears a temporal curse on its face and is heir to
Ham, from whom it is descended; thus it was born for slavery
from father unto son, and to eternal servitude" (M. de St.-Michel,
Voyages des îles Camercanes, 1652, as quoted in Sala-Molins,
Le Code Noir, p. 22. See also Ch. 1, p. 35 and n. 64; p. 168 and
n. 165 in this chapter.

155 Robert Pogue Harrison, *Forests*, pp. 61–62.

156 "Panic" refers to the irresistible fear provoked by Pan's apparition.

157 Boumediene, *La Colonisation du savoir*, p. 408. In this quotation
from the Inquisition's records, *Coca mia*, "my *coca*," refers to
the ritual use of *Erthroxylaceae* by indigenous cultures of the
Andes.

158 Alejo Carpentier, *Kingdom of This World*, pp. 23–24, 36.

159 Stefania Capone, *Searching for Africa in Brazil*, p. 79.

160 These ambiguous figures are found in tales as well as in mythologies: Loki (Scandinavian mythology), Anansi (the spider of
Caribbean tales), Coyote (in the tales of Amerindians of North
America), Sun Wukong (divine monkey of a Chinese novel who
became a figure in popular culture), etc.

161 The title of the legendary song "Cross road blues," composed by
Robert Johnson in 1937, evokes precisely this pact that its author
supposedly made with the devil in order to be able to play like a
god. See Bruce Conforth and Gayle Dean Wardlow, *Up Jumped
the Devil*.

162 After an insurrection of slaves, freedmen, and maroons, slavery
was effectively abolished: most plantations were raided and
burned, many colonists massacred. The abolition of slavery was
first decreed in Saint-Domingue in 1793, then by the Convention

in Paris in 1794. It was Napoleon's effort to re-establish slavery on the island in 1802 that provoked the future Haiti's war of independence.

163 Édouard Glissant, *Poetics of Relation*, pp. 5–6; translation modified.

164 After the Valladolid debate (1550–1551), "Indians" were recognized as having souls, and a papal bull forbade their reduction to slavery. How, then, was the enslavement of *nègres* justified? Through "blackening," which was equated with "blackness" via the renewal of a Biblical myth, namely the curse of Ham, quoted earlier (see Ch. 1, p. 35 and n. 64; also p. 164 and n. 155 in this chapter). The color of 'black' skin became the stigma of slavery, the very mark of infamy which no emancipation will be able to erase.

165 In the religions of Palo Monte, Santeria, etc.

166 Audre Lorde, "A litany for survival," p. 255.

167 *Ponto riscardo, vèvè, firmas* are all terms indicating the image, the signature, the seal by which divinities are invoked and rendered present. They also provide diagrams or a kind of cartography for ritual performance; see Julien Bonhomme and Katerina Kerestetzi, "Les Signatures des dieux."

168 Lydia Cabrera, *La forêt et les dieux*.

169 This is a gesture repeated in very different modalities, by Toussaint Louverture on the slave labor island of Saint Domingue and by Rosa Luxembourg in Germany at the start of the twentieth century (in the Spartacist uprising of 1919).

170 James C. Scott, *Domination and the Arts of Resistance*, p. 162.

171 In Greek mythology Arachne was a young weaver whom Athena punished for her excellence and pride by transforming her into a spider.

172 African–American transcription of Ananzé, a name found among the Akan peoples of the Côte d'Ivoire–Ghana region.

173 Breleur et al., *Manifeste pour les "produits" de haute nécessite*; see p. 2. See also p. 147 (full quotation) and n. 101 in this chapter.

174 Walter Benjamin, "Theses on the Philosophy of History," p. 257.

175 Michelle Mattiuzzi, Jota Mombaça, and Sara Elton Panamby, "Le Mandiguêt."

176 Ernst Bloch, *The Principle of Hope*, pp. 8–9.

177 Benjamin, "Theses on the Philosophy of History," p. 254.

178 David Abram, *The Spell of the Sensuous*, p. 19.

179 Roland Bacon, "Les premières images de la toile cosmique."

180 Jakob von Uexküll, *A Foray into the Worlds of Animals and Humans*, p. 53.

181 With respect to the themes of netting, *lyannaj*, and intertwined memories, see in particular the choreographic creations *Démayé*, by Florence Boyer (Figure 7), *S/T/R/A/T/E/S Quartet*, by Bintou Dembélé, and *White Dog*, by Latifa Laâbissi.

182 "Each and every living thing is a subject that lives in its own world, of which it is the center. It cannot, therefore, be compared to a machine, only to the machine operator who guides the machine" (Jakob von Uexküll, *A Foray into the Worlds of Animals and Humans*, p. 45).

183 He inspired thinkers as different as Deleuze and Heidegger and was the first biologist (ethologist) to consider the animal as a subject, on the basis of its lived world, its perspective.

184 Von Uexküll, *A Foray into the Worlds of Animals and Humans*, pp. 42–43.

185 In line with Einstein's general relativity or with quantum physics which emerged in his time.

186 See "Les Savanturiers."

187 This is the source of Fernand Deligny's interest in aboriginal worlds, as well as in those of spiders; see Deligny, *L'Arachnéen et autres textes*.

188 Paul Valéry, "Philosophy of the Dance," p. 74; translation modified (so much as to be completely different…).

189 See Fernand Deligny, *Cahiers de l'immuable*.

190 Tim Ingold, *Making*, p. 88.

191 There was constant police pressure after the riots of 1992, which ignited this working-class neighborhood of Los Angeles. The riots themselves were a movement of popular revolt provoked by the Rodney King affair in 1991, when a video revealed systemic racism, and particularly the racism lurking in American police departments, to the general public.

192 The source of this quotation is the choreographic creation of Heddy Maalem, *Éloge du puissant royaume*.

193 I mean here the perpetuation of slavery via the US penitentiary system. On this subject, one can read the dense and brilliant analyses by Michelle Alexander, *The New Jim Crow*. See also Ava DuVernay, *13th* (a documentary distributed by Netflix).

194 Expressions such as "Negro spirituals," "soul music," or "soul sisters" continually contest the degradation in humanity to which African–Americans were always the target: a systemic racism that arises when someone destined for the status of expiatory victim is reduced to an organ-body, a tool-body, a black matter-body.

195 Audre Lorde, "Poetry is not a luxury," p. 37.

196 Fanon, *Black Skin, White Masks*, p. xii.

197 To be visible is to be able to be seized, captured. It is also a trap
    for recognition, respectability, and the "whitening" that these
    presuppose.
198 Fanon, *Black Skin, White Masks*, p. xii.

Works Cited

Abram, David. *The Spell of the Sensuous: Perception and Language in a More-Than-Human World.* New York: Vintage, 1997.

Agamben, Giorgio. *Homo Sacer: Sovereign Power and Bare Life*, trans. Daniel Heller-Roazen. Stanford, CA: Stanford University Press, 1998.

Agier, Michel. *Vivre avec des épouvantails: Le monde, les corps, la peur.* Paris: Premier Parallèle, 2020.

Alexander, Michelle. *The New Jim Crow: Mass Incarceration in the Age of Colorblindness*, rev. edn. New York: New Press, 2012.

Alexis, Jacques Stéphen. *Romancero aux étoiles.* Paris: Gallimard, 1988 [1960].

Amelot, Xavier. "La Forêt primaire, image et imaginaire de la forêt pluviale," in *Atlas critique de la Guyane*, ed. Matthieu Noucher and Laurent Polidori. Paris: CNRS Éditions, 2020.

Amos, Jonathan. "America colonization 'cooled Earth's climate,'" BBC News, January 31, 2019. https://www.bbc.com/news/science-environment-47063973.

Anonymous, "La Meuse: Ses vaches, ses éoliennes, ses flics," in *Plus Bure sera leur chute…* Blog, vmc.camp, August 8, 2016. https://vmc.bureburebure.info/2016/08/08/la-meuse-ses-vaches-ses-eoliennes-ses-flics/index.html.

Armand, Margaret Mitchell. *Healing in the Homeland: Haitian Vodou Tradition.* Plymouth: Lexington Books, 2013.

Autres Brésils. "À propos de l'incendie au Musée National."

September 3, 2018. www.autresbresils.net/A-propos-de -l-incendie-au-Musee-National.

Azihary, Mahmoud. *Mayotte en sous-France: Mensonges et manip-ulations d'état au service des intérêts des amis de l'Entre-Soi.* Paris: L'Harmattan, 2016

Bâ, Amadou Hampâté. "La Notion de personne en Afrique Noire," in *La Notion de personne en Afrique noire*, ed. Roger Bastide and Germaine Dieterlen. Paris: L'Harmattan, 1993 [1973].

Bacon, Roland. "Les premières images de la toile cosmique révèlent une myriade de galaxies naines insoupçonnées." CNRS, March 18, 2021. https://www.cnrs.fr/fr/les-premieres-images -de-la-toile-cosmique-revelent-une-myriade-de-galaxies-naines -insoupconnees.

Bakhtin, Mikhail. *Rabelais and His World*, trans. Hélène Iswolsky. Bloomington: Indiana University Press, 1984 [1965].

Banks, Russell. *Cloudsplitter: A Novel.* New York: HarperCollins, 1998.

Barad, Karen. *Meeting the Universe Halfway: Quantum Physics and the Entanglement of Matter and Meaning.* Durham, NC: Duke University Press, 2007.

Barthélémy, Gérard. *Créoles–Bossales: Conflit en Haïti.* Cayenne: Ibis rouge, 2000.

Barthélémy, Gérard. "Le rôle des Bossales dans l'émergence d'une culture de marronage en Haïti," *Cahiers d'études africaines*, 37.148 (1997): 839–862.

Bastide, Roger. *Images du Nordeste mystique en noir et blanc.* Arles: Éditions Actes Sud, 1995 [1978].

Bataille, Georges. *Erotism: Death and Sensuality*, trans. Mary Dalwood. San Francisco, CA: City Lights, 1986 [1957].

Baudelot, Alexandra, ed. *Latifa Laâbissi: Grimaces du réel.* Dijon: Presses du réel, 2016.

Benjamin, Walter. "Critique of violence," in his *Reflections: Essays, Aphorisms, Autobiographical Writings*, ed. Peter Demetz, trans. Edmund Jephcott. New York: Harcourt Brace Jovanovich, 1978.

Benjamin, Walter. "Theses on the philosophy of history," in his *Illuminations: Essays and Reflections*, ed. Hannah Arendt, trans. Harry Zohn. New York: Schocken Books, 1969.

Binctin, Barnabé. "À deux pas de 'la Jungle' des migrants, Calais prépare un parc de loisirs." *Reporterre*, October 27, 2016. https://reporterre.net/A-deux-pas-de-la-Jungle-des-migrants -Calais-prepare-un-parc-de-loisirs.

Blanc, Guillaume. *L'Invention du colonialisme vert: Pour en finir avec le mythe de l'Éden africain*, with Preface by François-Xavier Fauvelle. Paris: Flammarion, 2020.

Bloch, Ernst. *The Principle of Hope*, vol. 1, trans. Neville Plaice, Stephen Plaice, and Paul Knight. Cambridge, MA: MIT Press, 1986 [1959].

Boclé, Jean-François. *The Tears of Bananaman*. Installation, 2009–2012. Galeria Passage Crista, Puerto Limon, Costa Rica, 2021. http://jeanfrancoisbocle.com/works/installations/the-tears-of-bananaman/05.html.

Bolsonaro, Jair. "What Brazil's president, Jair Bolsonaro, has said about Brazil's Indigenous Peoples." Survival International, https://www.survivalinternational.org/articles/3540-Bolsonaro.

Bonhomme, Julien, and Katerina Kerestetzi. "Les Signatures des dieux: Graphismes et action rituelle dans les religions afrocubaines." *Gradhiva*, 22 (2015): 74–105.

Borges, Jorge Luis. *Labyrinths: Selected Stories and Other Writings*, ed. Donald A. Yates and James E. Irby. New York: New Directions Books, 1964.

Boumediene, Samir. *La Colonisation du savoir: Une histoire des plantes médicinales du "Nouveau monde" (1492–1750)*. Vaulx-en-Velin: Éditions des Mondes à Faire, 2016.

Boutang, Yann Moulier. *De l'esclavage au salariat: Économie historique du salariat bridé*. Paris: Presses Universitaires de France, 1998.

Bouyer, Frédéric. *La Guyane française: Notes et souvenirs d'un voyage exécuté en 1862–1863*. Paris: Hachette & Cie, 1867.

Boyer, Florence, choreographer. *Démayé*. Dance duo, Companie Artmayage, 2021. https://www.lalanbik.org/article/1509-demaye-florence-boyer-compagnie-artmayage.

Bradbury, Ray. *Fahrenheit 451*, 60th anniversary edn. New York: Simon & Schuster, 2013 [1953].

Breleur, Ernest et al. *Manifeste pour les "produits" de haute nécessite*. Paris: Institut de tout-monde/Éditions Galaade, 2009. Reprinted in Édouard Glissant and Patrick Chamoiseau, *Manifestes*. Paris: La Découverte, 2021, 135–157. https://www.editionsladecouverte.fr/manifestes-9782348060595.

Burroughs, William S. *Naked Lunch: The Restored Text*, ed. James Grauerholz and Barry Miles. New York: Grove Press, 2001 [1959].

Cabrera, Lydia. *La Forêt et les dieux: Religions afro-cubaines et médecine sacrée à Cuba*, trans. from Spanish by Béatrice de Chavagnac. Paris: Jean-Michel Place, 2003.

Canetti, Elias. *Crowds and Power*, trans. Carol Stewart. New York: Farrar, Straus, & Giroux, 1984 [1960].

Capone, Stefania. *Searching for Africa in Brazil: Power and Tradition in Candomblé*, trans. Lucy Lyall Grant. Durham, NC: Duke University Press, 2010.

Carayol, Rémi. "Chasse à l'homme à Mayotte." *Plein droit*, 82 (2009): 19–23. http://www.gisti.org/spip.php?article1742.

Carpentier, Alejo. *The Kingdom of This World*, trans. Harriet de Onís. New York: Collier Books, 1970 [1949].

Césaire, Aimé. *Discourse on Colonialism*, trans. Joan Pinkham. New York: Monthly Review Press, 1972 [1950].

Chamoiseau, Patrick. *Slave Old Man*, trans. Linda Coverdale. New York: New Press, 2018 [1997].

Citton, Yves. "Cartographies lyannajistes et politiques monadistes," in *Le Pouvoir des liens faibles*, ed. Alexandre Gefen and Sandra Laugier. Paris: CNRS Éditions, 2020.

Clastres, Pierre. *Society against the State: Essays in Political Anthropology*, trans. Robert Hurley and Abe Stein. New York: Zone Books, 1989 [1974].

Claudel, Paul. *Poetic Art*, trans. Renee Spodheim. Port Washington, NY: Kennikat Press, 1969 [1907].

Coccia, Emanuele. *The Life of Plants: A Metaphysics of Mixture*, trans. Dylan J. Montanari. Cambridge: Polity, 2019.

Le Code noir ou Edit du roy, servant de reglement pour le gouvernement & l'administration de justice & la police des îsles françoises de l'Amerique, & pour la discipline & le commerce des negres & esclaves dans ledit pays: donné à Versailles au mois de mars 1685, avec l'Edit du mois d'aoust 1685 portant établissement d'un conseil souverain & de quatre sieges royaux dans la coste de l'Isle de S. Domingue. Paris (au Palais): Claude Girard, 1735 [1685]. https://archive.org/details/lecodenoirouedi00fran/page/8/mode/2up.

Comaroff, Jean, and John L. Comaroff. "Naturing the nation: Aliens, apocalypse, and the postcolonial state," *Journal of Southern African Studies*, 27.3 (2001): 627–651.

Condé, Maryse. *I, Tituba, Black Witch of Salem*, trans. Richard Philcox. Charlottesville/London: University Press of Virginia/Caraf Books, 1992 [1986].

Confiant, Raphaël. Interview, *Télérama* 2273 ("La Martinique de Raphaël Confiant"), August 4, 1993.

Conforth, Bruce, and Gayle Dean Wardlow. *Up Jumped the Devil:*

The Real Life of Robert Johnson. Chicago, IL: Chicago Review Press, 2019.

Conrad, Joseph. *Heart of Darkness*, ed. Owen Knowles and Allan H. Simmons. Cambridge: Cambridge University Press, 2018 [1899].

Corten, André. *Misère, religion et politique en Haïti: Diabolisation et mal politique*. Paris: Éditions Karthala, 2001.

D'Estaing, Valéry Giscard. "Giscard D'Estaing sur Mayotte." Declaration, 1974. https://soundcloud.com/muzdalifahouse /giscarddestaingsurmayotte.

da Cunha, Euclides. *Rebellion in the Backlands (Os Sertões)*, trans. Samuel Putnam. Chicago, IL: University of Chicago Press, 1975 [1902].

Dambury, Gerty. "Guadeloupe: Le créole, langue de la mobilization," *Le Nouvel observateur* (special issue *Rue 89: Penser l'écologie*). November 4, 2016. https://www.nouvelobs .com/rue89/rue89-nos-vies-connectees/20090216.RUE8506 /guadeloupe-le-creole-langue-de-la-mobilisation.html.

Davis, Angela Y. *Blues Legacies and Black Feminism: Gertrude "Ma" Rainey, Bessie Smith, and Billie Holiday*. New York: Pantheon Books, 1998.

de Certeau, Michel. *The Practice of Everyday Life*, trans. Steven F. Rendall. Berkeley: University of California Press, 1984.

Deleuze, Gilles, and Félix Guattari. *A Thousand Plateaus: Capitalism and Schizophrenia*, trans. Brian Massumi. Minneapolis: University of Minnesota Press, 1987 [1980].

Deleuze, Gilles, and Claire Parnet. *Dialogues*, trans. Hugh Tomlinson and Barbara Habberjam. New York: Columbia University Press, 1987 [1977].

Deligny, Fernand. *L'Arachnéen et autres textes*. Paris: L'Arachnéen, 2008.

Deligny, Fernand. *Cahiers de l'immuable*, vol. 1: *Voix et voir*, special issue of *Recherches* 18 (1975).

Dembélé, Bintou, choreographer. *S/T/R/A/T/E/S: Quartet*. Performance art, Companie Rualité, 2016. https://www.facebook .com/Strates-Quartet-Avignon-203159100081711.

Déribéré, Maurice. *La Couleur*. Paris: Presses Universitaires de France, 1964.

Descartes, René. "Meditations on first philosophy," in his *Philosophical Writings*, vol. 2, trans. John Cottingham, Robert Stoothoff, and Dugald Murdoch. Cambridge: Cambridge University Press, 1984.

Devin, Christine. *Hanuman or the Way of the Wind*, trans. Roger Harris. New York: Discovery Publisher, 2020 [2001].

Diop, Birago. "Spirits" [1947], in *The Negritude Poets: An Anthology of Translations from the French*, ed. Ellen Conroy Kennedy. New York: Viking Press, 1975, pp. 152–154.

Dorlin, Elsa. *Black Feminism: Anthologie du féminisme africain-américain, 1975–2000*. Paris: L'Harmattan, 2008.

Dorlin, Elsa. *La Matrice de la race: Généalogie sexuelle et coloniale de la nation française*, preface by Joan Wallach Scott. Paris: Éditions la Découverte, 2006.

Dorlin, Elsa. *Se défendre: Une philosophie de la violence*. Paris: La Découverte, 2017.

Douglas, Mary. *Purity and Danger: An Analysis of the Concepts of Pollution and Taboo*. London: Routledge, 1995 [1966].

DuVernay, Ava, dir. *13th*. Documentary, Forward Movement and Kandoo Films, 2016.

Elbadawi, Soeuf. *Un dhikri pour nos morts: La rage entre les dents*. La Roque d'Anthéron: Vents d'ailleurs, 2013.

Ellison, Ralph. *Invisible Man*. New York: Vintage Books, 1972 [1952].

Fairbank, Calvin. *During Slavery Times: How He "Fought the Good Fight" to Prepare "the Way": Edited from His Manuscript*. Chicago, IL: R. R. McCabe & Co, 1890.

Fanon, Frantz. *Black Skin, White Masks*, trans. Richard Philcox, rev. edn. New York: Grove, 2008 [1952].

Fanon, Frantz. *The Wretched of the Earth*, trans. Richard Philcox, with introductions by Jean-Paul Sartre and Homi K. Bhabha. New York: Grove, 2004 [1963].

Federici, Silvia. *Caliban and the Witch: Women, the Body and Primitive Accumulation*. New York: Autonomedia, 2004.

Ferdinand, Malcolm. *Decolonial Ecology: Thinking from the Caribbean World*, trans. Anthony Paul Smith. Cambridge: Polity, 2022.

Fisher, Mark. *Capitalist Realism: Is There No Alternative?* Winchester: Zero books, 2009.

Fleischer, Alain. *La Traversée de l'Europe par les forêts*, Paris: Éditions Virgile, 2004.

Foucault, Michel. "Different spaces," in his *Aesthetics, Method, Epistemology*, vol. 2 of *Essential Works, 1954–1984*, ed James D. Faubion, trans. Robert Hurley et al. New York: New Press, 1998.

Foucault, Michel. "The subject and power," in his *Power*, vol. 3

of *Essential Works, 1954–1984*, ed. James D. Faubion, trans. Robert Hurley et al. New York: New Press, 2000.

Foucault, Michel. "What is critique?" trans. Lysa Hochroth, in his *The Politics of Truth*, ed. Sylvère Lotringer and Lysa Hochroth. New York: Semiotext(e), 1997.

Foucault, Michel. *Discipline and Punish: The Birth of the Prison*, trans. Alan Sheridan. New York: Vintage Books, 1979 [1975].

Foucault, Michel. "Preface to *Anti-Oedipus*," in his *Power*, vol. 3 of *Essential Works, 1954–1984*, ed. James D. Faubion, trans. Robert Hurley et al. New York: New Press, 2000.

Fouchard, Jean. *The Haitian Maroons: Liberty or Death*, trans. A. Faulkner Watts. New York: Edward W. Blyden Press, 1981 [1972].

Frankétienne. *Les Affres d'un défi*. Paris: Éditions Jean-Michel Place, 2000.

Gell, Alfred. *Art and Agency: An Anthropological Theory*. Oxford: Clarendon, 1998.

Glissant, Édouard. *Caribbean Discourse: Selected Essays*, trans. J. Michael Dash. Charlottesville: University Press of Virginia/Caraf Books, 1999 [1981].

Glissant, Édouard. *Le Discours antillais*. Paris: Gallimard, 1997 [1981].

Glissant, Édouard. *Introduction to a Poetics of Diversity*, trans. Celia Britton. Liverpool: Liverpool University Press, 2000 [1996].

Glissant, Édouard. *Poetics of Relation*, trans. Betsy Wing. Ann Arbor: University of Michigan Press, 1997.

Glissant, Édouard, *Treatise on the Whole-World*, trans. Celia Britton. Liverpool: Liverpool University Press, 2020 [1997].

Glowczewski, Barbara. *Rêves en colère: alliances aborigènes dans le Nord-Ouest australien*. Paris: Plon, 2004.

Good, Chris. "Why did the CDC develop a plan for a zombie apocalypse?" *Atlantic*, May 20, 2011. https://www.theatlantic.com/politics/archive/2011/05/why-did-the-cdc-develop-a-plan-for-a-zombie-apocalypse/239246.

Guattari, Félix. "Le Capitalisme Mondial Intégré et la révolution moléculaire," lecture delivered at the Centre d'Information sur les Nouveaux Espaces de Liberté (CINEL), 1981. http://www.revue-chimeres.fr/drupal_chimeres/files/cmi.pdf (last accessed on December 2021).

Gumbs, Alexis Pauline. *Undrowned: Black Feminist Lessons from Marine Mammals*. Chico, CA: AK Press, 2020.

Haeckel, Ernst. *Generelle Morphologie der Organismen:*

Allgemeine Grundzüge der organischen Formen-wissenschaft, mechanisch begründet durch die von Charles Darwin reformirte Descendenztheorie, vol. 2. Berlin: G. Reimer, 1866.

Han, Byung-Chul. *The Transparency Society*, trans. Erik Butler. Stanford, CA: Stanford University Press, 2015 [2012].

Haraway, Donna J. *Staying with the Trouble: Making Kin in the Cthulucene*. Durham, NC: Duke University Press, 2016.

Haraway, Donna. "Race: Universal donors in a vampire culture: It's all in the family: Biological kinship categories in the twentieth-century United States," in *The Donna Haraway Reader*. New York: Routledge, 2004.

Haraway, Donna. "Teddy bear patriarchy: Taxidermy in the Garden of Eden, New York City, 1908–1936," in *The Haraway Reader*. New York: Routledge, 2004.

Harrison, Robert Pogue. *Forests: The Shadow of Civilization*. Chicago, IL: University of Chicago Press, 1992.

Hawad, Mahmoudan. *Furigraphie: Poésies, 1985–2015*, trans. into French by Hélène Claudot-Hawad. Paris: Gallimard, 2017.

Helg, Aline. *Slave No More: Self-Liberation Before Abolitionism in the Americas*, trans. Lara Vergnaud: Chapel Hill, NC: University of North Carolina Press, 2019.

Hitchcock, Alfred, dir. *Vertigo*, restored by Robert A. Harris and James C. Katz. Universal City, CA: Universal Studios, 1998 [1958].

Hobsbawm, Eric. J. *Bandits*, rev. edn. New York: Pantheon Books, 1981 [1969].

Hoppin, Richard H. *Medieval Music*. New York: W.W. Norton, 1978.

Horton, Richard. *The COVID-19 Catastrophe: What's Gone Wrong and How to Stop It Happening Again*. Cambridge: Polity, 2020.

Hurault, Jean. *Africains de Guyane: La vie matérielle et l'art des noirs réfugiés de Guyane*. La Haye: Mouton, 1970.

Hurault, Jean. "Histoire des noirs réfugiés Boni de la Guyane française," *Revue Française d'Histoire d'Outre-mer*, 47.166 (1960): 76–137.

Hurbon, Laënnec. *L'Insurrection des esclaves de Saint-Domingue, 22–23 août 1791: Actes de la table ronde internationale de Port-au-Prince: (8 au 10 décembre 1997)*. Paris: Karthala, 2000.

Hurbon, Laënnec. *Le Barbare imaginaire*. Paris: Éditions du Cerf, 2007 [1988].

Infante, Guillermo Cabrera. *View of Dawn in the Tropics*, trans. Suzanne Jill Levine. New York: Harper & Row, 1978.

Ingold, Tim. *Lines: A Brief History*. London: Routledge, 2007.

Ingold, Tim. *Making: Anthropology, Archaeology, Art and Architecture*. London: Routledge, 2013.

Jones, LeRoi (Amiri Baraka). *Blues People: Negro Music in White America*. New York: Harper Perennial, 2002 [1963].

Kanor, Véronique, dir. *Broyage de cannes* (film), DVD video, 6 min, La Noiraude et Compagnie, 2010.

Klein, Naomi. "Screen New Deal: Under Cover of Mass Death, Andrew Cuomo Calls in the Billionaires to Build a High-Tech Dystopia." The Intercept, May 5, 2020. https://theintercept.com/2020/05/08/andrew-cuomo-eric-schmidt-coronavirus-tech-shock-doctrine.

Klemperer, Victor. *LTI: Lingua Tertii Imperii (The Language of the Third Reich): A Philologist's Notebook*, trans. Martin Brady. London: Bloomsbury, 2013 [1957].

Klotz, Nicolas, and Elisabeth Perceval, dirs. *L'héroïque lande, la frontière brûle*. Documentary. Shellac Productions, 2018.

Kopenawa, Davi, and Bruce Albert, *The Falling Sky: Words of a Yanomami Shaman,* trans. Nicholas Elliott and Alison Dundy. Cambridge, MA: Harvard University Press, 2013.

Krause, Bernie. *The Great Animal Orchestra: Finding the Origins of Music in the World's Wild Places*. New York: Little, Brown, 2012.

Krenak, Ailton. *Ideas to Postpone the End of the World*, trans. Anthony Doyle. Toronto: Anansi International, 2020.

L'Isle-Adam, Auguste, Comte de Villiers de. *L'Ève future*, ed. Nadine Satiat. Paris: Garnier-Flammarion, 1992 [1886].

La Boétie, Étienne. *Anti-Dictator: The Discours sur la servitude volontaire*, trans. Harry Kurz. New York: Columbia University Press, 1942.

Laâbissi, Latifa, choreographer. *White Dog*. Dance, Centre Pompidou. https://www.festival-automne.com/en/edition-2019/latifa-laabissi-white-dog.

Lagnau, Laurent. "Pourquoi il faut s'intéresser aux îles Eparses." Blog. Zone militaire, July 19, 2014. http://www.opex360.com/2014/07/19/pourquoi-il-faut-sinteresser-aux-iles-eparses.

Las Casas, Bartolomé de. *An Account, Much Abbreviated, of the Destruction of the Indies, with Related Texts*, ed. Franklin W. Knight, trans. Andrew Hurley. Indianapolis, IN: Hackett, 2003 [1552].

Latour, Bruno. *Down to Earth: Politics in the New Climatic Regime*, trans. Catherine Porter. Cambridge: Polity, 2018.

Lazar, Florence, dir. *Tu crois que la terre est chose morte.* Documentary. Paris: Sister Productions, 2019.

le Bris, Michel. *Le Grand Dehors,* Paris: Payot, 1992.

Le Namouric, Patrice, dir. *Caligula.* Compagnie TRACK. Tropiques Atrium/Scène Nationale, Martinique, 2019.

Le nouveau petit Robert. Le Robert: Paris, 1994.

Lhamon, William T., Jr. *Raising Cain: Blackface Performance from Jim Crow to Hip Hop.* Cambridge, MA: Harvard University Press, 1998.

Lienhard, Martin. *Le Discours des esclaves: De l'Afrique à l'Amérique latine,* trans. into French by Beatriz Lienhard-Fernández and Martin Lienhard. Paris: L'Harmattan, 2001.

Linebaugh, Peter, and Marcus Rediker. *The Many-Headed Hydra: Sailors, Slaves, Commoners, and the Hidden History of the Revolutionary Atlantic.* Boston, MA: Beacon Press, 2013.

Lorde, Audre. "Poetry is not a luxury," in her *Sister Outsider: Essays and Speeches.* Freedom, CA: Crossing Press, 1984.

Lorde, Audre. "A litany for survival," in her *Collected Poems.* New York: W.W. Norton, 1997.

Maalem, Heddy, choreographer. *Éloge du puissant royaume / Praise of the Mighty Kingdom.* Krump Contemporary Dance Show, Maison de la Dance de Lyon. 2017. https://www.numeridanse.tv /videotheque-danse/eloge-du-puissant-royaume.

Malcolm X. "Message to the Grass Roots," in *Malcolm X Speaks: Selected Speeches and Statements,* ed. George Breitman. New York: Grove Weidenfeld, 1965.

Manning, Erin. *The Minor Gesture.* Durham, NC: Duke University Press, 2016.

Martin, Nastassja. *Les Âmes sauvages: Face à l'Occident, la résistance d'un people d'Alaska.* Paris: La Découverte, 2016.

Marx, Karl. *Capital: A Critique of Political Economy,* vol. 1, trans. Ben Fowkes. New York: Vintage Books, 1977 [1867].

Mattiuzzi, Michelle, Jota Mombaça, and Sara Elton Panamby. "Le Mandinguêt: Écriture performative message ancestral," *Multitudes,* 65.4 (2016): 128–133.

Maximin, Daniel. *Lone Sun,* trans. Clarisse Zimra. Charlottesville: University Press of Virginia, 1989 [1981].

"Mayotte: La Chasse aux étrangers par la population est ouverte... et couverte." Blog Mediapart de la Cimade, April 21, 2016. https://www.lacimade.org/mayotte-la-chasse-aux -etrangers-par-la-population-est-ouverte-et-couverte/?fbclid

=IwAR0RjeHbl2c4UQFPh-U8-cRanZ9Pn54lkN3-R6bxu
FXuv6P6l9qQNDetK5c.

"Mayotte: Mort de 7 migrants dans un naufrage," *Le Figaro*,
February 10, 2014. https://www.lefigaro.fr/flash-actu/2014/02
/10/97001-20140210FILWWW00105-mayotte-mort-de-7
-migrants-dans-un-naufrage.php.

Métraux, Alfred. *Voodoo in Haiti*, trans. Hugo Charteris. New
York: Oxford University Press, 1959.

Miano, Léonora. *Afropea: Utopie post-occidentale et post-raciste*.
Paris: Grasset, 2020.

Mohamed, Isabelle. "Les Comores existent-elles?" *Revue
Maadzishi*, 3 (2000), n.p. [Moroni, Union of the Comoros:
Éditions Komedit.]

Montaigne, Michel de. *The Complete Essays of Montaigne*, trans.
Donald M. Frame. Stanford, CA: Stanford University Press, 1958
[1580–1588].

Morrison, Toni. *Beloved*. New York: Vintage Books, 2004 [1987].

Naipaul, V. S. *The Middle Passage: Impressions of Five Societies
– British, French, and Dutch – in the West Indies and South
America*. New York: Macmillan, 1963.

Ndagano, Biringanine. *Nègre tricolore: Littérature et domination en
pays créole*. Paris: Maisonneuve & Larose, 2000.

Neyrat, Frédéric. *The Unconstructable Earth: An Ecology of
Separation*, trans. Drew S. Burk. New York: Fordham University
Press, 2019.

Niccol, Andrew, dir. *Gattaca*. Culver City, CA: Sony Pictures Home
Entertainment, 2021 [1997].

Nietzsche, Friedrich. *On the Genealogy of Morals* [1887] and *Ecce
Homo* [1908], trans. Walter Kaufmann and R. J. Hollingdale.
New York: Vintage Books, 1989.

Nietzsche, Friedrich. *Beyond Good and Evil* [1886], in *Basic
Writings of Nietzsche*, ed. and trans. Walter Kaufmann. New
York: Modern Library, 1968.

Nolan, Christopher, dir. *Inception*. Burbank, CA: Warner Brothers
Entertainment, 2017 [2010].

Noucher, Matthieu. "Le Blanc des cartes: Entre soif d'aventure,
désir de connaissance et appétit de conquête," in *Atlas critique
de la Guyane*, ed. Matthieu Noucher and Laurent Polidori. Paris:
CNRS Editions, 2020.

Odin, Pierre. *Pwofitasyon: Luttes syndicales et anticolonialisme en
Guadeloupe et en Martinique*. Paris: La Découverte, 2019.

Pattée, Estelle. "Nouvelle-Zélande: Les droits et devoirs du fleuve Whanganui," *Libération*, March 28, 2017.

Peck, Raoul, dir. *I Am Not Your Negro*, text by James Baldwin. New York: Magnolia Home Entertainment, 2017 [2016].

Péret, Benjamin. *La Commune des Palmares*, trans. from Portuguese by Carminda Batista. Paris: Syllepse, 1999.

Perrot, Michelle. "Faire exister les acteurs de l'ombre." Interview with Michelle Perrot conducted by Dénètem Touam-Bona and Sylvain Marcelli. *Ban public*, May 8, 2004. http://prison.eu.org /spip.php?page=imprimer_article&id_article=4639.

Anne Perzo, "'Décasages,' ces chasses aux clandestins condamnées par le tribunal administratif," *Journal de Mayotte*, June 4, 2016. https://lejournaldemayotte.yt/2016/06/04/les-chasses-aux -clandestins-condamnees-par-le-tribunal-administratif.

Pierre-Petit. "Fugue," in *Encyclopaedia universalis*. France, 2022. https://www.universalis.fr/encyclopedie/fugue.

Pichel, Irving, and Ernest B. Schoedsack, dirs. *The Most Dangerous Game*. Los Angeles, CA: RKO Radio Pictures, Kanopy Streaming, 2018 [1932].

Plato, *Phaedo*, trans. Hugh Tredennick, in *The Collected Dialogues of Plato*, ed. Edith Hamilton and Huntington Cairns. Princeton, NJ: Princeton University Press, 1973 [1961].

Police, Gérard. *Quilombos dos Palmares; Lectures sur un marronage brésilien*. Cayenne: Ibis rouge, 2003.

Price, Richard. *First-Time: The Historical Vision of an Afro-American People*. Baltimore, MD: Johns Hopkins University Press, 1983.

Price, Richard. *Maroon Societies: Rebel Slave Communities in the Americas*, 3rd edn. Baltimore, MD: Johns Hopkins University Press, 1996 [1973].

Price, Sally, and Richard Price. *Maroon Arts: Cultural Vitality in the African Diaspora* Boston, MA: Beacon Press, 1999.

Putnam, Hilary. *Reason, Truth, and History*. Cambridge: Cambridge University Press, 1981.

Raynal, Abbé (Guillaume Thomas-François). "Present state of Peru," in his *A Philosophical and Political History of the Settlements and Trade of the Europeans in the East and West Indies*, trans. John Obadiah Justamond, vol 4 (Book VII, ch. 28). London: W. Strahan, 1783 [1780].

Ribeiro, João Ubaldo. *An Invincible Memory*. London: HarperCollins, 1989 [1984].

Roumain, Jacques. *Masters of the Dew*, trans. Langston Hughes and Mercer Cook. Oxford: Heinemann, 1978 [1944].

"Run, nigger, run," African–American folk song, c. 1851. Roud Folk Song Index 3660.

Saint-Méry, Moreau de. *Description topographique, physique, civile, politique et historique de la partie française de l'Isle Saint-Domingue*, vol 1. Paris: Société française d'histoire d'outre-mer, 1984 [1797].

Sala-Molins, Louis. *Le Code noir ou le calvaire de Canaan*. Paris: Presses Universitaires de France (Quadrige), 1987.

Sarkozy, Nicolas. "Le Discours de Dakar de Nicolas Sarkozy," *Le Monde*, November 9, 2007. Delivered July 26, 2007. https:// www.lemonde.fr/afrique/article/2007/11/09/le-discours-de-dakar _976786_3212.html.

"Les Savanturiers: Musique de toile d'araignée," France Inter, April 25, 0221. https://www.radiofrance.fr/franceinter/podcasts /les-savanturiers/musique-de-toile-d-araignee-1291767.

Schoelcher, Victor. *Des colonies françaises: Abolition immédiate de l'esclavage*. Paris: Éditions du Comité des travaux historiques et scientifiques, 1998 [1842].

Scott, James C. *Domination and the Arts of Resistance: Hidden Transcripts*. New Haven, CT: Yale University Press, 1990.

Severi, Carlo. *The Chimera Principle: An Anthropology of Memory and Imagination*, trans. Janet Lloyd. Chicago, IL: Hau Books, 2015.

Souriau, Étienne. *The Different Modes of Existence*, trans. Erik Beranek and Tim Howles. Minneapolis: Univocal Publishing, 2015 [2009].

Stedman, John Gabriel. *Narrative of a Five Years' Expedition against the Revolted Negroes of Surinam*. Amherst: University of Massachusetts Press, 1972 [1796].

Tansi, Sony Labou. *The Seven Solitudes of Lorsa Lopez*, trans. Clive Wake. Oxford: Heinemann, 1995 [1985].

Tansi, Sony Labou. "Lettre fermée aux gens du Nord et Compagnie" [1992], in his *Encre, sueur, salive et sang: Textes critiques*, ed. Greta Rodriguez-Antoniotti. Paris: Seuil, 2015.

Thompson, E. P. *The Making of the English Working Class*. New York: Pantheon Books, 1964.

Thoreau, Henry D. *Walden*, ed. J. Lyndon Shanley. Princeton, NJ: Princeton University Press, 2016 [1854].

Tocqueville, Alexis de. *Democracy in America*, trans. and ed. Harvey

C. Mansfield and Delba Winthrop. Chicago, IL: University of Chicago Press, 2006 [1835–40].

Tonda, Joseph. *Afrodystopie: La vie dans le rêve d'Autrui*. Paris: Karthala, 2021.

Tonda, Joseph. "En Afrique, l'argent se mange." Interview with Laurence Caramel. *Le Monde*, August 15, 2021.

Touam Bona, Dénètem. "'Écrire' Haïti…" Interview with Frankétienne, Lyonel Trouillot, Gary Victor, *Drôle d'époque*, 14, 2004: article 3419. Republished in *Africultures*, May 24, 2004.

Touam Bona, Dénètem. "L'Espace d'une fugue… Éthique et esthétique du marronage," *Drôle d'époque*, 17 (2005): n.p.

Touam Bona, Dénètem. "Mayotte: Peau comorienne, masques français," *Jeune Afrique*, June 13, 2016. https://www.jeuneafrique.com/333052/societe/mayotte-peau-comorienne-masques-francais.

Touam Bona, Dénètem, dir. *Spectrographies: Contes de l'île étoilée*. Compagnie Les Écorcés and Compagnie Carole Chausset, Centre International d'art et du paysage de l'île de Vassivière, France, 2022. https://vimeo.com/733156310?fbclid=IwAR1NCcENgexLAK61jslfr4WqlMNGnefS_Wnt633kWfnpQQVR9Vk8_tc0SME.

Triay, Philippe. "Mahmoud Azihary: Mayotte est 'complètement en marge de la République.'" Interview on Francetvinfo, April 7, 2016. https://la1ere.francetvinfo.fr/mahamoud-azihary-mayotte-est-completement-en-marge-de-la-republique-347765.html.

Trouillot, Èvelyne. *The Infamous Rosalie*, trans. M.A. Salvodon. Lincoln: University of Nebraska Press, 2013 [2003].

Tsing, Anna Lowenhaupt. *The Mushroom at the End of the World: On the Possibility of Life in Capitalist Ruins*. Princeton, NJ: Princeton University Press, 2015.

Tsing, Anna Lowenhaupt. "A Threat to Holocene Resurgence Is a Threat to Livability," in *The Anthropology of Sustainability: Beyond Development and Progress*, ed. Marc Brightman and Jerome Lewis. New York: Palgrave Macmillan, 2017, 51–65.

Tsing, Anna Lowenhaupt. "La Vie plus qu'humaine." *Terrestres*. www.terrestres.org/2019/05/26/la-vie-plus-quhumaine.

Tsing, Anna Lowenhaupt, Jennifer Deger, Alder Keleman Saxena, and Feifei Zhou, eds. *Feral Atlas: The More-than-Human Anthropocene*. Stanford, CA: Stanford University Press. https://feralatlas.org/#.

Twain, Mark (Samuel Clemens). *The Adventures of Huckleberry Finn*, ed. Henry Nash Smith. Boston, MA: Houghton Mifflin, 1958 [1885].

Valéry, Paul. "Philosophy of the Dance," *Salmagundi*, 33/34 (1976): 65–75.

Van Dycke, W. S., dir. *Tarzan the Ape Man*. Burbank, CA: Turner Entertainment, distributed by Warner Brothers Home Entertainment, 2017 [1932].

Van Peebles, Melvin, dir. *Sweet Sweetback's Baadasssss Song*. New York: Criterion Collection 1095, 2021 [1971].

Vergès, Françoise. *The Wombs of Women: Race, Capital, Feminism*, trans. Kaiama L. Glover. Durham, NC: Duke University Press, 2020 [2017].

Virilio, Paul. "Citoyens de la ville-monde." *Le Monde diplomatique*, June 28, 1992.

Virilio, Paul. "Je ne suis pas un révolutionnaire, mais un révélationnaire." Interview compiled by Jean-Claude Raspiengeas, *La Croix*, September 18, 2018. https://www.la-croix.com/Culture /Paul-Virilio-Je-suis-pas-revolutionnaire-revelationnaire-2018-09 -18-1200969633.

Von Uexküll, Jakob. *A Foray into the Worlds of Animals and Humans, with A Theory of Meaning*, trans. Joseph D. O'Neil. Minneapolis: University of Minnesota Press, 2010 [1934].

Wachowski, Lily, and Lana Wachowski, dirs. *The Matrix*. Burbank, CA: Warner Brothers Entertainment, 2020 [1999].

Wachtel, Nathan. *The Vision of the Vanquished: The Spanish Conquest of Peru through Indian Eyes, 1530–1570*, trans. Ben Reynolds and Siân Reynolds. New York: Harvester Press, 1977 [1971].

Warburg, Aby. "A lecture on serpent ritual," trans. W. F. Mainland, *Journal of the Warburg Institute*, 2.4 (1939): 277–292. https:// www.jstor.org/stable/750040.

Weber, Max. "Science as a vocation," in his *The Vocation Lectures*, ed. David Owen and Tracy B. Strong, trans. Rodney Livingstone. Indianapolis, IN: Hackett, 2004 [1919].

Westphal, Bertrand. *The Plausible World: A Geocritical Approach to Space, Place, and Maps*, trans. Amy D. Wells. New York: Palgrave Macmillan, 2013.

Wright, Lawrence. "One drop of blood," *New Yorker*, July 25, 1994: 46–55.

Wright, Richard. *Black Boy (American Hunger): A Record of Childhood and Youth*, Foreword by John Edgar Wideman, Afterword by Malcolm Wright. Text restored and established by the Library of America. New York: Harperperennial/Modern Classics, 2020 [1945].

Zhuangzi. *The Complete Works of Zhuangzi*, trans. Burton Watson. New York: Columbia University Press, 2013.

Zonca, Vincent. *Lichens: Toward a Minimum Resistance*, trans. Jody Gladding. Cambridge: Polity, 2022.

Zuboff, Shoshana. *The Age of Surveillance Capitalism: The Fight for a Human Future at the New Frontier of Power*. New York: Public Affairs/Perseus Books, 2019.

Index